SOCIAL LEARNING TECHNOLOGIES

Social Learning Technologies

The introduction of multimedia in education

Edited by
MARC VAN LIESHOUT
TINEKE M. EGYEDI
WIEBE E. BIJKER
University of Maastricht, The Netherlands

Ashgate

Aldershot • Burlington USA • Singapore • Sydney

Published by
Ashgate Publishing Limited
Gower House
Croft Road
Aldershot
Hampshire GU11 3HR
England

Ashgate Publishing Company
131 Main Street
Burlington, VT 05401-5600 USA

Ashgate website: http://www.ashgate.com

British Library Cataloguing in Publication Data
Social learning technologies : the introduction of
    multimedia in education
    1. Education - Data processing 2. Multimedia systems
    I. Lieshout, Marc van II. Egyedi, Tineke M. III. Bijker, Wiebe
    E.
    371.3'34

Library of Congress Control Number: 00-135324

ISBN 0 7546 1409 3

Printed and bound in Great Britain by Antony Rowe Ltd., Chippenham, Wiltshire

Contents

List of Figures	vii
List of Tables	viii
Contributing Authors	ix
Preface	xiii

PART I: CONCEPTUAL FRAMEWORK

1. Introduction
   Wiebe E. Bijker, Tineke M. Egyedi, Marc van Lieshout   3

2. Multimedia in Education
   Anneke Eurelings   11

3. Social Learning
   Marc van Lieshout, Wiebe E. Bijker, Tineke M. Egyedi   37

PART II: CASE STUDIES

4. Multimedia and Education as a Marketing Strategy
   Ruth Mourik   63

5. Learning in Cable-School: The Use of Networked ICTs in an Educational Context
   Roger S. Slack   83

6. From 'Spice Girls' to Cybergirls: The Role of Multimedia in the Construction of Young Girls' Fascination for and Interest in Computers
   Hege Nordli   110

7. Distance Teaching on Bornholm
   Finn Hansen, Christian Clausen   134

v

8. Teaching Transformed? The Appropriation of Multimedia in
    Education: The Case of Norway
    Margrethe Aune, Knut H. Sørensen   159

9. A Project Adrift: Mechanisms of Multimedia Innofusion in
    Education
    Tineke M. Egyedi   190

10. Telepoly: The Risk of Creating High-End Expectations
    Pierre Rossel, Martine Buser   206

11. Diversified Hypermedia Use: An Experiment with Dis-closure
    Tineke M. Egyedi   226

PART III: COMPARATIVE ANALYSES

12. Setting of Multimedia Use
    Tineke M. Egyedi, Marc van Lieshout, Wiebe E. Bijker   251

13. Multimedia Innofusion
    Tineke M. Egyedi, Marc van Lieshout, Wiebe E. Bijker   264

14. Social Learning in Educational Multimedia
    Marc van Lieshout, Tineke M. Egyedi, Wiebe E. Bijker   281

15. Conclusions and Recommendations
    Wiebe E. Bijker, Tineke M. Egyedi, Marc van Lieshout   313

Bibliography   *319*

List of Figures

Figure 10.1   Telepoly scenario according to TIK, ETHZ   212

Figure 11.1   A Storyspace document view in figurative mode with in the foreground two opened information entities   234

Figure 11.2   A Storyspace document view in the chart mode   235

Figure 11.3   A Storyspace document view in the outline mode   236

Figure 13.1   The time perspective (t) of the concepts of configuration, translation and appropriation   266

Figure 14.1   Dimensions of mode of experimentation vis-à-vis mode of control   289

Figure 14.2   Presentation of the modes of control versus experimentation on the axes of the five project dimensions   290

Figure 14.3   Language Course – "Controlled experimentation"   291

Figure 14.4   Cable School – "Submissive experimentation"   293

Figure 14.5   Bornholm teleteaching "Controlled experimentation"   294

Figure 14.6   Telepoly – "Controlled experimentation"   296

Figure 14.7   "IMMICS the course" – "Submissive experimentation"   297

Figure 14.8   Visualisaton of all cases in one figure, showing the prominence of either the mode of control or the mode of experimentation in each case   300

Figure 14.9   Dimensioning of good practices   309

List of Tables

Table 2.1   Relationship between the learning theory and
             characteristic application features   20

Table 2.2   The areas of implementation related to the characteristic
             features of educational applications   22

Table 6.1   Frequency of use of different computer applications
             among the seven computer fascinated girls   119

Table 9.1   Evaluating parties and their interest with regard to one
             pilot project   192

Table 12.1   Overview of cases   252

Table 15.1   Summary of conclusions   314

Contributing Authors

Margrethe Aune is an associate professor at the Department of Interdisciplinary Studies of Culture, the Centre for Technology and Society, at the Norwegian University of Science and Technology in Trondheim. She has a PhD in sociology; her thesis was based on a study of energy consumption and everyday life. Her research interests focus on lifestyle and energy consumption, information and communication technologies and social studies of medicine.

Martine Buser is a sociologist who graduated from the University of Lausanne. She has obtained a Master's degree at the European Master in Science, Society and Technology course at the Swiss Federal Institute of Technology in Lausanne and has started her PhD research on telework studying the complementarity of physical and virtual moving in the field of enterprises. She is currently working as scientific collaborator at ESST-EPFL, mainly on the impact of new information technology on organisation in enterprises and is also involved in the assessment of teleteaching experiments inside and between the two Federal Institutes of Technology. She has written several reports and published articles related to both subjects.

Wiebe E. Bijker is professor of Technology & Society at the University of Maastricht. He was trained as an engineer in applied physics and studied philosophy. Bijker has been Dean of the Faculty of Arts and Culture (1995-2000), and chairs the board of the Netherlands Graduate School for Science, Technology and Modern Culture. He is also founding co-editor of the monograph series 'Inside Technology' of MIT Press. He recently helped to create the Maastricht McLuhan Institute for European Studies of Digital Culture.

Christian Clausen is associate professor at the Department of Technology and Social Sciences, the Technical University of Denmark. He is currently managing Danish and international research projects and programmes. He is a member of the international editorial board and referee for the journal *Technology Analysis and Strategic Management*, and a number of the

European Science and Technology Observatory (ESTO). Since 1987, his main research area has been in the field of the assessment of technology and work. Of special interest have been the Scandinavian experiences with action research on technology and work and workers' participation. Later, the focus of research shifted towards technology studies and the social shaping of technology. Current research themes: the social shaping of computer-aided production management and computer integrated manufacture, social shaping of management concepts as well as social learning in multimedia.

Tineke M. Egyedi is a research fellow at the department of Information and Communication Technologies, the Faculty of Technology, Policy and Management of the Delft University of Technology. She was trained as a social psychologist and acquired her Ph.D. degree on ICT standardisation (Delft UT). As a consultant for KPN Research, the Netherlands, she compared Internet and JTC1 standards. She did research on container standardisation at the Royal Institute of Technology in Stockholm, Sweden, and participated in the Mobile Multimedia Communication project (Delft UT), a study of multimedia-supported co-operative work. Her last assignment was at the Maastricht University, where she participated in two European projects addressing multimedia use in education (ELECTRA and SLIM). Her main interest is in standardisation and infrastructure development.

Anneke M.C. Eurelings is currently Executive Director of the Maastricht McLuhan Institute (MMI). She was trained as an electrotechnical engineer (medical engineering) at the Technische Universiteit Eindhoven. At MMI she is responsible for setting up, executing and managing research, education and external service in the fields of digital culture, knowledge organisation and learning technology. Since 1987 she has been involved with ICT and education at the Universiteit Maastricht as Director of the Computing Centre and as the University's co-ordinator in this field. She was also the initiator and co-ordinator of an EU project (ELECTRA) in which four universities in the Euregion Meuse-Rhine researched and developed electronic learning environments.

Finn Hansen is currently a part-time freelance teacher and consultant, until 1998 he held a position as Associate Research Professor (eng.sc.) at the Department of Technology and Social Sciences, Technical University of Denmark. Since 1983, he has been working on various research and development projects, mainly in system development, electronic media and the electronics industry. The basic theme in this work has been the study of developments in contemporary social practice related to the electronics industry, electronic media and computer technology. These analyses have been based on approaches adopted from the history of technology, sociology of technology and from a specific insight in technological knowledge and practice in the electronics and multimedia field. The research projects have reflected international trends in the electronic sector and its consequences on national and system levels.

Marc van Lieshout is senior researcher at the department of Strategy, Technology and Policy of the Dutch organisation for Applied Scientific Research (TNO) situated in Delft. His previous assignment was at the faculty of Arts and Culture at the University of Maastricht. He also had a position as assistant professor at the department of Informatics at the University of Nijmegen. He was trained as physicist. His research focuses on studying the combined technological and social processes of change related to the introduction of information and communication technologies in various social practices.

Ruth Mourik received her masters degree in Anthropology and Non-Western Sociology, with a specialisation in material culture, at the University of Amsterdam in 1996. In 1997, she received a masters degree in Science Society and Technology Studies at the University of Maastricht, after following the inter-university ESST programme European Studies on Science, Society and Technology. Her thesis discussed the social shaping and social learning processes in a multimedia distance education project, and forms the basis for her chapter in this book. Currently, she has a position as a PhD-student at the University of Maastricht, Faculty of Arts and Culture, Department of Technology and Society Studies. Her thesis will discuss the (de-)construction of risk in a technological culture, with respect to, amongst other things, a cattle disease and water management.

Hege Nordli (NTNU, Trondheim) is a PhD student in Sociology at the Centre for Technology and Society at the Norwegian University of Science and Technology. Her PhD project is about female hackers. She did her master thesis on young computer fascinated girls. Her contribution is based on this material.

Pierre Rossel studied at the University of Geneva and of Neuchatel, where he got his Ph.D in anthropology in 1990. A researcher at the Swiss Federal Institute of Technology in Lausanne since 1984, he developed assessing procedures in various situations where culture and socio-economics were related. After setting up a small research unit of Technology Assessment in this latter institution and directing the Tissot Economic Foundation for two years, he returned in 1992 to the Swiss Federal Institute of Technology in Lausanne to set up the Swiss chapter of a European Master in Science, Society and Technology post-graduate programme which he has been organising ever since. He has published some 100 articles, books, parts of books and reports, either as author or co-author, in the fields of interest mentioned, in particular the Technology Assessment of emerging technological systems, in NICT and high-speed transportation.

Roger S. Slack BA (Liverpool), PhD (Victoria University of Manchester) has taught sociology at the Manchester Metropolitan University and is currently a Research Fellow at the University of Edinburgh's Technology Studies Unit and Centre for Educational Sociology. His research deals with the development of Technologies from an ethnomethodological standpoint. He has interests in social theory, sociology of scientific knowledge (especially Artificial Intelligence), multimedia and CSCW.

Knut H. Sørensen is a professor of sociology at the Department of Interdisciplinary Studies of Culture, Centre for Technology and Society, the Norwegian University of Science and Technology in Trondheim. His research interests are in science and technology studies, in particular on information and communication technology, energy and the environment, and technology policy and transport.

Preface

This volume is one of the results of the European Union project "Social Learning in Multi-Media" (or *SLIM*, see Introduction of this volume, note 1). During four years we collaborated in such varied European university cities as København, Lausanne, Maastricht and Namur; concluded our workshops with singing in Dublin, dancing in Edinburgh, and nightlife in Trondheim.

This book, then, is very much the result of a collective endeavour. All SLIM members contributed to the discussions that shaped the chapters in this book, even though they may not be among the primary authors. In that sense, the volume bears witness of the truly enabling character of EU research funding in the social sciences. We thank all our SLIM colleagues and friends for the stimulating collaboration in this project. Special thanks go to Robin Williams for co-ordinating the overall SLIM project.

We particularly thank the authors of this volume for their patience in collaborating with the editors to mould this collection of, we think, original and thought provoking chapters into a coherent and focused book.

Finally, we thank Sabine Kuipers for managing the lay-out and production of the manuscript.

Marc van Lieshout
Tineke M. Egyedi
Wiebe E. Bijker

PART I
CONCEPTUAL FRAMEWORK

1 Introduction

MARC VAN LIESHOUT, TINEKE M. EGYEDI,
WIEBE E.BIJKER

Introduction

Most of us have been to school. We all know what it means to be educated. We have learned to read, write and do arithmetic (the famous 3Rs). An 'educated' guess would be that ninety percent of the readers will have become educated by means of traditional educational tools: blackboard, textbooks and classes. Even in the face of the broad spectrum of school systems world-wide, the basics of education have been rather consistent over the past decades. The advent of information and communication technologies, however, promises to disrupt the traditional concepts of education and training, of learning and teaching. It is often stated that the new learning tools will change our perspective on learning and teaching in less than a generation. Teachers will be replaced by advanced computer programmes, pupils will learn at home and there will be no need for them to meet in badly equipped classrooms. Everyone will profit from the opportunity of being taught by the best of all teachers by means of distance learning through electronic networks. School boards will be able to follow the progress of their pupils online. Teachers do not have to spend hours and hours painstakingly correcting their pupils' work. The burden of teaching and learning will be lessened and will be replaced by a more cheerful, pleasant *and* effective form of teaching and learning.

Although this vision is a highly technological utopian one, parts of it have appeal and can not be easily dismissed as apparent mismatches with present-day developments in education and training. Political slogans such as 'lifelong learning', 'the knowledge society', etc., focus on societal changes in dealing with knowledge and learning. The traditional view on learning, as being located primarily in the first phase of one's life and organised in concrete buildings for most of one's young years, gives way to a disembedded form of learning, at any time, at any place, and in a manner of one's own choosing. The emergence of electronic networks, the seemingly unlimited opportunity to share content with everybody, everywhere, feeds the view that everybody will become master of his or her

3

own educational biography. Although we could easily dismiss such views as being grounded in a too deterministic approach of technology, we also have to recognise that, first, these visions – including their ideological base – pop up every now and then and, secondly, that they do form part of the push to re-organise our educational system. We do not deny the high and forceful pace with which new versions of software applications, next generation PCs, etc. are released (regrettably, often without genuine quality tests). Neither do we deny that the convergence of various kinds of information representation (such as text, data, stills, movies, images) with various kind of information carriers (fixed, mobile, terrestrial and space-based telecom infrastructures, CD-ROMs, floppy disks, DVDs) gives rise to an unprecedented myriad of rich information contexts. This by itself, however, does not provide a rich environment for educational uses. There is more at stake. Extra work has to be done in order to create useful multimedia uses in education. A more elaborate view is needed to understand what happens when new multimedia applications and tools are introduced in educational contexts. In this volume we shift the focus from the technology itself to the social practice in which the technology is expected to function. Both technology and social practice need to change in order to establish a good match. In this view, introducing technology is a mutual and simultaneous reshaping of technology and the social context in which it has to function. The introduction of multimedia in educational settings no doubt offers very interesting examples of this process of mutual determination. For one thing, as indicated, because the educational system is in a phase of change. There is a lot to learn from how this process takes place, and which factors determine perceived success or failure. For another, multimedia is *hot*. Both its content and its carriers(what kind of information is presented, is it static or dynamic, what kind of communication processes are supported, etc.) are of interest. Multimedia pops up in quite different guises. It is increasingly becoming part of daily practice. All the more surprising that the uptake of multimedia in education is still modest.

Social Learning in Multimedia

The central questions in this volume are: In what manner is multimedia used in the education sector? Which mechanisms affect the introduction, development and diffusion of innovative multimedia uses in the field of education? This volume aims to contribute to a better understanding of the problems and mechanisms that determine the uptake of multimedia in the field of education. Multimedia practices, projects and policies are presented to illustrate different aspects of the uptake of multimedia. Case studies highlight the problems that occur when multimedia is introduced in new educational settings. The cases demonstrate the need to adapt both the educational setting and the technology. They show how innovative multimedia uses develop and what mechanisms lead to diffusion of multimedia in education. Furthermore, a conceptual framework is developed to interpret and compare the cases. This provides a more general insight into practices and policies. Together, the case studies and the comparative analyses contain recommendations for 'good practices', hints to be taken into account and pitfalls to be avoided when implementing multimedia in education, and innovation and diffusion policies. With our analyses and recommendations, we address educational technologists, project managers who deal with educational multimedia, teachers, school boards, and policy makers in this field.

Most studies that deal with the introduction of Information and Communication Technologies (ICTs) in education have a narrow managerial, organisational perspective. They focus on implementation problems and view the ICT tool as a static object. Specific aspects of the educational setting, processes of mutual adaptation between technology and its setting, and mechanisms that underlie multimedia diffusion in the education sector remain underexposed. The contributors to this volume have a different approach. Our main expertise lies in the field of the innovation and diffusion of technology. We emphasise the importance of the broader social setting in which a technology, an artefact or a technical system is implemented. It is a sociotechnical approach. We apply this approach to innovation and diffusion processes. Our approach is unusual for the multimedia field in education and our focus is new. However, we share our focus with colleagues researching other sectors of society: our SLIM partners.

This volume is one of the spin-offs of a European project called *Social Learning In Multimedia* (SLIM[1]). The focus in SLIM is on how society learns to use multimedia in different areas of society, such as education, the public sector, and the arts and culture sector. That is, how does the uptake of multimedia proceed in these sectors? Important topics are the identification of factors that enhance learning and the appropriation of innovations, and the transferability of experiences across sectors: that which is useful in one situation may not necessarily be so in another one.

These questions and topics are also addressed in this volume. The 'spirit of SLIM' inspired us in the way we deal with them.

Outline of the Book

The volume consists of three parts: an introductory part, in which the state-of-the-art of multimedia in education is examined and the conceptual framework is discussed; an empirical part, in which eight case studies are presented; and an integrative part, in which the case studies are compared and analysed. Although a tight relationship exists between the conceptual framework in Part I and the analyses in Part III, and cross-references are made between chapters, all chapters can be read separately. They stand in their own right, and have their own focus and line of argument. Each chapter starts with an abstract. To allow the reader to choose his or her own way through the volume, we briefly highlight the content of each chapter.

Part I: Conceptual Framework

Chapter 2 provides an overview of current use of multimedia in education. Relevant concepts are introduced, such as the distinction between learning about, with and through ICT. The author discusses the main trends in multimedia use and pedagogy. She indicates ways in which new developments in teaching and learning can profit from ICT, and provides guidelines for incorporating pedagogy and instructional engineering in multimedia use and project design.

In chapter 3, the theoretical background of the studies is introduced. It builds mainly on theories from the fields of Social Studies of Technology and sociology. Briefly, these argue that technology cannot be isolated from the practices into which it is introduced, and that technology itself is a social practice. A conceptual framework is developed to help understand processes of multimedia diffusion in education. *Innofusion* (a combination of innovation and diffusion) and *social learning* are two leading concepts. They are explained and further elaborated in the comparative analyses of chapter 13 (Innofusion) and chapter 14 (Social Learning).

Part II: Case Studies

The second part of the book consists of eight empirical studies, carried out by SLIM researchers in several European countries. Most of the cases focus on a multimedia project. They cover a variety of issues, educational settings, and multimedia uses. The 'learners' addressed range from children to adults; the educational settings vary from primary school to the home and the university setting; the initiators of multimedia use are educational institutes, government bodies and, sometimes, commercial companies; the multimedia used ranges from stand-alone software for private use to communication technologies for distance teaching; and the issues of concern range from gender aspects to economic issues. Together, they offer a heterogeneous picture of multimedia use in education. We briefly outline each of the studies.

Multimedia and education as marketing strategy (chapter 4) describes how a telecom company attempts to broaden its playing field. A distance-language course for children is set up. Children are chosen because they are likely to bring favourable public exposure. Ten children from different European countries are connected by means of extended ISDN facilities. The author uses theories from the social studies of technology (SCOT and the notion of inscription). She analyses the manner in which the children are made to fit the technology. She describes how teachers abandon their initial aims and adopt the company's aims, and shows how the public success of the project is manipulated.

Learning in Cable-School: the use of networked ICTs in an educational context (chapter 5) describes a project initiated by a cable company to connect schools to the Internet with cable modems. The company sees it as a stepping-stone for contracts with local government. The aim of the project is that teachers from different schools share their teaching material via the web. The author analyses why this does not happen. He examines the partner relationships in the project and the working context of teachers, and addresses the emergence of other multimedia uses. He introduces the term 'social learning of independence'.

From Spice-girls to Cybergirls: the role of multimedia in the construction of young girls' fascination for and interest in computers (chapter 6) follows a number of computer-fascinated girls in order to understand and increase young females' multimedia use. The study summarises Norwegian policy on this matter. A discussion of gender theories is included. The author examines home and school computer use. She analyses the girls' learning strategies and describes developments in their computer use. The chapter ends with a number of clear and useful policy recommendations on how education should go about increasing girls' interest in computing and computers.

Distance teaching on Bornholm (chapter 7) describes a trial initiated by the Danish government. Because of the lack of suitable educational possibilities on the island of Bornholm, a distance teaching set-up is organised with educational institutions on the mainland. Video-conferencing technology is used. The authors critically examine the political context of the project, and its technical and pedagogical basis. Project developments are analysed on the degree of symmetry between sending and receiving institutions and the centre-periphery debate on economic development and education.

Teaching transformed? The appropriation of multimedia in education: the case of Norway (chapter 8) addresses Norwegian policies and experiments on multimedia in education. The authors use the concepts of 'learning economy', 'domestication' and 'social learning'. The study discusses the role of ICT as it is perceived and shaped at different levels in education. In government scenarios, the availability of computers is a major concern. However, the study illustrates considerable differences in the way schools exploit the computer capacity available and 'domesticate' ICT. In order to learn from these practices, the authors plead for effective local learning economies within and between schools.

A project adrift: mechanisms of multimedia innofusion in education (chapter 9) follows the institutional wanderings of a project (IMMICS) in a Dutch university faculty. The author adopts the theoretical framework of chapter 3 and focuses on mechanisms that lead to the diffusion of innovative multimedia uses. The study shows that the project's meaning and locus within the faculty change until it becomes associated with a specific course. The actor network involved expands, implodes and re-emerges. Some actors in the faculty are meaning brokers, others are intermediary multimedia users and producers combined. The author notes mechanisms that propel faculty-wide multimedia innofusion.

Telepoly: the risk of creating high-end expectations (chapter 10) describes a broadband real-time distance teaching project between three Swiss institutes for technical education (i.e. three different language areas). The study discusses the Swiss public policy debate on the use of new ICT-related educational tools. It shows the project's initial emphasis on realising a stable technological infrastructure (ATM). When new strategic actors become involved, these prioritise educational issues. Telepoly illustrates the difficulty of matching changing priorities, and the importance of adapting teaching strategies to the requirements of distance teaching.

Diversified hypermedia use in education: an experiment with dis-closure (chapter 11) describes the use of hypermedia software in a university course (IMMICS, see chapter 9). The teachers do not prescribe how hypermedia should be used in the course. Indeed, they encourage innovative uses. The author uses the term 'diversification experiment' to contrast their approach with 'verification experiments'. She examines which limits the educational setting poses on user experimentation and to what degree innovative uses emerge. Using concepts discussed in chapter 3, she analyses the experiment as an attempt to postpone consensus about the meaning of hypermedia (i.e. prolong *dis-closure*).

Part III: Comparative Analyses

In Part III, we analyse and compare the findings of the case studies in order to determine which mechanisms affect the introduction, development and diffusion of innovative multimedia uses in the field of education. We compare the educational settings in which multimedia is used, and subsequently apply and elaborate the two key notions of the conceptual framework: *innofusion* and *social learning*. A table is added at the beginning of Part III, which summarises the features of the cases that are relevant in respect to innofusion and social learning.

Chapter 12 addresses the setting of multimedia use. The leading question here is which features of the educational and project settings clarify the lagging-behind in the use of multimedia. Different angles are taken. The cases are examined on incentives for multimedia use, the role of teachers, the significance of education for the kind of multimedia used, and the locus of learning. The comparison points to several problems in the educational and project setting that hamper the uptake of multimedia in this sector. They range from the marginalisation of teachers in projects to too narrowly defined policies on educational multimedia.

Chapter 13 examines how multimedia innofusion takes place. Three concepts are used to analyse innofusion processes: 'appropriation', 'configuration' and 'translation'. First, their relationship is specified. Subsequently, the concepts are used to examine the cases. The focus is on mechanisms that promise to lead to more widespread use in education. Overall, the degree of innofusion is modest. But the cases nevertheless indicate ways in which this may be improved. The findings illustrate that innofusion occurs along lines of multimedia production as well as multimedia use. Policy should address both. Examples are discussed in which mechanisms, intrinsic and extrinsic to the setting at hand, propel multimedia innofusion.

In chapter 14, the empirical material is analysed once more, but now from the perspective of social learning. The two empirical manifestations of social learning, the *mode of experimentation* and the *mode of control*, are further elaborated. These concepts and the notions of perceived success and failure are applied to the cases. The analysis shows that all multimedia projects are characterised by aspects of the 'mode of control' while only a few also show aspects of the 'mode of experimentation'. Multimedia practices are focused too much on technological results alone, bypassing broader educational implications. 'Failure' is usually neglected as source of social learning, and thus neglected as an outcome that might further the successful introduction of multimedia under different circumstances.

In Chapter 15 we draw conclusions about the mechanisms that affect the introduction, development and diffusion of innovative multimedia uses in education. We recommend ways to improve the uptake of new learning technologies. The recommendations address praxis and policy. They aim to assist educational technologists, teachers, school boards, and policy developers in making optimal educational use of multimedia.

Note

1   The SLIM project was funded by the European Union under the programme of Targeted Socio-Economic Research (TSER), 1996-1999. Participating universities were: University of Edinburgh (UK, co-ordinator), University of Dublin (Ireland), University of Trondheim (Norway), Technical University of Denmark (Denmark), University of Maastricht (The Netherlands), Facultés Universitaires Notre Dame de Paix de Namur (Belgium), Ecole Polytechnique de Lausanne (Switzerland).

2 Multimedia in Education

ANNEKE EURELINGS

Abstract

The innovations in education using the new possibilities of information and communication technology, such as interaction and multimedia, involves a complex process with many impediments. Information technology provides learning situations that give students more control. This coincides with a shift in paradigm from a teacher-oriented to a more student-oriented learning approach that many educational institutions are already willing to adopt. However, changing both the learning approach as well as the means to support it increases the complexity of the design and implementation process. The limited knowledge of the relationship between instruction, learning and learning technologies further hinders an efficient and effective design of learning applications. However, based on qualitative analyses it can be stated that learning applications do seem to favour active learning behaviour and promote the development of skills that will be needed in the future. Multidisciplinary development teams, applying a principled design approach, and strong user involvement are key factors for success. It is expected that the development of a framework for evaluation and ongoing research in cognitive science and instructional design will in, the longer term, provide education with more guidelines for the effective implementation of information technology. In addition to this, the new generation of software tools that facilitates the development process of electronic learning environments will have a positive impact on teachers who are striving to overcome the impediments and change their teaching courses into learning environments.

Introduction

The role of multimedia in education is often referred to as the role of information and communication technology in education. This second definition has the advantage that it links the major issues in education,

11

namely the processing of information in an interactive communication process with peers, tutors and experts, with the major characteristics of the technology under consideration. From this perspective it is clear that the rapid developments in the ICT sector will have implications for teaching and learning.

Since the late eighties, governmental and educational institutions have made substantial investments in the integration of technology in the curricula. In Europe many programmes have been started up to bring computers into the school environment, to train the teachers and to promote the production of new learning materials and innovative approaches to teaching and learning. However, the results are difficult to assess and, compared to the integration of technology in the workplace, it seems that progress is rather slow. This overall view is more diverse once we take a closer look at the decade itself. Until the first half of the nineties the major output of the technology push was computer-based training and simulation programmes. Teacher-student interactions were replaced by computer-student interactions. Although learning can be improved by these types of applications, the integration of these applications in educational practice has been very limited. The high investment beforehand and the limited stimulus for learners has restricted the usefulness to the more simulation-oriented type of applications.

The ICT developments in the second half of the nineties renewed the interest in the possibilities of technology for the curriculum. The world-wide web, video conferencing and groupware opened up the possibility for students to access information and to have interaction with others through electronic communication even on a global scale. These technological developments coincided with a shift in the educational approach from a teacher-oriented to a more student-oriented approach. This new approach, aimed at activating students by creating a rich information environment where peers, tutors and experts interact concerning situated learning materials, seems to be favoured by the new technological features. A new awareness has stimulated educational and governmental institutions to invest again in infrastructure and to address the meaning of technology for education. At present we are at the middle of an exciting, exploratory period of assessing the value of these new ICT tools for education.

The next section describes the general framework of the relationship between learning theory, instructional design and the role of information and communication technologies. Educational applications based on various uses can be ordered. The relationship between learning theory and instructional design is of such a nature that only global guidelines can be formulated as a basic principle for the design of applications. In the third section a closer examination of the major characteristics of educational applications is derived from a historical perspective of the different areas of implementation. What benefits can be expected from technology enhanced instruction? The differences in educational context, the differences in type of applications as well as the diversity in evaluation approaches, make it difficult to generalise on project outcomes. Only on a general level can indications be given of the added value that one may expect from information and communication technology enhanced learning. Integrating technology in the curriculum results in new, innovative ways of teaching and learning. Designing applications in this stage of development is complicated as only limited knowledge is available. Project outcomes are strongly influenced by the design process. Key factors in this process that are prerequisites for usable products are described in the fifth section.

The objectives for applying ICT in education are driven by technological developments and a general awareness that these developments will have an impact on teaching and learning. The community has tried to explore the potential of these new developments through projects and has subsequently gained an intimate knowledge of the impediments that will have to be overcome. What strategy should be defined to progress from exploration to a more structural approach for integrating ICT in the curriculum, and how can we apply the knowledge gained?

General Framework

ICT in Teaching and Learning

Multimedia stands for the (simultaneous) use of different types of (electronic) media, such as text, sound and (moving) images. The developments in the domain of information and communication technology have enabled computers to present information in a multimedia format, but have moreover provided the desktop with access, search and retrieval possibilities to global (multimedia) resources as well as interaction with peers, tutors and experts all over the world. Multimedia and ICT have become umbrella terms for a number of different technologies that can be used to collect, store, process and distribute information of different types. When discussing the meaning of multimedia for education, I want to focus on the meaning of information as well as interaction, communication, for the learning process, and I therefore use the terms ICT and multimedia simultaneously and without further differentiation.

In teaching and learning ICT can be put to various uses. A practical and often used order (Moonen & Kommers 1995) is:

- learning about ICT (ICT as an object of study);
- learning with ICT (ICT as a tool);
- learning through ICT (ICT as an independent learning resource that replaces activities of the teacher, peers, readers, etc.).

Teaching students *about* computers is the most straightforward means of addressing the need for computer literacy. Students learn how ICT works and what they can do with it. Although it may seem very easy to do, it is not without obstacles. The shelf-life of any information on computers that we impart to the students is disappointedly short – technology is changing so rapidly that there is little we can say about computers today that will not be obsolete by the time the students graduate. Furthermore, learning about computers in the abstract, with no particular orientation or purpose, will produce an inflexible form of knowledge that will be difficult to apply in practice. However, this approach is often considered as a requirement for learning *with* ICT.

Learning *with* ICT as defined by Moonen and Kommers stands for the support of students during their searching, processing and storing of information on issues related to learning. By doing so the student will develop the necessary ICT and information skills. In this approach students use word processors, spreadsheets, access the internet and use e-mail and news groups. Learning with computers engages students in authentic activities that correspond to the way in which technology will be used in later practice. Learning in this way appropriates the notion of personal computing from professional settings and introduces it into instructional practice. Moonen and Kommers have defined ICT in learning *with* ICT, as a tool designed independent of the process it supports. However Koschmann (1995) reports that 'problem-based learning curricula that utilise electronic resources in significant ways are subtly altered by the introduction of technology leading to the emergence of new instructional forms'.

The third approach, learning *through* ICT, relates to technology as a tool for instructional delivery. The general definition presupposes that technology can be used as an independent learning resource that replaces the activities of the teacher, peers, readers, etc. It will be clear that this type of technology involvement changes the teacher role from being a primary knowledge source and knowledge transmitter to that of a guide and mentor in learning processes. This will lead to major changes in the pedagogical setting. This changing learning approach, often introduced in combination with the technological possibilities to enhance this shift, introduces a complex situation that requires professional change-management capabilities.

Often, a fourth functionality of ICT in education is distinguished. It addresses the support of organisational and logistical interactions between students and the educational institution. This type of functionality does not interact with the core of teaching and learning, but, as just mentioned, it is sometimes a facilitator for the introduction of other approaches.

In this chapter I will concentrate on the domain of learning *with* and learning *through* ICT. In order to get a deeper insight into both the functionality and the features of applications supporting teaching and learning, we have to go back to the basic principles that underlie the design of these systems: learning theories and their implications for instructional design.

Learning Theory and Instructional Design

The developments in cognitive science and learning theories indicate a shift from a behaviourist approach to a more constructive approach. This means that knowledge is no longer regarded as an objective representation of the external world, but that knowledge is the result of interpreted information in the context of experiences. These insights are built upon the ideas of Dewey, who wrote extensively on the nature of knowledge, how people come to 'acquire' it, and what teachers can do to foster this process (Dewey 1933).

From the beginning of this century, experimental education has been considered a 'linking science' in the sense of Dewey, with its source domain in experimental psychology and its target domain in the educational practice of instruction and teaching. Dewey, who can be characterised as an educational philosopher, held a pragmatic view that was continually informed by 'observation and experiment' and by which 'ideas are only tentative or working hypotheses until they are modified, rejected or confirmed by the consequences produced by acting on them'. For Dewey the ultimate goal of instruction is to encourage students to adopt an attitude that accepts and even embraces the condition of uncertainty and doubt. At the beginning of this century the mainstream of educational theories and instructional programs clearly consisted of the 'reform pedagogy' with its foundation in anthropological and philosophical ideas (Seel & Dijkstra 1997). The 'progressive education' of, among others, Dewey dominated the educational thinking in North America for the first half of the 20th century. Instructional design (ID) consisted then mainly of creating concrete instructional materials and environments in which students can learn effectively.

After the Second World War behaviourism and systems theories heavily influenced the approaches to instructional design and the development of educational technology. As a result, the view on instructional design became one of a deterministic and rational process. However, several investigations (Kerr 1983; Rowland 1992) indicate that even experts who regularly designed instruction did not apply the 'scientific principles based on behaviourism' but followed rather more or less stereotyped expectations and routines. In conventional terms instructional systems development is considered a linear process. However, this linear approach fails to adapt to the increasing complexity of advancements in learning theory offered by cognitive psychology or of those that are the result of emerging technologies or the specific needs of individual situations. The developments in cognitive science that relate to the ideas and theories of Dewey have brought about new theories in learning often referred to as constructivism. In the constructive approach learning can no longer be considered a mapping of external information into memory, but rather as a process through which the learners systematically construct mental models. From this perspective the objective of instructional design should be to support (cf. Koschmann, in press):

- learners to become increasingly active;
- teachers to become increasingly collegial;
- materials to become increasingly authentic.

Instructional attempts to simplify, interpret or illustrate complex concepts using concrete representations may actually contribute to, or reinforce erroneous understanding due to an oversimplified view of how complex concepts are applied in practice. As reality has many faces which change in the course of time, Koschmann states that instructional environments should foster termlessness. He defines this as follows: 'instruction should instil a sense of tentativeness with regard to knowing, a realisation that understanding of complex material is never 'completed', only enriched, and a lifelong commitment to advancing one's knowledge'. Information-rich environments are the key elements of an environment that fosters termlessness learning.

The implications of the shift in learning theory and instructional design for the learning environment are situated in the strengthening of student activities and improving the authenticity of the learning environment. Educational institutions are trying to redesign their curricula in such a way that student-centred learning is favoured. The new ICT tools seem to provide the students with possibilities for taking more control over their own learning. After all, students can have access from their home environment to global information resources, experts and learning applications independent of their regular curricula. Educational institutions try to find ways if and how ICT can enhance the implementation of student-centred learning. This often results in a new teaching and learning environment of which both the learning approach as well as the means of teaching are changed. This double change process results in a very complex situation that is extremely difficult to assess in respect to added value for teaching and learning.

Educational Technology

In the past, there has been experience in the use of technology in different educational settings. These historical areas of implementation differ in respect to underlying assumptions, or show a change in the approach to learning in the course of time. In order to make a comparison possible I have looked for the ways in which the major design criteria of learning environments, as described above, are translated into characteristic system features. These characteristic features of educational applications will then be used in later sections when comparing the project outcomes.

Areas of Implementation

Looking back upon the developments in educational technology over the last ten years, separate forms of implementation dependent on the institutional objectives, the learning theory and the technology used can be distinguished. They can be described as follows:

- Global, open and distance education;
- Computer supported individual learning environments;
- Computer supported collaborative learning environments.

Distance education has the longest history when it comes to looking for means to overcome the physical distance between learner and the educational organisation. Its model of instruction was originally based on notions of delivery or transmission that treat the learner as a passive recipient of knowledge. Although in primary and secondary education this was often restricted to an add-on such as school television, in higher education, especially in the USA and Australia, it was implemented as a basic carrier for transmitting education. Open Universities belong to the early adopters of computer mediated communication for this purpose. Due to the fact that large-scale ICT-services have become available in all higher education organisations, they too are investigating ways to reach new target groups with post-academic education, applying the concept of distance education. But as the governing learning theory in higher education is still very teacher-driven, the tele-learning approach also reflects this. Video conferencing and (interactive) computer based teaching are means to implement the traditional mode of instruction with learners at a distance. When comparing the different initiatives, a more and more diversified approach due to differences in underlying principles can be observed.

The computer supported individual learning applications date back to the late eighties when computer based training and individual tutoring systems were started. The main idea behind this development was that (some of the) teachers and their knowledge could be replaced by computer systems. Drill and practice programmes and simulations were the first results but the fact that the products were very much under computer control limited the learners' possibilities and therefore the usefulness of the programmes. The new possibilities for interaction and communication have renewed the interest in computer based training. At present, many projects try to create a learning environment for individual learning that contains (part of the) teacher's knowledge while at the same time giving the learner more control. While the original instructional model was strongly related to the "transmission" model, the present instructional model tries to make the student more active by giving him some more control over his learning. In addition to this, information and communication technology is also often used to increase the authenticity of the instructional material as multimedia and hyperlink technology can bring content more in context.

Computer supported collaborative learning has a much shorter history then the other two categories. A limited number of educational institutions started in the '90s to investigate what the possibilities of computer mediated communication (CMC) could mean for their existing educational mission. The intention was not oriented to bridging distances, but was oriented to see if new methods of working (viz. computer mediated communication) could provide added value for the learners. This approach found much support in educational institutions that favoured student centred learning and that recognised the importance of social interaction between peers and between peers and their tutor as an important element of the learning environment. At present this category of applications is often referred to as computer supported collaborative learning.

A categorisation based on a historical perspective is due to become obsolete. However it reflects the present situation as it can be found in literature describing project results. Over time it can be observed that the differences between the educational applications in each of the three categories becomes more and more diffuse once information and communication technology becomes integrated in the curricula both for regular and for life long learners. It is expected that educational institutions, due to competitive forces, will have substantial differences amongst themselves with respect to educational approach and their target groups. To be able to judge what kind of educational applications will meet their requirements, I will describe below how major design criteria of learning environments are translated into characteristic application features.

Characteristic Features of Educational Applications

As stated earlier, design criteria are defined dependent on the governing learning theory, behaviourism or constructivism. These different instructional design criteria will have consequences for how information and communication can contribute to the learning environment. Table 2.1 describes the role of ICT in the light of the most striking features. From a technological perspective, independent of the learning approach, ICT offers possibilities for both synchronous and a-synchronous communication. This time related characteristic feature of educational applications should be added to table 2.1.

Table 2.1   Relationship between the learning theory and characteristic application features

Instructional design criteria derived from:		Characteristic application features	
Behaviourism	Constructivism	Behaviourism	Constructivism
Transmitting knowledge	Constructing knowledge	Filled application	Empty application
Teacher oriented	Student oriented	Teacher/programme controlled	Student controlled
Individual learning	Group learning	Student-computer	Student-group interaction
Abstract knowledge	Knowledge in context	Limited information environment	Rich information environment

I will now review the features of educational applications are explained in more detail.

Filled versus empty applications The paradigm shift in learning theory has changed the role of the computer in the classroom from a 'teaching machine' to a 'learning tool' (Zucchermaglio 1993). In the function of a teaching machine all the elements for a learning environment are embedded in the computer software: subject matter and didactical method. In the learning tool approach these two elements are disconnected: the didactical method is only reflected in the design of the electronic learning environment, while the subject matter is brought into the environment by the learners themselves. Applications that contain the teacher's knowledge, often called courseware applications, are considered as *filled* applications. While, on the contrary, word processors, databases for processing information and groupware applications are examples of *empty* software: they function as generic tools for users, and allow the user self to bring information into the application. Collaborative learning environments that can be described as a framework in which learning can take place can be supported by groupware, which are described as 'empty' software applications. They function as learning tools in a specific instructional setting. In these applications the content is the shared knowledge that is the result of the interactions between peers and their tutor.

Teacher- versus student controlled applications Instructional design based on behaviourism contains elements as stimulus, response and reinforcement. This leads to the development of drill and practice applications and tutorials. The teacher control over the students learning is built in through programme controlled learning. Cognitive learning theories are more dominant in actual design activities. Simulations in which students can work with complex multimedia information and communication software (such as groupware) for interactions in collaborative learning, are just a few examples of applications that are open and can be used flexibly in student-centred learning arrangements. Control is given to the user or shared between peers, while the teacher guides the learning process.

Individual versus group applications Student-centred education puts an emphasis on the student being in control over his/her own learning. self-direction is an important feature, as well as the active role that the learner has in the learning process. The process of transferring external information to internal knowledge can be put in a sequence of logically ordered activities by the learner: search for information, processing, understanding, integrating and elaboration. This situation can be realised in an educational setting were the machine – student interaction favours this approach. This category is often referred to as courseware applications. These types of application should be based on a profound approach to study and a high level of inter-activity. In social constructivism, however, knowledge building is not regarded as an isolated individual process.[1] Jonassen, Mayes and McAleese (1993) state that cognitive development in terms of construction of knowledge can only take place in a collaborative working environment where common understandings result from the social negotiation of meaning. In the analysis of the learning process communication appears to be equally important as working with information. Applications that support collaborative learning, such as in problem-based learning or in project-based learning are called computer supported collaborative learning applications (CSCL).

Limited- versus rich information environments Learning takes place in a constructed learning environment instead of in the real world where the to-be-acquired knowledge and skills have to be used. This constructed environment has the advantage that information and problem-solving can be studied independently, although there is always the danger that the relationship between the information presented and the real world becomes disconnected. Knowledge and skills cannot then be used adequately. For each instruction the designer always will try to create situations that resemble the actual situations. The decision is often guided by the economic feasibility of the presence and use of the real situation for purposes of instruction (Dijkstra & Merrienboer 1997). In the constructivistic approach media cannot be the main influence on learning directly, but can only have an indirect and subsidiary influence. But when the available domain-specific knowledge is not sufficient to construct a mental model, the learner will extract the necessary information from the environment. To foster termlessness learning, as defined by Koschmann, information-rich environments are a prerequisite.

Synchronous versus a-synchronous applications The dominant instructional environments are founded on simultaneous interactions of tutor and students, thus allowing interactions between them to occur. Only in limited situations like television was this simultaneousness abandoned, but, as a consequence, it was not possible to have interactions between tutor and student. In distance education a long history of the use of technology in a simultaneous setting exists. Synchronous communication over distances, such as video conferencing, requires an additional procedure to regulate the interaction and communication and due to this it is often regarded as inferior compared to life communication. Still, this type of application is able to support processes that require instantaneous feedback from the group. Collaboration without simultaneous presence is relatively new. The advancement in electronic communication facilities such as e-mail, bulletin-boards and groupware have introduced the possibility of collaboration between peers and tutors in an a-synchronous way. This type of communication makes it possible to disconnect the need to be simultaneous at the same time and place.

Table 2.2   The areas of implementation related to the characteristic features of educational applications

Feature / Area of impl.	Filled / Empty	Teacher / Student	Individual / Group	Info limited / Info rich	Synchrone / A-synchrone
Global open & distance learning	Filled	Teacher	Group	Info limited	Synchrone
Computer supported individual learning	Filled	Teacher	Individual	Info limited	-
Computer supported collaborative learning	Empty	Student	Group	Info rich	A-synchrone

In order to compare project outcomes it is relevant to relate areas of implementation to the characteristic features of educational applications as described above (see table 2.2).

Environments instead of applications   In the general framework section a distinction was made according to Moonen and Kommers (1995) between:

- ICT as a tool to support learning (*learning with ICT*), and
- ICT as an independent learning resource that replaces teacher- and peer activities (*learning through ICT*).

However, the analysis of the most striking features of applications for teaching and learning reveal that the definition of this distinction must be more differentiated. After all, software products such as groupware allow the development of tools that have incorporated pedagogical design issues. These applications support both individual learning activities as well as learning in a group. Tools that support group interaction and collaboration by bringing in peers, teachers and experts in an instructional setting, can best be defined as enablers of learning, as an integral part of the learning environment of students, staff and learning materials. These types of collaboration tools, learning tools, are equivalent to the workflow systems in the work environment: workflow systems steer and support the work process based on management principles, while the learning tools steer and support the learning process based on pedagogical principles. Learning *with* information and communication technology has an impact on the instructional setting, especially when tools are designed from a pedagogical perspective. Learning tools can enable students, peers and tutors to become engaged in each others learning process as a guide as well as a learner. For this reason I prefer, in addition to Moonen and Kommers' approach, to make a distinction between generic ICT-tools and pedagogically informed ICT-tools.

A second observation can be made: A different and new method of working has become visible; designing learning environments instead of learning applications. The term 'learning environment' is very widely used yet rarely defined. Goodyear (1998) defines the learning environment as 'a complex set of nested structures which provide the physical setting for the work of a community of learners'. This physical setting can include all sorts of learning resources, generic and pedagogically informed ICT tools, specific applications and other knowledge objects produced through interactions between members of the learning community. Both ICT developments as well as changing design perspectives have caused this shift.

Curricula consist of a number of different instructional settings: lectures, skill training, group activities, testing and library activities. Innovating education with ICT/Multimedia usually starts at course level not at curriculum level. At present, students often become engaged in using ICT/MM for their learning due to individual teacher initiatives. Integrating ICT at the curriculum level requires more; it requires thinking in terms of creating a consistent learning environment that has both physical and virtual components. From this point of view an electronic learning environment will consist of generic tools in combination with pedagogically informed ICT/MM tools. Both support the learners with their learning activities. Dillemans et al (1998) even consider the development of appropriate learning environments as a basic condition for usable and effective innovation. In their approach they distinguish three major elements that define (technological) learning environments: interaction environments, exploratory environments and tutorial environments.

This changing perspective, from course design to curriculum design, is facilitated by a new generation of software tools, such as learning space and virtual classroom. These tools are being promoted as blueprints for electronic learning environments where tutors only need to tune to specific instructional settings. Some of these new-generation tools provide semi-finished products for learning environments. Business claims that, in a specific teaching and learning situation, tailoring of this type of products will result in effective learning environments.

Innovative Projects

In the nineties, many European countries introduced high-investment programmes on national and institutional level for the development of innovative ways of using ICT in education. In 1992, the UK started the Teaching and Learning Technology Programme for higher education, which invested NLG. 22.5 million in the first three years. In 1998, the Netherlands started a NLG.800 million project to provide primary and secondary education with computers and network facilities (cf. Chapter 1). What are the results of this type of programmes, what added value can be expected from the introduction of technology for teaching and learning?

First of all an outline is given of the evaluation mode, followed by a global outline of the project outcomes.

Evaluation Mode

The parallel developments in recent years of ICT/MM on the one hand, and instructional models on the other hand, tend to favour a role of information and communication technology that supports interaction. This interaction can take place between students, between students and teachers or experts, or between students and a diverse set of learning materials. From stand-alone oriented drill and practice to an open communication environment with control to the learner. The general assumption being that multimedia-tools can enable learners to become active learners, not only in their regular phase of education but life-long. In this section, an overview will be given of the added value for learning that can be expected from ICT projects that have focused on information access, communication and interaction.

Salomon states: 'Projects often entail changes that far transcend the sheer introduction of computers. Almost everything has changed: curriculum, activity, engagement in learning, instruction, social interaction, teacher's role, mode of student evaluation. A lesson learned from this is that a systemic rather than an experimental-analytic paradigm for the study of system-wide changes is beneficial. A systemic paradigm uses whole systems as its unit of analysis, assumes that variables and events are inseparable from each other, and that they are in constant flux' (Salomon 1992). Project outcomes as presented below are based on a literature survey performed in 1994 by Eurelings and Ronteltap (1996). The outcomes of the projects will be presented in terms of:

- Pedagogical issues related to skill development, motivation, and meta-cognitive skills such as learning to learn;
- Socio-technical issues related to characteristics of interaction, user awareness of system functionality, extent of user control and technical usability.

Project Outcomes

Cognitive and meta-cognitive skills On average, students do not perform better in electronic learning environments but the social context of the self-directed learning does offer opportunities to support and strengthen the metacognitive activities of the learner (Pugh 1996; Scardamalia & Bereiter

1992). The regular tests are often not designed to assess this learning outcome. It is often argued that communication and information exchange with other students does have a positive impact on learning, with respect to student activeness, writing skills, and debating skills (Scardamalia & Bereiter 1996). The a-synchronous mode of CSCL applications enhances the possibility for reflection. But, as Rockman states: 'Because no one technology can do everything..., educational technology is most effective when used in that specific combination with other technologies and instructional approaches' (Rockman 1992). Students like to use new technology, overall, they experience joy, excitement and pleasure with electronic learning environments is general. It is expected that the new generation of students who do not find learning technologies integrated in their curriculum will regard the learning organisation as out-dated.

Added value of multimedia and information skill development   The added value of multimedia resources for learning is beyond doubt, both for teachers and for students. For teachers it means that the richness of the available information sources creates possibilities to design more authentic learning material. This development increases the possibilities for creating cognitive conflicts, an important stimulus for active learning. Oshima, Bereiter and Scardamalia (1995) state: 'Advancement of individual knowledge relies much on distribution of information and active interaction among information sources'. Another side-effect of this development is the further enhancement of information handling skills. Many students become more successful in searching the web for additional information or illustrative material, often creating information rich documents. Until now, the development of these skills has recieved little attention. Holden and Wedman (1994) state: 'The technology, while providing access to information, does not provide the ways to use that knowledge', while labour-market requirements will stress the importance of these skills in the Information Society.

Control and the changing role for teachers   Due to the fact that the original learning situation was often teacher-oriented, the impact of this type of applications is often very fundamental. Not only does the new situation require new skills of the teacher with respect to creating and using electronic learning environments, but also expects a different attitude: 'From sage on the stage, to guide on the side'. Electronic learning environments offer students the opportunity to become more responsible for their own learning, but this often leads at first to a need for an active moderator in the learning environment; after some time, when students and teacher are sufficiently comfortable with the new setting, the students take over. Only limited information is available on the experiences of teachers in performing this guiding role. Literature (Hammond 1992; Hansen & Perry 1993; Holden & Wedman 1994; Boettcher 1993) indicates that many teachers implementing tele-learning applications will encounter many problems; their changing role, the need for more authentic learning resources, the ICT skills needed, as well as budgetary problems, while a positive reward system for teachers is often missing.

Motivation and participation Students feel comfortable in an electronic learning environment and they experience their activity in a virtual environment as part of a group process. The possibilities for social interaction are felt to be an important stimulus, an enhancement of their own learning. It is often reported that student participation is higher than expected in an electronic learning environment compared to the regular instructional setting. As students stated: 'It is hard to get your opinion stated, either because someone else may say what you wanted to say or your thoughts just get stirred up in your head and you cannot express verbally what you are thinking. It is much easier to write down your thoughts' (Pugh 1996). For the teacher the electronic learning environment provides more information on the learning behaviour of the students and this information can be used to provide a more learner-oriented guidance.

Flexible and open systems The above-mentioned change is only possible when learning applications allow role change of the users, and systems are flexible in respect to user functionality (Rockman 1992). Only very seldom do projects report on user involvement during the developmental process. It appears that projects do not involve users in the set-up of the system, but that they incorporate the user experiences with the system in the real instructional environment in a second or later version of the application. Scardamalia *et al* (1998) argue that educational applications should be aimed at developing the intelligence of the user: 'Educationally irrelevant burdens should be minimised but not in ways that deprive students of occasions to develop the planning, monitoring, goal-setting, problem-solving and other higher-order abilities that are important objectives of education' (Scardamalia 1988). In general, the technical usability of applications is not simple. Projects often use the latest state-of-the-art technology, probably afraid that with less they will soon be obsolete. But the latest technological state-of-the-art often provides an unstable working environment. Although many projects report a moderate to low level of performance, project results do not seem to be influenced by the minor performances.

The Added Value of Learning Applications

Thus I did present a general account of the 'added/value' of ICT projects that have focused on information access, communication and interaction. The 'added-value' of learning applications was only discussed in a descriptive and qualitative way. The present state of the art, the exploratory phase in which we are at present, does not provide us with adequate hard data. The intertwining of learning theory and technology support, combined with the fact that both learning theories, as well as their derived instructional principles, are often of a qualitative nature, make it very difficult to make statements concerning the cost-effectiveness of learning applications based on the evaluation of project outcomes. From a more qualitative evaluation and a trend analysis of different evaluation resources, it can be stated that learning applications seem to favour active learning behaviour and promote the development of skills that will be needed in the future.

Instructional Design as a Complex System

The Need for a Principled Approach

Although many instructional design modes exist, I would like to argue that the efficiency and effectiveness of the design process of educational multimedia is questionable. This argument is based on the following observations:

- The relationship between learning theory, instruction, and the design of learning applications is weak. Design criteria are too general and can only guide system design to the level of major functionality and usability criteria.
- The environment becomes increasingly complex when both the learning approaches and the supporting tools are changed. The difficulty of learning from past experiences due to the fact that

comparison is limited as a result of differences in underlying principles, differences in technology used, as well as context and content-dependent solutions.

This gives rise to an important risk factor in the efficiency and effectiveness of the design process. The concept of instructional design should, therefore, at least be regarded as a complex system (Tennyson 1997; Koschmann *et al.* 1994). Strengthening the involvement of the user and his/her knowledge can set off this uncertainty in the design process. Two major perspectives can be distinguished in recent developments which define a more principled approach for designing learning applications: organising in phases and focus on usability.

A common approach underlies many instructional design models: the solution of an instructional design problem is usually characterised by a number of phases (Dijkstra & Merrienboer 1997; Goodyear 1997). Smith and Mayes (1995) take the following planning phases into account:

- Identification of user needs: user requirement analyses;
- Definition of the functional specifications;
- Building of the demonstrator;
- Verification and validation of the demonstrator;
- Implementation and exploitation.

During the phases, several formative evaluations take place in order to optimise the instruction developed. Although the phased developmental process guides the designer in his design process, it does not support the designer in his redesign issues; what criteria should be used in order to make the learning environment more efficient or effective?

Based on the evaluation of the DELTA programme, a research programme of the European Union on the use of telematic applications for education in the beginning of the nineties (cf. Chapter 1), a usability guide was developed by Smith and Mayes (1995). Usability was recognised as a vital determining factor in the success of any new learning technology. They found out that designing highly usable applications requires an intimate knowledge of its users and their activities, and constant redesigning and testing to ensure user needs are met. Usability engineering is concerned with:

- user involvement throughout;
- iterative design;

- usability testing;
- usability treated alongside functionality.

Rip, Misa and Schot (1995) and Jacobs (1996) give another reason why involvement of users, teachers is a key factor for success. Especially in situations when the role of technology is not restricted to 'doing the same things with different means' but 'when things may be done in different ways', it is difficult to grasp the user requirements. Investigations show (Jacobs 1996) that the unfamiliarity of users with the new services and products and, as a consequence, a changed learning situation, inhibits users when they are stating their needs. This requires a different approach for the detailed design. Building examples of major system functions and having them tested by students and staff provides feedback on the usability and can guide the further design of the system. Rapid prototyping is becoming a dominant mode of design and development, but it is still often restricted to the interface aspects, especially the 'look and feel' of the system instead of the testing of major system functionality and its effectiveness. The involvement of users serves more objectives: it also ensures the integration of (user) expertise and it creates a consensus for a new, redesigned, learning process.

Koschmann (1994) argues that from its inception the design should be provided with a model of learning and instruction and that the designer should be able to articulate these educational considerations from the earliest stages of the design. He proposes a four-step principled approach to the design of computer support for collaborative learning:

- making explicit the instructional requirements that serve as design goals for the project;
- performing a detailed study of current educational practice with regard to these tools;
- developing a specification based on the identified requirements/limitations of the instructional setting and the known capabilities of the technology, and
- producing an implementation that allows for local adaptation to instructional practice.

Integrating the first three steps of the principled approach of Koschmann in the user requirement phase as mentioned before, provides the designer with more information on the why and how of changes in the learning environment. While the requirement that allows local adaptation provides the user with the possibilities to adapt the tool to individual needs.

Key Factors for Success

It will be clear that research on instructional design and educational technology has a long history. Many publications and research programmes have focused on how to develop effective and efficient educational technology in teaching and learning. However, the results of this research as presented in the preceding paragraph are difficult to apply in day-to-day educational practice. At present many tutors and information technologists have become actively engaged in designing and developing innovative applications for the curricula of their own schools and faculties. Tutors and technologist have taken up the challenge to try to integrate ICT in their curricula, however limited their prior knowledge may be. Despite their goodwill and hard work they are often faced with considerable problems. These problems can be categorised as follows:

Need for multi-disciplinary development teams Designing applications and tools for teaching and learning require a knowledge of pedagogy, technology and the design of applications as well as user interfaces. Although it is possible to support regular staff in gaining a better understanding of the factors involved in the realisation of a successful application, it requires substantial investments. And staff are often only temporarily involved in projects that concern the development of educational applications. When the project is finished they usually return to their regular activities and the knowledge gained during the developmental process becomes dormant. Coopers and Lybrand (1996) found in their review of the TLTP programme, that multidisciplinary teams more often designed innovative applications in contrast to teams that took a more mono-disciplinary project approach. If a structural approach to educational innovation with technology is to be considered, staff must be supported by multi-disciplinary development teams.

Need for user involvement Although it is often well known to staff and technologists that user involvement from the start improves the project results, the involvement is often restricted to the level of testing the applications. This is often a consequence of the fact that in many educational institutions students are not involved in the quality cycle of improving the curricula and their instructional setting. This inhibits the willingness of staff to involve students in the developmental process. The impact of this weak user-involvement is less (Egyedi, this volume, chapter 11) when the instructional setting is mainly tutor-controlled, as in an electronic testing environment or when interactive courseware is used. But when the application is mainly concerned with supporting the activities of the learner a strong user-involvement is essential. The earlier-mentioned phased project approach enforces the theory that major issues are indeed taken into account during the developmental process. As each phase is concluded with a report, an extra stimulus is provided to create opportunities for feedback from experts, users and stakeholders. It cannot be too strongly stressed that prototyping provides a very reliable instrument for obtaining feedback from the users themselves. And finally, developing a system isolated from the organisational and cultural habits of the educational organisation, might result in low acceptance by teachers and students when implementation starts. Involving staff and students in the developmental process favours adaptation of the design to the 'couleur locale' and stimulates a positive attitude and willingness of staff and students to f the new learning approach.

Need for design guidelines   The state-of-the-art of the instructional design theory is not yet able to provide the guidelines that guide designers through their design decisions in such a way that enables them to come up with the most effective solution. The different perspectives of experts on how learning takes place, the complexity of the issues involved in what learning is about, the domain specific features as well as the mental models of those involved in the design process, are reflected in the outcomes of a design process. This leads to a situation in which the redesign of a specific instructional setting can result in a broad spectrum of different educational technology solutions. As a consequence we see that organisations are trying to look for best practices as examples to guide and accelerate the design process for their own organisations (Committ 1996). But it must not be forgotten that it is difficult to assess whether the added value of a learning tool from elsewhere has the same impact in another daily educational practice. This means that in addition to the best-practice results from elsewhere a heavy investment must still be made in the design process and the analysis of the user requirements in order to realise an effective application in one's own situation. Adopting a phased development process increases the chance that sufficient attention will be paid to the usability aspects. In addition to this approach 'best practices' can be used as an excellent tool to support users in making their user requirements more explicit.

With respect to the design process of learning environments, as mentioned previously, there has been no experience and no additional guidelines exist. It is expected that, in the coming period, exploratory research will take place to try to get a grip on how to design learning environments that meet the requirements of the learners. One interesting option will be to see if applying techniques from business process re-engineering to the design and management of learning environments will increase the pace of developments.

Need for staff development Bringing technology into the curricula has an impact on both learners and teachers. Even in traditional teacher-oriented learning environments the possibilities of communication between peers and between peers and their tutor often results in adding some interaction flavour to applications that are content oriented. However, these small changes already change the position of the tutor and place more control in the hands of the learner. In higher education pedagogy is often part of an implicit process, where individual teachers and their prior knowledge are major components. Changes in this educational setting from a teacher-controlled to a more student-controlled learning process requires explicitness and change management. Staff development is essential in realising the innovation of education in the long run. This means not only installing supporting resources, but also the development of a reward system that favours active the participation of staff in innovation of the curricula.

Need for an evaluation framework Until now programmes at national and institutional levels that provide additional funding, have been the motor for stimulating the information technology innovations in the curricula. This resulted in an exploration phase in which a large number of staff and students became involved in learning and grasping the potentials of ICT to innovate teaching and learning situations. Many expect that the results will provide guidance to a more strategic approach to the integration of technology in teaching and learning in the long run (Eurelings *et al.* 1998). However, this assumes that individual project results can be transformed to other situations. Goodyear (1998) states that the lack of an appropriate framework for organising our thinking about what we are trying to achieve, and our lack of reflection on our progress, poses a major obstacle to the systematic sharing of experiences. Learning from each other requires an appropriate intellectual framework against which we can structure our experiences and render them mutually intelligible. A clear perspective must be developed concerning the major evaluation issues that need to be taken into account in order to provide useful information that can be adopted by stakeholders. Project reviews in literature never use the same format, blueprints for evaluation seem to be lacking. Although a number if evaluation models exist, each often cover only a part of what we need. Until now ICT-based educational innovation does not provide us with data on how we might engage in the complex, co-ordinated work activity which is entailed in designing and managing a learning environment in a systematic way.

Continuing the Innovation Process

Impediments to Technological Innovation

Observations show that the progress of the introduction of technology in education is rather slow. Overall agreement exists on the reasons for this relatively slow developing process (WTR 1995):

- Staff does not really need technology to provide education, only in certain domain specific areas are ICT applications needed to meet the skills requirements of end-terms of the curriculum.
- The technical infrastructure is often still insufficient or not stable enough. The number of computers per student at the institutes as well as at home is not enough to expect that students can work with computers every day. With respect to applications that require electronic communication facilities, it is even worse; primary and secondary education hardly have access to networked computers, and in higher education, student access from the home environment is still limited. In general, higher education is definitely ahead of primary and secondary education.
- Information technology facilitates learning situations that give more control to students. However, at present, control of the learning process of students often rests in the hands of the teacher. Although many institutions have already indicated a willingness to realise this paradigm shift, in practice, limited resources and insufficient knowledge often hinder this educational transformation.

- Limited knowledge exists on the relationship between instruction, learning and learning technologies. Although there are many research results, they are strongly locally coloured and therefore difficult to transfer to a different educational setting.
- Integrating technology in the curriculum requires substantial efforts in terms of human resources and equipment. At present national and/or institutional programmes provide the necessary financial means. However, hardly no institutions have made structural funds available for the future, while other incentives for innovation are lacking.

What does this mean? Can we expect that the process of introducing technology into the curriculum will slow down even more in the coming period? In his article on 'Understanding the innovation process' Goodyear argues that the colossal sum of £1 billion a year is being spent on ICT in the UK, without any clear or convincing educational rationale. Only few universities have an overarching ICT strategy which firmly links ICT investment to institutional goals (NCIHE 1997) and it seems as if education is buying and using ICT because it is there and because related areas of activity outside education are buying it. Are we entering a new phase of technological innovation of teaching and learning? A new phase that perhaps needs more detailed objectives, other stimuli and different organisational measures, or one that will be supported by forces outside of education?

Conclusions

In the nineties, many experiments and projects took place to research what can be expected of the integration of information and communication technology for teaching and learning. Although evaluation can only answer this question in a descriptive and qualitative way, it has become clear that learning applications seem to favour active learning behaviour and promote the development of skills that will be needed in the future.

I expect that the barriers to the implementation progress as, mentioned above, will be overcome in due time. The speed with which ICT/MM becomes more and more visible in society, as part of existing products and services or as new services, will also act as a driving force behind its involvement of education. Soon, incoming students acquainted with ICT and well provided with the required infrastructure, will demand that education uses these tools for teaching and learning. This development will promote technology enhanced learning as a competitive issue for the teaching and learning market, where not only regular education but also electronic global newcomers will be providers.

However, this still leaves us with the problem of how to develop technology enhanced curricula that meet the user needs in an efficient and effective way. I see two important challenges for those involved in the research and implementation of learning technologies:

- The educational technology research community will have to take up the challenge of defining an appropriate intellectual framework against which the community and the implementers can structure and exchange their experiences. Developments in cognitive science, the principled approach as defined earlier, and strong user involvement are expected to have a positive impact on the effectiveness of the design process.
- The development process of learning technology applications should use a design-cycle approach with a strong accent on assessment, to ensure that an ongoing process of improvement will take place.

These challenges will not result in concrete guidelines in the short term, however I expect that the new generation of software tools that help teachers to develop learning environments and pedagogically informed learning tools will have a positive impact on the willingness of teachers to become engaged in rethinking education.

Note

1   There is an interesting merging of defining concepts in pedagogy and in the theoretical framework to be developed in chapter 3. Both pedagogy and the sociology of technology use the concept of social constructivism. The reader will easily differentiate by means of the context which of both tems is to be applied.

3 Social Learning

MARC VAN LIESHOUT, WIEBE E. BIJKER,
TINEKE M. EGYEDI

Abstract

In this chapter a theoretical framework is developed for the study of the societal introduction of educational multimedia. It is argued that a change in perspective on what precisely constitutes this introduction will support a better understanding of the perceived processes of change. Social studies of technologies have proved to be useful as explanatory framework for how processes of (socio-technical) change can be understood. A short introduction in the basics of these theories (under the heading of "social shaping of technology") is followed by the development of an evaluation framework for a proper analysis of the introduction of educational multimedia. *Innofusion* is the leading concept to cover this introduction process. This concept is heading a framework that entails three – mutually interchangeable – concepts: *appropriation, configuration* and *translation*. Then, we elaborate upon the concept of *social learning*. We introduce two interpretations of social learning: an analytical interpretation (that builds upon the social shaping approach) and an action-oriented or pro-active interpretation (that is related to *constructive technology assessment*). We introduce two empirical manifestations of social learning: the *mode of experimentation* and the *mode of control*. Having analysed the respective cases with respect to the presence of both modes, we pay attention to the identification of success and failure, and to the constitutive elements of good practices.

Introduction

The introduction of multimedia in education falls short on expectations. Educational multimedia (and ICT in more general) qualify for a quantum jump in teaching and learning. The potential of educational multimedia is however only marginally realised. Factors that contribute to the gap

37

between promises and reality have been identified in the preceding chapter, with emphasis on the learning process. In this chapter we continue the search for good educational practices surrounding the introduction of multimedia by turning to the technology at stake. Key issue is the concept of 'social learning', building upon two traditions of thought. The first is the social shaping approach in social studies of technology. The second is the sociological analysis of modern societies, particularly as presented in the work of authors such as Ulrich Beck and Anthony Giddens.

The social shaping approach grew out of a critical assessment, by historians and sociologists of technology, of accounts of technical development in society as these were predominant in the 1960s and 1970s and mainly entertained by economists. These economists understood technological innovation as bringing new artefacts to the market. The market was the central unit of analysis, while the artefact itself remained immune to further investigation – technology was an exogenous variable. Evolutionary economics[1] and social studies of technology then took up technology as an endogenous variable. The sociologically inspired models first took the artefact as their unit of analysis, and studied how it was socially constructed. The constructivists then proceeded to question a priori distinctions between social and technical aspects of change, and moved on to more heterogeneous units of analysis: socio-technical systems, networks or ensembles.

The second root of 'social learning' is in the concept of 'reflexivity' as coined by Beck (Beck 1992; orig. 1986) and Giddens (Giddens 1990). They both argue that social practices are inherently reflexively ordered and organised. Analysing social practices might thus focus on the role of reflexivity in shaping these practices. We take up the challenge to explore the fruitfulness of this assumption in analysing the introduction of new technologies. We do so by adding one element to the social shaping of technology approach: the reflexivity of social practices. This leads to a crucial refinement of the perspective of social shaping of technology.

Though the concept of social learning does not directly relate to general notions of learning and to developments in the educational sector (as discussed in the preceding chapter), it is obvious that social learning and learning are related to each other. After the concept of social learning is introduced we explore this relationship in more depth.

We proceed by briefly discussing the limitations of the traditional view of technology, and then continue to introduce the social shaping approach. The fourth section summarises our social shaping framework in four key concepts. Then we connect this analysis with the work of Giddens and

Beck, and finally present the social learning framework by identifying distinct modes of social learning.

Innovation and Diffusion: The Standard Image of Technology

Traditional innovation theories highlight the developmental process of artefacts as a sequence of spatio-temporally ordered events in which a number of separate phases can be identified: an *invention* is subsequently transformed in an *innovation* that is *diffused* under users who *implement* the innovation (artefacts) in their daily practices. These innovation theories originate from classical economic approaches in which analyses in terms of product-life cycles give developments a kind of 'natural trajectory': a *promising technology* is brought to the market; then, *product innovations* improve ('mature') the product while increasing its market potential; when saturation of market share is reached, *process innovations* contribute to efficiency procedures that enable a steady though declining growth in market share. Finally, the decline and withdrawal of the (improved) product has become inevitable and the product will be replaced in due time by a new product based on other technological core elements (Freeman & Perez 1988). The model is refined for the cycle we experience today (the information-communication cycle) in an alteration of the subsequent phases, but the spatio-temporal characteristics of the life-cycle remain the same (Barras 1990).

Instead of analysing isolated technologies one could also look at clusters of innovation. Schumpeter analysed the emergence of new technologies in different eras and came to the conclusion that each era could be identified by a key technology (in the previous era this was oil/energy, in the contemporary cycle this is the microchip/information) that satisfied a specific set of criteria (decreasing cost-performance characteristics, universal availability, universal applicability) and that led to a class of related technological systems in various social settings (Freeman & Perez 1988, pp. 48ff). As an illustration we could point at the key technology of the present situation: the microchip, that indeed has universal availability and universal applicability, and that still exhibits a growing performance at reduced prices. The cluster of related technological innovations is not very difficult to find either, be it in digitisation of artefacts or in the combined infrastructural and service innovations (customised services like tele-learning on newly developed information infrastructures like the Internet). The transformation from one cluster of innovations to the next one is characterised by what Schumpeter called 'creative gales of destruction': the old is destroyed in order to make place for the new and unknown.

However interesting in themselves, these economically inspired models do not allow for a detailed understanding of processes of technological change. These models focus too much on the macro-level, and reveal trends and patterns on a high level of aggregation. They take the artefact – or cluster of related innovations – as starting point for their analysis. The models that have tried to overcome the rather straightforward modelling of innovation and diffusion patterns (as if both are strictly time-ordered events) have contributed to a better understanding of how processes of innovation and diffusion evolve. These models are known as the evolutionary (or: quasi-evolutionary) models since they explain innovation and diffusion patterns as a process of variation and selection (Nelson & Winter 1977; Dosi 1982). In these models diffusion channels relate innovation practices to the selection environment by way of a nexus. This nexus enables the flow of information about the selection environment to the locus of innovation. Variation of an artefact is thus influenced by *a priori* knowledge about the selection environment. But within these quasi-evolutionary models ('quasi' because variations are not at random, but are structured by knowledge about the selection environment) 'innovation' and 'diffusion' remain distinct concepts.

Another problematic element of economically grounded models of change is that they take successful innovations for granted, or rather: they do not ask the question of success and failure. These models are based on the presupposition that the dynamics of demand and supply will eventually determine which products survive and which do not. Knowing these dynamics reveals which practices will be successful and which will not. Under the condition of perfect transparency (in price-performance characteristics) the market organises the diffusion process itself in a manner that leads to the most satisfactory choices. Though this approach has some explanatory power, it leads to unsatisfactory accounts. It is especially difficult to explain failures of (presumably) technically sophisticated innovations, like the Stirling engine, or the Philips V2000 system, and to explain the success of (presumably) technically inferior products like the DOS operating system in personal computers. An extra complicating aspect of contemporary processes is the speed of technological change itself, resulting in new versions of products before the previous versions have reached market saturation. The very notion of success itself thus has become ambiguous and needs to be better understood if we want a better management of innovations and projects.

Social Shaping of Technology

The need for a different conceptual apparatus to explain and understand processes of technological change has led to a variety of sociologically inspired models. The models have yielded new insights in how technological change processes can be addressed best. They start by questioning the separate status of technology *per se*. Technology, artefacts, technological systems and so forth are part of the social world. This enables an approach of technology as social phenomenon that is intrinsically linked to all other kinds of social phenomena. So, instead of presuming artefacts to be isolated entities within a social environment, these perspectives view technology as being a non-distinguishable part of reality.

The phrase 'social shaping of technology' was coined by the agenda-setting volume edited by Donald MacKenzie and Judy Wajcman (1985). The first more precise formulation in the form of a broad research programme it received in 1987 (Bijker, Hughes & Pinch 1987). Three different theoretical approaches were then distinguished – the systems approach, the social construction of technology (SCOT), and the actor-network theory.[2] In this study we remain closest to the SCOT-approach (incidentally we 'hire' concepts from actor-network theory). For our purposes, we can summarize the common theoretical base of SCOT as this has evolved in the past decade in the following four characteristics.

- Technology can be studied as a social phenomenon. To do this, the social study of technology focuses on the meanings attributed to technological practices by the various relevant social groups.
- The description of a technology through the eyes of different social groups results in demonstrating this technology's interpretative flexibility: there is not one technology, there are many.
- The analysis should be symmetrical with respect to success or failure. We are not interested in success or failure per se, but in how technologies are defined into being successful or failing. Success and failure are to be explained by the same conceptual framework.
- The working of a technology thus is not an intrinsic property of that technology, but socially constructed in specific practices.

To illustrate the general requirements that form the kernel of theories about the social shaping of technology, the introduction of computers in a classroom offers a good example. In an economically inspired approach it could be argued that introduction of computers in a classroom is the result of demand and supply characteristics, whereas the computer itself is perceived as an innovation to be introduced in the teaching practice. It is an innovative tool for the teacher, and can be used for all kind of educational purposes. Success could be defined as the selling of the computer. Adopting the social shaping perspective changes the picture. The computer gets a very specific meaning in the classroom. It is part of the social practice of the educational setting. The computer is e.g. purchased since it may be used for remedial teaching. The meaning attributed to the computer will then be related to the ideas about remedial teaching. How the teacher perceives the computer is depended on the teacher's own presuppositions, thoughts and experiences with remedial teaching and of course with computers. He might feel threatened because part of his experience and knowledge is supposedly transferred into a machine. He also might feel threatened now he is pushed into the educational format that is put forward by the software on the computer. Or he is delighted since the computer enhances his status within the school. Or he feels delighted now the computer offers opportunities to experiment with methods that are difficult to exploit without this extra teaching aid. One and the same computer thus gives rise to a variety of interpretations, depending on the specific circumstances of the actor who imposes his (or her) meaning on the machine. Whether the introduction of the computer is (eventually) perceived as a success or a failure is not clear at beforehand. The notion of success or failure itself depends on expectations that the actors have of the teaching aid. Their expectations constrain their notion of success or failure. When the computer is rarely used, this may be called a success by those who reject these 'alienating teaching tools' while those who embrace the machines will call the abstinence of use a failure, and vice versa. The school board might have a quite different 'definition' of success: it might declare the introduction a success when, for instance, more than half of the teachers use the computer in classroom situations.

So, responsible actors (teachers, parents, students, the school administration, etc.) will negotiate the meaning of the computer in the educational context. This negotiation comprises social and technical factors alike. The impossibility to discriminate *a priori* between social and technical aspects of this specific socio-technical constituency (i.e. the introduction and use of and attribution of meanings to the computer in the educational context) is explicated in the metaphor of the *seamless web*. The seamless web stands for a web of relations that connects all constitutive elements without further differentiation. It draws attention to how these constituent elements within a process of socio-technical change relate to each other. Processes of change are identified by changing relations within the web. There may be a process of 'hardening' specific relations, by which specific meanings become (at least temporarily) fixed. The result of these processes of stabilisation, closure or hardening (three concepts that relate to the same phenomenon) may be that a technical artefact or system gets a very specific meaning in a specific setting that is subsequently difficult to change.

We illustrate the combined socio-technical characteristics with the on-going debate about learning strategies and cognitive theories and the role of ICT within these strategies and theories. These debates determine (at least partly) how computers in educational settings are perceived: are they merely educational tools that may be used in the context of drill and practice exercises, or are they to be perceived as essential elements in learning students how to learn (recall the distinction made in chapter two between 'learning with ICT' and 'learning through ICT')? The pedagogical elements, together with the technical specifications of the configuration, form the socio-technical constituency that is introduced and that form the kernel of a web of manifold relations. Since these configurations are embedded in change processes themselves (i.e. the learning environment of a school that experiences continuous updating and adaptation) the configurations may become entrenched within the school system (i.e. get a specific meaning/function). These processes of change may lead to a very specific meaning of e.g. educational software (for instance that it is perfectly suitable for remedial teaching but that it should not be used in classroom situations). It might be that, when these fixed meanings have crystallised ('hardened' or 'stabilised'), and no matter whether these crystallisation's are perceived as rational or 'irrational', it becomes increasingly difficult to alter the practice of use, since new releases might be interpreted with the old software in mind.

These examples hopefully raise awareness for the specifics of this approach: we need a more integrating perspective when analysing processes of socio-technical change. If we are to understand the specifics of successful introductions of educational tools, we simply must take more into account than the mere technology that is at stake, or its price-performance characteristics. We need more sophisticated approaches. We have to re-construct the process of technology-in-the-making. In this reconstruction we have to be aware of a number of theoretical and methodological constraints in order to make our approach valid. Most of these constraints have been addressed in the foregoing. To summarise them once more:

- there is no *a priori* demarcation between 'technological' events and 'social' events, as if both relate to distinct domains of reality; technology-in-the-making should be seen as a social practice;
- within this social practice, there are many relations to discern; they span up a seamless web of relations; technology-in-the-making is not a deterministic or causal process;
- we must be able to explain change as well as continuity; when all remains the same, it must be able to understand why; when situations suddenly change it must be able to explain this change as well;
- success and failure must be explained in a symmetrical way; we must remain unbiased vis-à-vis whether a development will be signified as a successful one or whether it will be signified as a failure.

Framework to Analyse the Processes of Change

We now address the concepts that together form the core of a heuristic framework that guides our analysis of the respective cases. The concepts we present are general concepts, i.e. they are not specifically developed for the educational field. We start with an overall concept: *innofusion* (Fleck 1988). This concept stands for the combination of innovation and diffusion practices. Innofusion is a very useful concept within the context of our study, since it enables a comprehensive analysis of change processes that are usually addressed as distinct spatio-temporal practices, namely innovation and diffusion. By combining these practices in one, it enables a more encompassing approach of a socio-technical practice. We consider innofusion to consist of three distinct concepts: *appropriation*, *configuration* and *translation*. These three concepts form the kernel of our approach, and combine different perspectives on social shaping in one heuristic framework. We start with discussing the appropriation of a socio-technical practice, for instance the appropriation of a multi-media learning environment. User innovation is a very important characteristic of appropriation. In the process of appropriation the innovation itself may be adapted to 'local circumstances'. We continue with a concept that emphasises the other side of the coin: configuring the user. In developing multimedia, it is (usually) hoped that the user uses the product in the way as envisaged by the designer. In order to facilitate this, users are configured, i.e. they are enforced to follow the (mostly implicit) guidelines that are embedded in the design of the practice. The third concept is translation: a specific practice is transformed into another one. This translation may be rhetorically (by changing problem definitions), it may be literally (by changing words) or physically (by replacing objects).

Innofusion

Detailed studies of the construction of socio-technical practices have shown that the previously used demarcation between the process of innovation and the process of diffusion does not hold (cf. for instance (Bijker 1995) for a classical study of the development of the bicycle). Though innovation activities and diffusion activities can be demonstrated in the spread of educational multimedia, they can not be isolated from each other. The usual demarcation between a process of innovation, including a demarcated *locus* of innovation and a specific group of innovators, and a process of diffusion, including a *channel* of diffusion and specific diffusion characteristics, does not lead to an accurate description of practices that we experience. For one, processes of innovation continue during the process of diffusion. The user may be involved in changing the design of an artefact or changing the rules of use of an artefact. The user also may reject or withhold specific forms of using. A famous example of ongoing innovations during the stage of diffusion is provided by the introduction of a new telecom service in France, called Minitel. Minitel is the user-terminal that gives access to the Télétel-network. Minitel was dispersed for free. The telephone directory was to be replaced by an electronic directory that was available on the Télétel-network. So, it was launched as an information network, that enabled all French subscribers to search for phone numbers and for information that was put on the network (like information about public transport, etc.). The success of Minitel (as the entire network became popularly known) however, only started when some users innovated the network by using the network protocols in order to *communicate* with each other. They created small user-groups that could 'chat' with each other. This user-led innovation was quickly spread over the network and led to the emergence of a variety of 'chatboxes'. It opened the way to all kind of commercial services (including the well-known 'messagerie rose'). This process – in which innovation and diffusion aspects are indistinguishably intertwined – is best described as a process of *innofusion* (Fleck 1988). User innovation, which implies the open-endedness of a technical design, is fundamental to innofusion. On-going innovations alter the imposed *script* of a design, alter its meaning, transform its forms of use, and sometimes transform its physical appearance.

Appropriation

One perspective on the process of innofusion is the manner in which users *appropriate* a specific practice. Literally, this appropriation means that the user becomes the owner (in mental or in financial terms) of a specific practice. Buying a computer, or buying a CD-ROM that entails educational courseware, could be seen as a form of appropriating the commodity. But appropriation is a more encompassing concept. In order to familiarise a tool, or to familiarise with a practice, a novice has to gain skills, experience and knowledge about how and when to use a tool. Like in a play, a user has to become familiar with the *script* that is basic to the specific practice. But contrary to a play, the script can be adapted, it can be localised. The adoption of an artefact (for instance the adoption of a teaching aid containing spelling exercises, or the adoption of an ATM-network to transport real time video images) may lead to adaptation of the teaching practice to encapsulate norms and values of the new situation (it may lead to another style of teaching). This may infer that physical properties of the artefact change, it may be that the rules of use – and of non-use – will be accommodated. Sometimes, elements to be accommodated are prescribed in the artefact (like facilities as 'calling line identification' in modern telephone equipment to which users may 'opt in' or 'opt out'), sometimes local characteristics enable specific uses (like the answering machine that in the American situation became a machine to control entrance to the private sphere of the home). Some argue that this process of appropriation is as if the technologically determined and defined apparatus (a computer, or a multimedia course), must be 'tamed' to the local circumstances in which it will be used (must be domesticated) (Lie & Sørensen 1996). Styles of appropriation differ between different situations. They no doubt are culturally laden, and are inscribed with local norms and values.

Configuration

The process of appropriation is influenced by scripts that are embedded in the artefact or practice and that stem from the design process. Designers try to *configure the user* by their design. The artefact or practice is pre-structured by designers. Designers embed norms and values, knowledge and experiences into the design. Specific uses are preconceived, for instance through articulation of user requirements. These user requirements encompass rules to be followed, they promote specific user behaviour. They configure the user. Sometimes designers use formal models to design a tool, or artefact or practice, like prototyping. These models themselves reflect norms and values, knowledge and experience. They may be formulated in general terms, like the requirement of platform independence, or they may be very specific, and constrain uses to specific settings.

With respect to multimedia this configuring process is very difficult. The variables to be constrained are numerous. In the preceding chapter, for instance, it was mentioned that an ICT-based educational environment may be either filled or empty, rich or limited, teacher centred or student centred, and individual or group based. All these constraints add up to gross variety in configurational choices. The kind of uses that evolve around these educational tools or practices is *a priori* unpredictable. Standardisation is one of the means that designers may strive for to enframe new products. In an interesting study Woolgar shows how this process of configuring the user evolves (Woolgar 1991). His study relates to the design of a PC. The configuration of a PC is of course crucial to how it will be used, and whether users will judge its use satisfactory. Users communicate with a PC through the user interface. This interface embeds a myriad of design choices. Woolgar shows how the designers try to implement their notions of the 'ideal' user into the design.

Woolgar's study has been influential in getting the problem of design into the study of socio-technical practices. Woolgar revealed an interesting aspect, that he however did not identify as such. He drew attention to the meanings that designers attribute to the user. By this process, laden with both interpretations and organisational aspects as internal ranking of designers, 'the' user is configured. This gives rise to the apparent paradox that by focusing on a design strategy that incorporates *the* user, no user at all is configured. Consumer related studies have shown the variety in user behaviour and in diversity of users. Categorisation of users according to different sets of user characteristics have not been very convincing. It is very difficult to identify mutually independent variables (like age, education, gender) that may lead to a typology of users. Designers face a *dilemma of design*: making a customised and personalised design implies a myriad of possible design strategies and solutions; making only one design implies loosing sight on the – heterogeneously constituted – user (cf. Lieshout 1998, p. 5). Woolgar demonstrates in his study that it is typically the last strategy that is at work: designers use some kind of an ideal-type of user (that is based on personal preferences and styles) and use this ideal-typical user as model for configuring the tool or artefact or practice they are working at.

In educational practices this design dilemma is evident. Differentiation between 'classes' of users is necessary in order to make educational tools useful. But this implies that designers must be aware of the kind of users they are going to configure in their tools, artefacts or practices. And this presupposes knowledge of or insight into these distinct classes.

Translation

A final concept that we want to put forward as element of our approach is the concept 'translation'. This concept has its roots in studies of Latour in which he identified processes of translation (Latour 1987). Latour identifies several processes of translation, i.e. ways in which original intentions or objectives are redirected in order to gain impact. Though this seems as if processes of translation are conscious activities that need conscious actants to activate them, this is not what Latour thinks.

Latour identifies several forms of translation that all relate to attempts to re-direct existing networks in the way that is most desired by the translator. It may be by re-defining the objectives of the tool or practice, by trying to change the perceived needs of the users, by trying to turn the tool or artefact into an obligatory element for the user. All these forms are translations of meanings. For our purposes the translation of a PC into a multimedia-PC may be identified as a form of translation that Latour points at. The translations may have physical elements as well. The multimedia-PC, for instance, may have a CD-drive installed. It may also be equipped with a modem. Both physical extensions translate the meaning of the former PC into a device that is communicative, interactive and multimedia-based.

Another strong use of translation is the use of metaphors (Lieshout 1998). A metaphor translates the meaning of one concept into the meaning of another concept. A metaphor can be used to raise awareness for new phenomena: by means of the metaphor the meaning of the new phenomenon can be made better understandable. A metaphor triggers specific ways of thinking about its content, and contributes to smoothen the uptake of new concepts. Since the metaphor 'stands for' something else, there is always a chance of mismatch between the metaphor and the phenomenon it stands for: it is a form of translation that is based on a script that prescribes how the translation must be performed. This is not without problems, since this prescription can not be unambiguous either (otherwise there would be no need for a separate concept). The metaphor of the 'electronic highway' is a typical example of the strength of using a metaphor for guding processes of change.

Once More: Innofusion

The three concepts, introduced in the foregoing subsections, all enable a description of the innofusion process. The use of only one of three would suffice to describe the development of the innofusion process. Each concept, however, emphasises a different aspect of the change process, regarding the actors involved, the time frame and the kind of processes involved. Together they add up to a comprehensive analysis of the process of change in which parts of the analysis overlap. By this they enable a broader understanding of the dynamics that give rise to the process of change. We postpone further elaboration of the three concepts (and specifically how they relate to actors involved, to the time frame of the innofusion process and to the kind of processes they highlight) until chapter 12.

Social Learning: Reflecting on Social Shaping

In this section we proceed from the perspective of innofusion to the perspective of social learning. We follow Ulrich Beck and Anthony Giddens in their analysis of modern practices as *reflexive* practices; the dynamics of science and technology have given rise to an organisation of modern society that is inherently reflexive, i.e. that is characterised by a permanent process of evaluation, monitoring and feedback, consciously and unconsciously. *Social learning* is introduced as concept to cover the specifics of an analysis of reflexivity within contemporary socio-technical practices. The notion of *social learning* has an intuitive appeal. It builds on the key role of learning and education in modern society, expressed by phrases such as 'learning society', 'learning economy' and 'education permanente'. We will then stipulate the similarities and differences between the more general concept of learning and the concept of social learning. They both relate to learning, but they not necessarily share the – intuitive as well as conceptually grounded – meaning of learning. Finally, social learning is deconstructed into two dominant modes: the *mode of experimentation* and the *mode of control*. These modes are ideal-typical manifestations from social learning in practice. Both modes form extremes on a scale that relates the various dimensions of both modes to each other. We finally argue that a balance between both modes is needed in order to realise optimal benefits from the on-going changes.

Reflexive Modernisation

In his seminal work 'Risk society: towards a new modernity' (first published in Germany in 1986) Ulrich Beck takes a systemic position towards the organisation of scientific and technological knowledge. Contrary to philosophers who proclaim the end of ideology and the end of modernism, Beck assumed that present-day changes should be perceived as inherently related to the dynamics of scientific change. Basically, these dynamics have not changed since the inception in what is usually called the programme of Enlightenment: human race would profit from the benefits of a rational response to Nature and Culture; progress in scientific knowledge would enable progress in society. While in the past decades various scientific thinkers proclaimed the end of the dominance of scientific thought within the organisation of society (due to social problems like environmental degradation in combination with internal quarrels about the validity of scientific truth claims), Beck took a different route and came to the conclusion that the internal 'rules of the games' of science still hold. He did not deny that science was in a crisis. In his view, there was a crisis in science, that nonetheless provided the means itself to overcome this (socially and epistemologically rooted) crisis: 'Not only does the industrial utilisation of scientific results create problems; science also provides the means (...) to recognise and present the problems *as* problems at all, or just not to do so. Finally, science also provides the prerequisites for "over-coming" the threats for which it is responsible itself.' (Beck 1992, p. 163). It does so, because scientific activity may become the object of scientific scrutiny, just like any other societal activity. This in itself leads to dismantling scientific 'upholds', attempts to cover socially problematic results (like environmental degradation, due to overusing pesticides, or 'side-effects' of the Green Revolution like increasing dependency of indigenous population due to the introduction of yield mono-cultures) that resulted from scientific interference with social domains. Scientific scrutiny is recursively applied to science, thus yielding an internal dynamics to science that provides for legitimisation of scientific activities for years to come. This is not meant to be cynical, but only to point at the internal dynamics of science that promote a self-conscious and critical attitude towards outcomes of scientific activities. This is also not to imply that for instance nuclear scientists will perform a critical analysis of nuclear waste disposal in order to internally criticise their own efforts. The differentiation within science leads to differentiation of criticism as well. Scientific expertise is not limited to the constraints of the scientific laboratories any more, but is embedded in a wide variety of societal practices. The recursive application of scientific criticism to methods and results of scientific activities gives science an inherently reflexive aspect. From the outside, this reflection may be seen as intrinsically linked with science itself. From the inside, it is a differentiated and dispersed process.

Anthony Giddens takes a somewhat different perspective. He presents a sociological perspective on the organisation of modernity. For Giddens, modernity is based on features that are distinct from previous cultures. What must be shown, or developed, is the mechanisms and processes that contributed to the organisation of modernity. It is in this respect that Giddens emphasises the space-time distanciation as one of the characteristics of modernity. Giddens formulates the question of order (i.e. that which binds a society) as 'a problem of how it comes about that social systems "bind" time and space. The problem of order is here seen as one of *time-space distanciation* – the conditions under which time and space are organised so as to connect presence and absence' (Giddens 1990, p. 14). According to Giddens 'The dynamism of modernity derives from the *separation of time and space* and their recombination in forms which permit the precise time-space "zoning" of social life; the *disembedding* of social systems (a phenomenon which connects closely with the factors involved in time-space separation); and the *reflexive ordering and reordering* of social relations in the light of continual inputs of knowledge affecting the actions of individuals and groups' (Giddens 1990, pp. 16-17).

Just like Beck, Giddens points at the build-in reflexivity in societal activities.[3] Giddens adds to this reflexive element that social sciences have contributed to a better understanding of social processes but at the same time (might) have influenced the organisation of these processes by introducing the knowledge about these processes into society (a phenomenon usually termed *double hermeneutics*). This built-in reflexivity has become part of the embedded mechanisms of society as well, and has led to institutionalised reflexive practices that are based on scientific knowledge related to method and theory (what and how) to organise and structure social activities.

Both writers address contemporary processes of change within society on a high level of aggregation. Their approach is one way to bridge the gap between detailed studies of how projects and experiments find their place, and addressing the broader trends that form part of the process of change. Educational multimedia is no exception in this respect: it follows broader societal trends (related to societal changes in the role and function of education) while daily practice reveals a different kind of dynamics ('struggling' with day-to-day opportunities and challenges). Having presented this highly theoretical and abstract presentation of the ideas of Beck and Giddens in a nutshell, it is now possible to elaborate their thoughts within the social study of technology, into the concept of social learning.

From Social Shaping towards Social Learning

The social study of technology considers technology to be a social practice. It does not presuppose any specifics on the practice under study: technology can be studied just like any other social practice. We have introduced a conceptual framework that allows to take the specifics of the dynamics of change into account. Beck and Giddens have pointed at a typical feature of contemporary processes of change: they are reflexively constituted. Integrating this characteristic into the theories of social shaping changes the perspective from social shaping to *social learning*. This offers an interesting opportunity to further the understanding of the processes of socio-technical change. Social learning in the way we are going to use it, is not a univocal concept. It is a multi-layered concept, that falls apart into two distinct aspects: one that we label the analytical aspect of social learning (or: the weak form) and another that we label the action-oriented or pro-active aspect of social learning (or: the strong form). The first aspect focuses on the analysis of constitutive elements of contemporary practices. The second aspect builds on what is known as *constructive technology assessment*. Constructive technology assessment aims at improving the social embedding of new technologies. The purpose of our study is to better the understanding of the societal uptake of educational multimedia; social learning is a concept that furthers this understanding, but needs attention for some pitfalls on the road, like the problem of what precisely constitutes good practices.

Social-shaping studies, we might argue, take a rather detached position with respect to intervention in the world. The intention of contributing to the development of good practices only figures at the background. First of all, these studies want to contribute to a better understanding of processes of socio-technical change. Reflexivity is a necessary aspect of each theory on social change. Awareness of the complicated relation between the object under study and the concepts used, is a necessary element in social studies: the interpretation of the object under study may change due to results of former research. Analysis of the social practices under study reveals the kind of reflexive elements that constitute these practices and that give rise to specific dynamics within these practices. When studying how practices are configured, how they are appropriated and how they are translated, we have to pay special attention to elements that reveal the reflexive organisation of these processes. The assumption that reflexive aspects play a role, and may be identified with proper analytical means, grants social learning a status on its own.

The action-oriented approach of social learning has, at least implicitly, always been part and parcel of the study of technology. It focuses on how society could benefit from a better understanding of the process of socio-technical change. Society should learn how to introduce technology. This approach is typical for *constructive technology assessment*, whose promoters strive for a good entrenchment of technology in society. They perceive problems in how technology is on the one hand promoted (by innovators) and on the other hand regulated or controlled (by regulators or surveillance organisations). Society must learn to bridge the gap between promoters and controllers, and constructive technology assessment might be a way to proceed (Rip, Misa & Schot 1995). Arguments about the position of researchers with respect to 'social learning' are, amongst other provided by Brian Wynne, who points at the reflexivity that is needed on part of the researchers to enable learning by society. Critical awareness of the complicated relation between the different constituent elements in the web of socio-technical relations is necessary to unravel the quasi-causal relations between technology and society. Technology is not impartially imposed on society: power relations, institutional commitments, unilateral risk assessments, etc. constrain the introduction of technology and promote certain configurations while prohibiting others. Social learning is equal to critically examining these relations and opening debate about them (Wynne 1995, p. 31).

Social learning thus in the end stands for learning by society how to improve the innofusion process of (in our case) educational multimedia. The claim that there *is* something to learn and something to improve presupposes that two problems are adequately tackled: how to differentiate between good and bad practices, and how to differentiate between success and failure? Given the theoretical approach as presented above, tackling these problems is far from trivial. The notion of interpretative flexibility of technology and the requirement of a symmetrical explanation of success and failure seemingly contradict the existence of an objective tool or yardstick to differentiate between good and bad practices and success and failure. From this it is logical to analyse the social practices that are presented in part two in depth; the results of this analysis lead the way to identifying constituent elements of good practices and contributes to understanding what constitutes success and what constitutes failure.

Social Learning Versus (Individual) Learning

We must now clarify the relationship between social learning and (individual) learning, if only because we study in this volume the innofusion of multimedia in educational practices and therefor will relate to learning theories and practices.

Learning in general presupposes awareness for what is learned, and an awareness for how it is learned. Contemporary theories about learning emphasise the constructive foundation of learning: new knowledge is acquired in relation to what is already known and experienced (see chapter 2). Learning is situated learning; it only occurs when what has to be learned (skills, knowledge, attitudes) is connected to former knowledge, skills and attitudes. Learning in itself is positively valued in contemporary societies. Learning is often associated to an ideology of progress. It may thus be stressed that today's 'Information Society' calls for enhanced education and learning, as expressed in slogans like *education permanente*, and *life long learning*. The foundations of learning itself have changed, as was discussed in the previous chapter: a paradigmatic shift in learning strategies can be identified, in which the combination of changing psychological perspectives (about how people learn) and advanced ICT plays a significant role. Learning has become more reflexive in itself, by its emphasis on 'learning how to learn'.

The psychological theory that guides today's educational strategies – indicated as 'the constructivist model' in chapter 2 – emphasises situational and localised characteristics of learning. Social learning emphasises in a similar vain the importance of the local setting. Being conceived on the basis of social shaping theories, social learning presupposes local characteristics to be important for the process of change. But contrary to (individual) learning, 'social learning' does not presuppose an actor in which the learning is embedded. The everyday conception of learning presupposes someone learns: no learning without a student. Social learning (as analytical concept) however, does not relate to an actor, or a collective (or society at large). It simply equates the presence of reflexivity (some might say: intended or unintended feedback) within social practices with learning. Learning gets a metaphorical meaning in the sense of change over time (Sørensen 1996). Only when taking the action-oriented perspective on social learning, the correlation between ordinary learning and social learning is more intimate. Then, it refers to how society learns to improve the innofusion of educational multimedia. The intuitive notion of learning (that is open to criticism due to its unproblematic implicit notion that learning by itself is 'good') relates to the intuitive notion that by practising society learns how to improve the innofusion of educational multimedia. As stated before, but for the sake of its bearing repeated here, this idea of progress should not be taken on face value, but should first be critically analysed.

Social Learning: Taking up Reflexivity

In the preceding sections two levels of reflexivity have been discussed. The first level concerns the relation between the researcher and the object in social science, and is not typical for social learning *per se*. The second level concerns reflexivity as can be observed in all social practices. The analysis of this level of reflexivity contributes to our understanding of how socio-technical practices (e.g. the innofusion of multimedia in educational settings) evolve over time.

At the first level it is recognised that the mere analysis of social practices may influence these practices. This aspect of reflexivity is necessarily present in all theories about the social world. For example: the design of a multimedia package may profit from the findings of a researcher who researched configuration and appropriation processes in a variety of social settings and who reported on the terminology and strategies that she found. Her findings and subsequent proposals may contribute to changing the design practice.

The second reflexive layer is crucial to our study of social learning. Beck and Giddens describe how actors are involved in reflexive practices, and how these reflexive practices are crucial for contemporary processes of socio-technical change. Actors monitor and evaluate each step in constructing new socio-technical practices. These monitoring and evaluation procedures are institutionalised in the construction of a new socio-technical practice. Procedures and institutionalisation are crucial elements in the process of change. Social learning is directed at identifying reflexive aspects within a process of change. To be aware of these reflexive practices, and to analyse them with respect to these reflexive elements, is central to social learning. One of the case studies in this book shows how a project was accompanied by seven (!) layers of evaluation.[4] What remains to be shown (presupposing awareness for these evaluative layers) is how these evaluative practices contribute to the process of configuration, translation and appropriation of multimedia in the educational practice under study.

Now we can take a closer look at the constituent elements of social learning *per se*. How to use the concept in practice? Can we differentiate between various forms of social learning? What kind of dimensions of social learning should be distinguished? And do these dimensions relate to spatio-temporal aspects, organisational aspects, aspects regarding the content of the practice, etc.?

As a kind of first order approximation we propose a rather straight forward deconstruction of the concept. This deconstruction is guided by a common sense approach of relevant aspects of projects. A project for instance can be constrained by strict limits in time, in use, in users, it can have a very tight and bottom down organisational structure, it can have to realise very strict objectives, it can be very controlled and protected from its environment, it can have very strict financial constraints, etc., etc. This 'bag' of constraints controls the development of the project in a strict sense. These constraints – that may be intensively monitored and surveyed – condition the innofusion of educational multimedia in that apparently *a priori* goals and objectives have to be realised. These constraints condition the experimenting space and the room to explore and try out the multimedia applications in different educational settings. By constraining the development unforeseen uses will hardly emerge, and if they emerge they may be perceived as anomalies that must be neglected or played down. On the other hand, a tight control structure might enable the realisation of very clear and unambiguous objectives. When a project is only meant to validate previous experiences, the need to experiment or to explore may be negligible. We propose to call the ideal-typical representation of a strongly controlled project the *mode of control*.

The mode of control has a counterpart, that relates to an open structure, to uncertainty regarding the objectives to be met, uncertainty regarding the kind of uses to be exploited, etc. This uncertainty is part of emergent technological configurations that have not yet matured into standard ways of using and producing. Educational multimedia typically is such an emergent technological configuration. The socio-technical configuration is not fixed, but rather open. There is room to experiment, and to explore uses. There is no strict demarcation between producers and users. Both participate in a network in which ideas and practices are communicated. Guidelines can be process-oriented: who is going to participate, how to organise the decision making process, what kind of decisions to be made, how to balance content and conduit issues, what kind of evaluation and feedback be organised, what kind of supervision, etc. These process-oriented constraints condition the social space in which experimentation and exploration of the educational setting occurs. No strict objectives are posed on the process, though there is an open eye for what happens and how it happens. The evolving practice is monitored but there is no control structure that addresses the use of the gathered information. Actors learn by trying, by using, by exploring. We propose to call the ideal-typical representation of a project that is rather open in where it ends and how it ends and that is directed at exploring possible uses the *mode of experimentation*.

The educational practice itself poses its limits. A fully open and non-controlled experimentation is in conflict with an inherent characteristic of an educational practice: in the end it must be able to validate and to evaluate what is learnt. A totally free and unconstrained exploration of multimedia, indicated as a *laissez faire* approach is not to be expected within educational settings.

Finally, the issue of good and successful practices implies that within the specific context of a project a balance is found between experimentation and control, between slight indications of constraints and strict guidelines, between endorsed external objectives and intrinsic learning processes, leading to a co-evolution of technology and social practice.

Social Learning: Experimentation Versus Control

There is a great variety to be observed in how multimedia are introduced in educational settings. This is not only due to the variety of settings itself (for instance the differentiation between countries, school systems, and formal and informal modes of learning). The variety also illustrates the localised character of the introductory process. Traditional innovation and diffusion theories are too much focused on a macro-view and do not pay sufficient attention to the practice of 'technology-in-the-making', the permanent process of negotiations that accompany the reshaping of educational practices. A more satisfying approach is rendered by theories under the heading of social shaping of technology. This approach presupposes the heterogeneity of technology and society. Technology and society form a seamless web in which it is impossible to differentiate *a priori* between technical and social elements. The process of change is a *socio-technical* process of change. Technology is open to analysis as a social practice. Three key concepts have been introduced to guide this analysis: the process of *configuration*, the process of *appropriation* and the process of *translation*. These three concepts offer distinct views on the process of socio-technical change. In combination they offer a fruitful framework for an analysis of technology-in-the-making, for the *innofusion* of technology in a social practice. Chapter 12 explores the cases, presented in part two, on how they contribute to the innofusion process.

We then introduced an extra element into the analysis: modern societies are inherently reflexive. Recognising this reflexivity will eventually allow us to present recommendations on how the accompanying processes of change may best be guided. Since the processes of change are reflexive in themselves, we have coined the term *social learning* to indicate the character of these processes. The purposeful feedback, the permanent monitoring and the institutionalised forms of evaluation contribute to a process of change that may be termed 'learning'. Then we postulated two modes of social learning as empirical manifestations of social leaning: the *mode of experimentation* and the *mode of control*. Both modes can be observed in present-day educational settings. Both modes should be granted the status of 'ideal-type': real social practices comprise a mix of both modes. Style of management, attitude towards change, organisation of feedback, evaluation and monitoring processes, and the role of external and internal objectives determine the balance between both modes. Successful innofusion of multimedia into a specific educational setting presumes a proper balance between both modes. The notion of success (and failure) relates to the manner in which the process of change is incorporated into the social practice. How this relates to both modes is part of the analysis in chapter 13.

Notes

1   For an introduction and overview, see Dosi et al. 1998.
2   See for a more detailed historical review (Bijker 1995).
3   Especially in his contribution to 'Reflexive Modernisation' (Beck, Giddens & Lash, 1994) Beck takes reflexivity in a very literal manner: unconscious 'bouncing back' of a situation. He reserves the term 'reflectivity' for conscious monitoring and evaluating practices. Giddens takes a more relaxed position on the differences between both terms (and their subsequent practical interpretation). We follow Giddens.
4   See 'A promise adrift: mechanisms of multimedia innofusion in education' by Egyedi (chapter 9, this volume).

PART II
CASE STUDIES

4 Multimedia and Education as a Marketing Strategy

RUTH MOURIK

Abstract

In 1996, the marketing and communication division of a telecommunication company presented the results of a distance education project at a national fair on technological innovations. The project consisted of teaching children in different European countries a language via video-conferencing technology. The project was declared a (marketing) success, even though during the project the educational and marketing goals conflicted and the expected use and users of the technology did not match the actual use and users. By focusing on the interaction between the actors by means of a theory on the social construction of technology, SCOT, this case gives insight in the way educational objectives and content are sacrificed for other – in this case marketing – purposes and the reasons for this sacrifice. The teachers had their own interpretation of the project, but were forced to sacrifice their main requirement. When this requirement could not be met they abandoned the fight for the educational objectives. This meant the teachers were now more than ever subject to the micro politics and power structure of the dominant 'marketing' sociotechnical frame. SCOT also addresses the reason for the attribution of 'success' to the project. There occurred a closure as to the objective of the project in the interaction process. The actors adopted the marketing division's objective. Thus the project was a success in spite of all the problems and in spite of the fact that the educational and technical objectives were not met.

Introduction

April 1996: the marketing and communication division of a telecommunication company presents a distance education project at a national fair on success. In this chapter I will discuss the mismatch between the educational and the dominant marketing goals, the mismatch between the models of users, use and setting as envisaged by different actors. Furthermore I will address the reasons for the attribution of the predicate 'success' to the project. I will start this chapter with an elucidation of SCOT, I will then present the project chronologically, continue with a discussion of the social shaping processes in the project, and conclude with how success or failure are ascribed.

Conceptual Framework

The Social Construction Of Technology (SCOT) theory supplies me with a theoretical framework to explain the interaction between the actors in this project and the outcomes of this interaction in the project. I will not discuss the theory extensively but focus on those notions that I need to discuss my research question: How and why are educational objectives and content sacrificed for other purposes, in this case marketing objectives? The notions that I will discuss briefly here are the social shaping of technology, the notion of social actors, interpretative flexibility and the inclusion and harshness of technology.

In the SCOT theory, technological development is not seen as consisting of separate political, social, economical and technical aspects. These aspects are interwoven in a complex dependency and evolve simultaneously. Technological development does not determine society but is socially shaped and shaping (Bijker & Law 1992). Heterogeneous elements and activities are involved in a dynamic process of interaction and interaction. So, technological development is the outcome of social confrontations and interactions between all elements involved, human and non-human. Different social actors participate. The concept of 'relevant social actors' is used to denote institutions and organisations as well as unorganised groups of individuals. The main requirement is that all members of a certain group share the same set of meanings, with regard to a specific artefact (Bijker, Hughes & Pinch 1987). Relations between actors in the interaction process are not linear. Actors can change position according to the time or the actors with whom they are negotiating. Relations are not fixed entities. They can become stronger or weaker over time, or disappear altogether. To understand the development of a technology it is important to know the meanings given by relevant social groups to an artefact and to the process of development. The identification of relevant social groups is indicated by the actors themselves. The attributed meanings can be different, thus it might look as if there are more artefacts when in fact there is only one. This phenomenon is called interpretative flexibility. For example, in the marketing project discussed below multimedia is a marketing tool, an educational means, a technical learning object. Different objectives would create different desirable designs.[1] In demonstrating interpretative flexibility I want to clarify that the stabilisation of an artefact (closure) is a social process and hence subject to choices, interests and value judgements (Bijker 1995). Whether the stable artefact is 'working' or 'non-working'/ 'true or false' should not be judged by the researcher but by relevant social groups or actors. Every relevant social group has different solution strategies in the interaction process, has different objectives with the technological development and different theories. Also, capabilities, practical uses of the technology, and ethics in regard to a particular artefact differ. These aspects form a frame that shapes the thinking, handling and interaction of that relevant social group. Within the SCOT theory this frame is called a 'sociotechnical frame'. Depending on the position of a relevant social group in such a sociotechnical frame, the frame affects the action and behaviour of the group of actors strongly (high inclusion), or has little effect (low inclusion). Actors with a high degree of inclusion are closer to the inside of the frame than actors with a lower degree of inclusion. For actors with a high inclusion the artefact is unambiguous and constrains their actions. For actors with a low inclusion the artefact has a relatively undifferentiated, monolithic meaning. These actors have a 'take it or leave it' choice. Artefacts can have different shades of harshness for actors with different degrees of inclusion (Bijker 1995).

Description of the Project

The End of the Story: The Final Presentation at a National Fair for Technological Innovations

The project was presented at an annual fair for technological innovations. This project consisted of connecting several children from all over Europe with teachers in the country where the company was based in order to teach them a language. The project was a state-of-the-art technological project with educational purposes. In spite of the state-of-the-art technology, and the educational and technical expertise and experience the company said it had built up in the six months the project lasted, at the fair only five of nine children were connected. They were connected to each other through computers while they sat next to each other and to a teacher, it was claimed, elsewhere in the country. However, the teacher sat in the basement of the fair building! Another teacher was with the children to reassure them because in spite of the course they could hardly communicate with each other in the learnt language without computer mediation. They could only answer the most trivial questions like what their name was. At the fair nothing technologically new was presented in spite of the fact that the company had stated that their project was the fulfilment of the technological promise to multimedia distance education. This belief in the technological promise will be elucidated later in this section. In newspaper articles and radio editions, most of them national media, the project was depicted as a success with almost no problems and with great results on the educational and technological side. Why was the project at the fair set up in its most technologically simplified form? Why were the children so inadequate in communicating in the language they learned? To begin with, let me take you back to the beginning.

The Beginning of the Story: The Initialisation of the Project

The project was conceived at the Marketing Communication Division (MCD) of a telecommunications company.[2] Two of ten employees at the MCD handled the project. This telecommunications company is a division of a multinational European company. This multinational positions itself as a world-wide supplier of high-tech systems in telecommunications, electronics, information highway technology and electro-mechanics fields. There are more than 185,000 employees world-wide. Industrial installations are set up and local partnerships are forged in more than 20 countries; business dealings take place in 130 countries. One reason for initialising the project is to be found in the light of the future liberalisation of the European Telecommunications market.

This telecom division started positioning itself vis-à-vis the multimedia sector at the end of 1995. The country's telecommunication infrastructure and basic services (telephone, telex, radio-mail, telegraph and fixed lines) were a monopoly of the national telecommunication operator until January 1998. Then liberalisation of the alternative and traditional telecommunication infrastructure took place. Thus, the first objective of the MCD was to position the division in the multimedia field. To do so the MDC needed to change the image end-users had of the division and to associate the division with the technology beyond the telephone. The second reason was that the MCD felt the need to secure the role of the company internally. The company was one of three divisions in the country that were threatened in their existence. Of the three divisions one had been closed, another was heavily under fire and the position of the division involved was not secure either. The project was a means to profile the division internally and to show its capabilities to the headquarters that resided in a different European country.

When these two goals were set the MCD hired a marketing bureau to think about acceptable technological stunts that would get the attention of the public. Moreover, they had to do something that had not been done before in the multimedia field: to fulfil the technological promise to multimedia technology. This belief in the technological promise was that, with respect to technology, everything was possible, the sky was the limit. No matter how many connections, what kind of computers were used, what kind of multimedia, everything was possible. The marketing bureau hired came with two technical projects: a distance education project with children and a distance teleworking project with adults. I will only discuss the distance education project.

First, the MCD informed themselves about what was feasible within the time span they had (September-April) and what technology was needed to develop a new network. After the headquarters had given their approval to work out the plans, the MCD needed to find people who could manage the technical part of the project. Since it was a marketing project the MCD wanted to keep control. The telecom division financed everything. The MCD involved three people from their Education Centre, I will refer to them as the 'EC'. The EC is an internal training centre that has expertise and experience on the technical and social aspects of distance learning and video-conferencing. In September 1995, the MCD and the EC started working on the details of the project. With the earlier-mentioned objectives in mind the MCD fixed five important characteristics of the project: the time available, what kind of multimedia network would be used, what technology would be used, what test group would be used, what would be the educational curriculum. The first requirement the MCD set out, was the time that was available. More specifically, the date that the project had to be finished: April 15th. That was the first day of the fair where the project would be presented to the public. This was a hard deadline and, as will become clear, this deadline profoundly shaped the interaction between the actors. Secondly, the project had to concern telecommunication multimedia networks since one objective was positioning the company as number one in the multimedia field. Teleworking, telelearning and telemedicine applications received attention from the media and the public, which obviously were the targets for this marketing project. They started with telelearning and teleworking since these two applications would involve the least outsiders. Thirdly, the technology had to be state-of-the-art. Thus, a connection was made between ten Personal Computers and a Multipoint Control Unit (MPCU). Eight multipoint connections were possible, so to create ten connections was a realistic challenge from a technical point of view. The children and the teachers saw each other through video-conferencing on the computer screen. Furthermore, the traditional blackboard was replaced by a whiteboard that could be seen on every person's computer screen. Lastly, the applications were to run on an ISDN – Integrated Services Digital Network.

The choice to teach children of the age of ten was a marketing choice: children sell! Furthermore, children are playful, spontaneous and have a good ability to learn. This was important because, at the fair, actual results needed to be presented. Initially, the MCD wanted twenty children but the technology posed constraints. The multipoint connection for twenty children was not possible because there would not be enough time to create a stable connection at the fair. Once it had been decided to teach ten children, the question arose what to teach these children: when one has a group of children from different countries a common language in which to teach them is needed Thus it was decided to teach the children a language. At first, the MCD told me that a language was chosen because the project would be presented at a national fair. Later, I was told that a language was chosen because the company had to find a reason for the fact that the lessons would be given from the country where the company was situated. If they had chosen a different language the company would have lost its function as the centre of the project.

With the basic requirements set, a soft- and hardware supplier needed to be found that could meet the technical demands of the project. The EC had worked before with an American soft- and hardware supplier MW on a distance education project and therefore they contacted them again with the list of technical requirements. When MW assured they would have the network up and running in the beginning of January, the MCD contracted them. Soon after the contact with MW, the MCD asked the EC to search for teachers. The EC had connections with research centres on distance learning that had no commercial interests. This was important because the company had to be the only one that benefited commercially from it. That is how three teachers from a national University got involved. These teachers, whom I will refer to as U, were specialised in distance learning for adults throughout the world, especially Europe and Africa. At the same time that the EC searched for the teachers, the MCD was recruiting the test group: the children. Ten children were recruited within different company divisions all over Europe. These company children were chosen on the basis of several criteria: they had to be aged around ten: the age at which children are playful, fast learners and most receptive for language, but also mature enough. The preference was for children who were bilingual and had experience in working with a personal computer. The children were asked to participate through articles in the company newsletters, through posters and through the company radio advertisements. This did not work; no child responded. Children who were relatives of involved actors or of the people responsible for the recruitment in different company divisions were then asked. Later in the project three other children got involved because it appeared the initial group of children was a little reticent to talk in a strange language. It was believed that children who already had a knowledge of the language would make the first group feel more comfortable speaking the language. The children in this second group were relatives of the teachers or technicians. The parents saw the project as the perfect opportunity for their children to learn another language and about another country, meet people internationally and learn more about educational forms. The technical aspects did not interest them much.

The MCD and the EC searched for additional technical support and found it in the data networks technician (DNT) from the corporate business division. At the same time the MCD started the public campaign. In this campaign the MCD involved two groups of media. One group was paid by the MCD to write about the project. These media passed on the information as written in the folders and advertisement campaign by the MCD. The objectives of the project were learning about educational aspects, end-user aspects of distance learning, possibilities of enhancing the quality of distance learning and building-up technical and educational expertise concerning multimedia networks. The paid media issued advertisements and short articles in financial magazines, telecom magazines and radio messages aimed at the public. The media were the outlet for this division, the intermediaries between the MCD and the public. Before the project even started, the MCD already had the campaign up and running, making the public believe it was already taking place successfully. The other group of media, the unpaid, did not come up with other information articles than the paid media. Apparently they issued the press release delivered by the company, thus copying the success story without any critical reflection.

Once the teachers were involved, they started working on their curriculum. They set up a list for MW stating the basic requirements such as the necessary audio equipment, a video communication for 'lip synchronisation' so that they could practice audio and video pronunciation exercises. The teachers also needed a whiteboard and a flip-chart. MW promised that all these requirements would be fulfilled. Furthermore, the teachers asked the MCD and the EC for a pilot and control group of children to analyse the differences between a traditional classroom situation and this virtual classroom. In the course of the preparations of the educational curriculum, the teachers and the EC formulated some additional requirements. These requirements were the result of the fact that children would be the test group. This means that the chances of the children destroying an application by mistake or create other kinds of problems are much bigger and need to be controlled. Many of the additional requirements had never been developed before. Therefore, MW asked a delivery delay of two weeks: instead of the agreed 15th of January the installation would take place by the end of January.

The Big Turn Around in the Project

This probable delay shook up the project immensely. The MCD saw it as a breach of contract, lost confidence in the software company's capabilities and cut MW out of the project. The MCD believed beyond doubt in the technological promise that everything was possible, that their technical requirements were technologically feasible. They felt certain that they could get the requirements fulfilled before the 15th of January. Important is the fact that the MCD had already started their marketing campaign which stated up front that the project was a technical and educational success and that everything was going fine. The company, it said, was ready for the multimedia market and the distance education market. In other words, the project even though not yet started, could not be cancelled without the company losing face and thus clients.[3] The MCD demanded that the EC and the DNT come up with a solution within a week. The EC and DNT started building a multimedia network with the hard- and software they already had, and bought additional software from other software suppliers. Furthermore, the MCD assigned the EC and the DNT the task of adapting all the soft- and hardware in such a way that the project could be started around the 15th of January. But the EC and the DNT did not manage either and ended on the same date MW had said it would be ready with the implementation of the teachers' requirements. Nevertheless, the MCD was certain that MW too would not have delivered the required technology within these two weeks. By the end of January the EC and the DNT had built up a network as best as they could. The company installed the equipment at the end of January, gave the children and their parents a paper with instructions on how they should start up the computer and how they could set up an ISDN connection.

Teaching Multimedia Distance Education

Then the actual distance education part of the project started. But soon the problems piled up. The problems went further than the 'normal' bugs in software and some adjustments of the parameters for the hardware. According to the actors involved, several technical problems occurred due to MW dropping out. Because of the limited time available to find new soft- and hardware suppliers, the new material could not be tested thoroughly. There were many bugs and other problems related to the novelty of the technology. Technical problems occurred with the start-up and stability of the connection. The video-conference software failed more often than it worked. Sometimes children could not even participate in the lessons. The audio and data communication often dropped out, meaning that the children missed either parts of, or the whole lesson. The starting-up of the computers and the ISDN line often failed. Sometimes children were not connected at all. The technical side of the project was not at all ready when the project started. Whole computers had to be replaced. The microphones and loudspeakers could not filter out the background noise enough and echoed all the time. The logbooks state that the first weeks of the project problem after problem arose causing the lessons never to start on time.

The learning process suffered immensely from these problems, in a qualitative and quantitative sense. The search for a control group of children to compare a real and virtual classroom was put on a hold. When the project started again there was no time anymore to involve a control group. Secondly, the actors mention that because of the problems the project was delayed for more than two weeks and the time available for teaching was reduced from 60 to 40 hours. Subsequently, the curriculum would consist only of material that would be relevant. This meant they had to learn how to present themselves, how to tell something about the home country and how to tell if they thought the language was difficult or easy to learn. According to the teachers, if the fair had not been the end goal, the tutorial program would have been different. Much more fun things would have been taught. But the fun things that had no direct link with the presentation at the fair were left out. Learning how to speak the language gained priority. The children had to use this language to speak to the press; they did not need to know how to write or spell and so spelling was not taught at all. Furthermore, the technology needed for lip synchronisation could not be developed in time for the project. Therefore no phonetic rehearsals could be held to help the children to pronounce correctly. To avoid instability resulting from the multiple connections, the children had to be split in groups of three.

External factors also influenced the project, for example the ISDN communication protocols differed from country to country and in some countries such as Italy the telecom infrastructure was not adequate. There was no ISDN infrastructure to the home of a child. The video and audio connection was built up differently in countries. These were technical problems that, according to the DNT, even other technicians could not have foreseen. These are choices that were so transparent that they forgot to check them. Many of the technical refinements had to be implemented along the way.

In the initial video-conferencing try-out it appeared that in the case of one of the children, neither he/she nor his parents spoke English and a translator became necessary. The voice control functioned at that time. This means that the person speaking is in view. Since the translator was always translating he was in view all the time. This problem could not be resolved in time for the fair and the child was therefore taken out of the project. The MCD, the EC, the DNT were afraid the children would not stay motivated, would not co-operate, would be too tired after their own schooldays to be able to concentrate. The MCD therefore started a 'motivation campaign' during the first weeks of the actual teaching: postcards, small gifts like pens were sent to the children and little competitions, games were organised. Furthermore, they had to write down their experiences in a diary. Other than expected, the children used the multimedia network actively and creatively. They would be mischievous. For example, they would take away certain documents from the screen or place other documents on the screen. Another piece of mischief involved the voice-activated switch camera. A child could whistle and thus monopolise the screen but there was a time delay between the audio and video transfer. Thus, the child that had whistled would be seen later than being heard; in the meantime other children followed this example and the teacher was not able to detect which child was responsible. Furthermore, the children had found a way to play with the whiteboard and make it or parts of it, disappear. Although the DNT and the EC could not control the environment directly they tried to forbid the child and its family from using the computer in such a way that could cause damage to the project software. They also adjusted (read stripped) the whiteboard application. They removed unnecessary and uncontrollable applications. To control the whiteboard the teacher was given an 'undo delete' option. Apart from the removal of applications, the connection procedure was carried out from the home country, unless the specific national communications protocol were such that they did not permit the children to call in whenever they felt like it. In the course of the project the children developed practical wishes such as those concerning the times of the teaching hours. They also came up with a special wish: they wanted to use the multimedia network outside class hours. Towards the end of the project the technician and the EC tried out this option. The children remained connected after the class had finished, but the teacher was removed from the network. After two or three times this experiment was stopped because the technicians had to stay present all the time since the children had not enough technical knowledge to keep the network working and on-line. Also the MCD, the EC and the technician were afraid the children would damage the technology and the system if used for other purposes. Furthermore, the MCD could not afford it: the expected costs of the international telephone connections were high and their finances were limited.

The End of the Story: The Presentation of the Project at the Technology Fair

At the presentation at the fair, the MCD called the project a huge success, technically as well as educationally. With all the previous technical problems in mind, the EC and the DNT decided to play it safe. Therefore, they decreased the number of connections to five at a time, a number that has proven to be stable. Furthermore the teachers' computer was set up in the basement of the building instead of in another city or country, thus excluding the possibility of problems due to external factors and the line became more stable since it was only several metres instead of several hundred. After the fair, the files on the project were closed and it was declared a technical success from a marketing viewpoint. The technical problems that occurred during the project were not blamed on technical breakdowns or on the shortcomings of the belief in the technological promise, but on the limited time and on human factors such as organisational problems and MW's incompetence.

Social Shaping Processes in the Project

Educational and Other Objectives in Opposition

To avoid too much overlap with the previous section I focus here on a few examples of interaction. They demonstrate how and why the educational objectives and content were sacrificed for other – in this case marketing – purposes. Let me first rephrase the interaction process briefly in SCOT terms, and then present the overall line of argument before I turn to the tension between the marketing and educational objectives.

For the MCD the project was the solution to a marketing problem: changing the image of the company and, more importantly, securing the position of the company internally. This problem definition would become the most influential factor in the development of the multimedia network because of the decision power of the MCD I will argue that the MCD had a high inclusion in a specific sociotechnical frame, a marketing frame, which influenced its thinking and handling strongly. The 'marketing' sociotechnical frame of the MCD consisted of a preferable marketing design, a specific interpretative flexibility, that defined what was desirable and what was not with respect to social and technical decisions. Also, micro-politics with the headquarters, technicians, teachers, children, and macro-politics with respect to international competition were part of the 'marketing' sociotechnical frame, and, as will be demonstrated further in this section, the control over knowledge about the technical artefact. Even if they wanted to get out of this 'marketing' sociotechnical frame, they could not really do so since getting out of the 'marketing' sociotechnical frame meant packing up altogether. The choices they made constrained them for the rest of the process of developing the multimedia network. In the interaction process the MCD tried to draw the other actors inside this 'marketing' sociotechnical frame. A frame where they had control over one important interaction tool: the final decision power. Although the MCD delegated the responsibility to the EC, the EC did not have a great amount of control over what technology was to be used since the MCD already had formulated most of the requirements. I argue that the EC adopted the sociotechnical 'marketing' sociotechnical frame of the MCD. They had to act according to marketing objectives; although their objective was different from that of the MCD. They were content with the technical and educational know-how they would gain through the project. For the teachers however, it was important to learn about the educational aspects of the project. For them the project was the solution to an educational problem. This problem definition, and the subsequent 'educational' sociotechnical frame would come to be in direct opposition to the 'marketing' sociotechnical frame in the interaction about the development of the multimedia network. In the subsequent interaction process the educational aspects had to make way more than once for the marketing aspects of the project because of the deadline of the fair.

Let me now illustrate the way educational objectives were sacrificed for other – in this case marketing – purposes. The belief in the technological promise created expectations on the side of the EC,[4] the teachers and the MCD that otherwise probably would not have been formulated. This belief in the technological promise was often, although indirectly, used as a reason for the necessity of sacrificing the educational objectives in favour of other purposes. I will discuss this later in this section. The high inclusion of the MCD in the 'marketing' sociotechnical frame gave them no other choice but to exclude MW. Instead of adjusting the image of, or belief they had in the technological promise they adjusted reality by getting rid of the company and tried desperately to find a solution to fulfil the technological promise. Often that reality meant that the educational objectives had to be sacrificed for marketing purposes. One could think the company might have tried to change the project into something less difficult to realise. But they had put so much faith in this promise that they had started the commercial and promotional campaign of the project even before it had begun. They could not stop without a disastrous loss of face. According to Van Lente (1993), actors are often captured by expectations that lead a life of their own, independent of these actors. He analyses how this affects the development of technologies. In the case of this project the belief in the technological promise was not adjusted to the 'social or technical reality'. The MCD's 'marketing' sociotechnical reduced their room to manoeuvre. When the belief in the technological promise appeared to be a 'lie', they had no other way than to go forward and try to make the most of it. That reality was adjusted to the belief in the technological promise.[5] A manager of the company[6] mentioned that nowadays, due to the liberalisation of the market and thus the necessity of listening to the final user, the marketing departments have, everywhere, taken more and more power. The result is that the technicians serve the marketing people. Most of the time, the technologies developed do not work during presentations at fairs but 'you have to make people believe that it works'. The important thing is that the equipment will work some weeks or months later. The deadline posed by marketing divisions are usually too tight. Moreover, it appears to be common knowledge that companies announce the launch of a new technology without being able to deliver.[7] According to the manager, the reality is that if most people see an experiment as a success, it is a success. The final logic of this kind of firm is to make money and marketing is essential to raise money and awareness.

In the course of the project the other actors adopted (consciously or unconsciously) the 'marketing' sociotechnical frame, and changed or adjusted their objectives to the marketing design. Thus, the interpretative flexibility of the different actors with regard to preferable designs converged with the marketing interpretative flexibility. Closure occurred. The interaction process resulted in a technology set-up that was more capable of fulfilling the requirements of the MCD than those of the teachers or technicians. The MCD mentioned that the educational curriculum and requirements had to adjust to the technical aspects of the multimedia network. In fact, the MCD did not allow adjustment of the technology. Because of their high inclusion in the 'marketing' sociotechnical frame they could not adjust the belief in the technological promise so they moulded the less obdurate aspects: the humans in the 'marketing' sociotechnical frame, the working material, the content of the material and the pedagogical objective. The social reality was adjusted time after time to the belief in the technological promise instead of adjusting the belief in the promise to the reality. For example, the number of children put together in the class had to be adjusted to four or five. Although a small class of children was not what the MCD or the teachers had thought about when advertising for a class of children, they could not really change this decision. It was a technical decision, technically necessary and thus the MCD or the teachers would not want to contradict. Because of uncertainty about the new soft- and hardware that would be used, first, the search for a control group of children was put on hold. Later, there was no more time. The teachers had their own interpretation of the project, but lost their main requirement. When this requirement could not be met they abandoned the fight for the educational design. This meant the teachers were now more than ever subject to the micro politics and the power structure of the dominant 'marketing' sociotechnical frame.

Inscribing Artefacts and Users

Part of the social shaping of technology theory addresses how the end user is represented. The producers of multimedia technologies mostly have ideas about the end use and the end user of their technologies. They will base their designs of the multimedia technologies partly on these models. This representation or construction of the end user often does not correspond with the actual use and user of multimedia. This mismatch between the represented and actual user becomes apparent when the technology is actually diffusing and used (Akrich 1992).[8] To understand and analyse several conflicts in the project I would like to discuss a notion by Latour (1987): the inscription of technical artefacts. According to Latour, the process of interaction between the innovators and the potential users and the outcome of these interactions are 'translated' or inscribed into technical artefacts. The composition of technical objects constrains users and forces a certain behaviour on them. Latour believes that the use of a technical artefact will almost always result in a 'conflict'. Objects have an obduracy that is established in confrontation with users and which is a function of the distribution of competence assumed when an object is conceived and designed. In the project there were several mismatches between the real and the represented user. Although the children had been carefully selected within the company itself, and on the basis of several characteristics, they did not match the expectations of the MCD, the DNT and the EC. The children and their parents had not been included in the development of the technical and educational aspects of the project. The MCD controlled what was told to the children and the parents about the project. In this way the children and their parents were drawn into the 'marketing' sociotechnical frame. But they had a low inclusion and were not treated as central actors (i.e.) they had no power or much room to make choices.[9] By keeping them 'ignorant', the MCD probably thought they would not need to negotiate much with this group. Technical artefacts always undergo a degree of appropriation, meaning that users will try to domesticate the technical artefact to suit their needs. The MCD, the EC, the DNT and the teachers had a certain representation of the children whom they saw as the end-users. This representation was reflected in the selection of the children.[10] In spite of the careful selection, they displayed behaviour which the teachers, the DNT and the EC had not foreseen. As was hoped for the children used the multimedia network actively and creatively – but not in the way that was expected. They made mischief, as mentioned previously. Because the education took place at home the children were much more spontaneous and fooled around more than they would have in a classroom. The environment also negatively affected the concentration of the children. Sometimes a chair was found to be empty: the child had gone to the kitchen. At the end of the project the technician argued that, in future, a similar technological constellation should allow the controller to silence a child by turning off the microphone. The technician felt the teacher needed to be able to better control the behaviour of a child. Although the DNT and the EC knew the users would be children, they forgot one of the most obvious changes needed: the height of the computer screen and other features of the setting. The camera mounted on the computer showed only the top of the head of the children. This problem was solved with pillows and books on the chair. Designers often underestimate the complexity of the application area. As it turned out, the children were not the only ones using the computer. The parents and other family members sometimes had expertise in computer programming and would use the computer for their own purposes and re-programme it. That led to problems with the video-conferencing software. Other siblings used the computer to do their homework or to play games. The spontaneity and creativity of the children, although useful for marketing purposes, had to be controlled as well. To prevent any child from dominating the lesson by playing with the voice-switched camera, the EC and the DNT designed the network in such a way that the teacher could technically control who would be seen and heard. Furthermore, the children were asked to remain quiet during the lesson and only to talk when they were asked to. If they wanted to ask something they could press a button made especially for this purpose. When they pressed the button a hand with a colour representing the child would be raised on the teacher's screen.

The way the MCD and EC solved these mismatches between the represented and the actual uses and users was quite interesting. On the one hand, the MCD stated that the pedagogical aspects and the children's behaviour were shaped by the technology. Nevertheless the DNT, on the other hand, mentioned that the technology was adjusted to the logic of the users. The software applications were refined to meet the logical reactions of the users. He said that it was done because the children's reactions would probably be the same as those of children in future telelearning classrooms. He said that it would be easier to adjust the technology than the reactions of the children. The MCD, EC and DNT tried to adjust the behaviour of the children to the image they had of the supposed or represented user, instead of adjusting the technological constellations to the users. By means of technical changes or just prohibitions, the behaviour of the children was controlled. A paradox arises here: the DNT and the EC tried to control every aspect of the behaviour of the users that the MCD had, in fact, hoped for: creativity, spontaneity, playfulness and the ability to learn the ins and outs of the technological possibilities. Nevertheless, without this spontaneity the possibilities and limitations would not be learned and their initial publicly stated objective of learning about the end-user's uses and needs with regard to the technology could not be met. This behaviour would also attract the attention of the public. The EC, on the other hand, wanted to find out what it took, technically speaking, to get the multimedia network stable. The multimedia networks' technical constellation also participated in the interaction process. According to the EC, the DNT and the teachers the behaviour of the children would be sometimes controlled or defined by the technology. Behaviour such as dominance and competition had to adjust to the technology. The children were forced together because of the character of the technology: on the whiteboard everyone sees what the others are doing. So the control over behaviour is stricter and co-operation was imposed on the children. Teamwork and team spirit seems to prevail in this form of teaching. The children did not have a strong sense of competition. The technology also imposed harsh rules on the teachers. According to the teachers, the teaching itself changed. Instead of 'teacher-centred education' it became 'student-centred'. The teacher became a facilitator, a mediator between the surplus of electronic multimedia information available and the student. The student, in other words, defined what he or she would learn. The teachers had to find new ways of teaching since they could not demonstrate to the children what jumping is by jumping themselves. They had to use a film or drawing. The teachers could not teach individually because then the others would not be able to learn, so the only way to help the slower learning pupils was by giving them more instructions and less difficult assignments. Also, the class management had to adjust to the technology. A lot of additional material had to be made because the speed at which material was used differed (faster) from traditional distance learning.[11] Because of the time delay between audio and video, pronunciation exercises could not be held. The learning process suffered immensely from these technical problems.

Thus, due to the multimedia network important changes occurred in respect to the (re)definition of 'learning' and 'teaching'. In general, the teachers concluded that due to multimedia in combination with video-conferencing, the learning and teaching became more personal, interactive and active. Nevertheless, the learning environment was of crucial importance. At home, in a familiar environment, it is likely that children become distracted. The harshness of technology did not stem from the fact that the designers of that technology had certain ideas about its usage by children and thus had 'inscribed' that usage in the software. In the project the harshness of the technology had more to do with the fact that the technology consisted of bits and pieces. It was not specifically designed for the project. If it had been, as would have been the case if MW had stayed, the inscribed usage would be relevant. As it is, it was relevant for parts of the system. The user model was evident in the software written by the EC and the DNT for the project and in other measures to 'control' the users. The DNT and the EC had specific ideas about the behaviour of the children. The 'human' children, that is, the kinetic, spontaneous and creative ones were seen as 'bad'. They had to adjust to the technology and not scream or pull practical jokes. The more 'machine-like' children, the ones that were serious and quiet, were the good children. They were a good match for the technology. So the technology was used to control the 'human' children and 'match' them with the technology. The fair really was the end of the project. From one day to the other there were no more lessons. For the children the end of the project came as a shock.

Concluding Remarks: Ascribing Success or Failure

By focusing on the interaction process between the actors by means of SCOT, this case gives an insight into the way educational objectives and content are sacrificed for other – in this case marketing – purposes, and the reasons for this sacrifice. After the fair the files on the project were closed. It was declared a technical success from a marketing viewpoint. The technical problems that occurred during the project were not blamed on technical breakdowns or on the shortcomings of the belief in the technological promise, but on the limited time and on human factors such as organisational problems and incompetence on the part of MW. The SCOT approach highlights the fact that a technology is a social construction, that a development is the outcome of interactions between actors, that the success or failure of a technology is not an inherent characteristic of the technology itself, but a socially constructed fact. The project was a success according to the actors directly involved, although the initial objectives announced to the media were not met. The reason for the attribution of 'success' to the multimedia network is that a closure occurred with regard to the interpretative flexibility in the project. The actors adopted, sometimes entirely, the MCD's meaning and objective, along with their own goals, as far as these did not conflict. The marketing objective was met and, in addition, the other actors learned about the technical and educational problems involved in this kind of project. Thus, the project was a success. After the project was concluded the MCD received word from its headquarters that they had done a good job. The headquarters was proud. The MCD had been able to change the image the end users had of the company thus securing their position in regard to the competitors.

Notes

1   I do not wish to state that different technologies exist next to each other. Different opinions as to what the multimedia network had to look like technologically and educationally existed, but by the time the project was closed, only one meaning had remained and was developed into an artefact. The interpretative flexibility occurred in the developmental stage. Thus I prefer to speak about desirable designs instead of artefacts.

2   This information is retrieved from the internet. For reasons of corporate confidentiality the addresses are not given.

3   The EC and the DNT had mentioned that it would perhaps have been better not to start the project at all because of the limited time that would be left with the fair in sight. If the fair would not have been the end goal, the project could have been set up in less a hurry and subsequently with less technical problems.

4   The MCD mentioned that in the technological sphere technicians and others always say 'everything is possible, the sky is the limit'. The promise here is that whatever you come up with as a technological idea, it is possible to produce it some way or the other. Perhaps now, sooner or later but it is or will be possible. Nevertheless the EC and DNT mentioned that if they had known about the difficulties in implementing the needed technology at forehand, they would have started the actual part involving the teaching much later and probable even would have chosen for different technology to be used. However, they had a deadline that was set with the demonstration of the project at the fair 'if we would have had the time we would have waited for the right and expected software of MW'.

5   Lente (1993) argues that this flexible character of the ideograph allows for linkages with e.g. the past and the future. Historical evidence of progress through technological development is used to strengthen the promise of progress. Innovation is emphasised as the key to progress and therefore it must not be stopped according to innovators and inventors. In this notion there is the implicit assumption that progress is inherently good. Progress continuously is projected as the historic force in the shaping of Modernity and so has become a widely shared cultural value. Seen from this perspective trying to hamper innovation stands equal to killing Modernity. This self-justification of technological developments also emerges out of linkage with the future through the technological promise: the next product is always better than the existing one and can be achieved and

developed. Development is necessary since it is inefficient and irrational to put up with a lesser product. The promise of invention justifies invention itself.

6   The text below contains parts of an email Beatrice van Bastelaer send me after her conversation with a manager of the company in which the conclusions of my paper were discussed. The manager had some interesting remarks as to what happened at the fair and what happened in the project in general that should be mentioned here. Also the following remarks should lead to some reflexivity on the idea of the SLIM partners. As I argue that the actors were in pursuit of a technological promise and shaped their world in such a way to match the promise one could argue that I have naively been in pursuit of a social promise without eye for the harsh marketing world outside.

7   But what I am wondering then is, if it is so usual not to deliver on time, why then was the MCD so stressed out when MW could not deliver on time but with a delay of two weeks. Why then all the trouble of cutting out a software supplier and doing the work yourself?

8   Winner (1988) discusses a related notion of end-user representation: the context-dependency, or inherent politics of artefacts/technology. He points out that within the process of technological development already norms and values are integrated in the technology so that it can be used to settle certain political conflicts, or to in/exclude actors from particular activities. Artefacts/technological products are inherently political: technology is politics by other means.

9   It is wrong to assume that children are rational actors that act properly when having the appropriate knowledge. But I will argue later that by keeping the children and parents uninformed as to technical aspects but also the marketing objectives of the project, the children and parents were excluded from a real interaction. Their knowledge was not considered to be important enough to take into account in the interaction process.

10   The user representation and user innovation practices went deeper than can be described in this paper. But since the project had been finished I could not look at the 'domestication' of technology. I had to conduct my analysis through interviews and texts and 'virtual presence' though videotapes.

11   Valcke (1996) believes that next to educational concerns, the need for a more efficient design, production and exploitation of learning materials is growing: materials have a shorter life-cycle so they have to be developed faster, and be updated more regularly.

5 Learning in Cable-School: The Use of Networked ICTs in an Educational Context

ROGER S. SLACK

Abstract

The paper discusses the uses of multimedia in a number of schools, centring on one project – the 'Cable-School'. I have used this project as a predicate for gaining access to and understanding the uses of multimedia technologies in schools. The paper argues that there is a clear division between the provision of technological infrastructure and pedagogic content. In some cases this has led users to generate their own content and to use the technology in potentially unanticipated ways.

Introduction

The paper describes the contours of the 'Cable-School' project that took place within schools in a city in the north of Britain and an adjacent region. I will show how the project failed and how local use was made of its infrastructure in what I term 'the social learning of independence'. 'Social' in that groups as opposed to individuals took decisions. 'Learning' in that innovation using infrastructure was required of the participants. 'Independence' in that the users of the system moved away from the system as technology-content, orienting to it as a technology to achieve their own aims. In short, the separation of the social from the technical and the technical from the pedagogic led to the failure of the project that was designed to integrate technology and content. This led to innovations by teachers who used the infrastructure *irrespective* of the content to develop *local solutions* for ICT provision.

Methodological Issues

The interview extracts centre on the accounts of the system given in tape-recorded interviews by two teachers; one involved with the project *ab origine* and the other who became involved soon after.[1] The interviews took place in schools and took the form of open-ended discussions on the system, together with some 'scene-setting' questions. Towards the end of the research, one teacher was prepared to discuss the Cable-School project with us at length. This provided some interesting comments and reflections on previous discussions and some further suggestions as to the problems of Cable-School. The schools that took part were as follows:

- Glen Academy: A large and modern school situated twenty kilometres north-west of a city in the north of Britain.
- New School: A school similar in design and age to Glen Academy but situated ten kilometres outside this north British city.
- City Academy: an older school situated within the north British city
- Suburban Academy: Another, older school situated in one of the more affluent suburbs of the north British city.

'Barry', the manager of the project within the Cable Company, generously granted us a number of interviews over the space of one year. Towards the end of the research, he was keen to present a summary of the project from his viewpoint. It is rare for a researcher to be able to discuss a project with its developers and users *in vivo*. It is rarer still to discuss the unfolding dynamics with the key member of project personnel in a company. My aim was to examine these two accounts (the teachers and the developers) and to explicate their sense of the project and its natural history.[2]

Basic Dynamics of the System

The Cable-School was a cable-based Internet service aimed mainly at high schools but also at junior schools. Schools were to be connected by cable modem to a web server hosted by the North British Council for Educational Technology (hereafter NBET). The web server hosts a number of teaching resource pages; notably worksheets that can be used either on-line or printed out and copied for use in class exercises. These sheets are web-based and use the potentialities afforded by the web interface (radio buttons, check boxes and the like) for students to complete quizzes and to move through documents (in at least one case). However, there were some worksheets that simply asked students for essays based on a stimulus. For example, one page provided students with a map of First-World-War battlefields and asked them to name each and to write an essay on the experience of being in such a place. Each school has a web page on a common server that gives details of the school's address and telephone number, together with some details about the senior staff (head-teachers and the like). Schools also have their own web servers that, in some cases, contain more detailed information about the school – sometimes in the form of a prospectus for potential students and their parents.[3]

Beside these resources, a number of other features were to be a part of Cable-School:

- Web authoring tools were provided so that teachers could generate their own web pages – both worksheets and other substantive content.
- File Transfer Protocol (FTP) was also provided so that teachers could download resources such as HTML editors and the like from a central server, and to enable the upload of files to that server (and to the school web servers).
- Electronic mail was also to be provided by the Cable-School project. This was regarded as important in facilitating the development of inter-school co-operation and for communicating with the staff at CableCo responsible for the development of Cable-School. A number of discussion groups were established by Cable-School staff and teachers: however, there were only a few regular users of the service and the discussions tended to centre on technical issues such as the use of HTML.
- Finally, a number of meetings between teachers and the staff of CableCo were also established. These forums were understood *by teachers* to be for discussion of the system and to enable them to take part in its development. Additionally, they was a site which provided support from CableCo's personnel regarding technical questions and the like.

'Prehistory'

The Cable-School has its roots in the desire of *Glen Academy*, a school in Glen Region to be connected to the SuperJANET[4] network by way of "the University of North Britain". The SuperJANET (*J*oint *A*cademic *Net*work) network connects the majority of Universities and other higher education institutions (HEI's) through a high-speed optical fibre broadband network. JANET and SuperJANET are the primary means of connection to the information available in and through HEI's, which Glen Academy focused on as an important component of the development of computing provision in the school.

Glen Academy is situated in an area that has a high concentration of IT manufacturing companies, some of which were keen to donate equipment to local schools. For example, Sun Microsystems donated a workstation and some training at West Coast University to the school. The equipment and training enabled Joanne, the principal teacher of computing at Glen Academy, to secure a central place for computing technology in the school. She then established a school web page and the beginnings of a school Intranet. The support that Sun Microsystems provided to the school was initially very comprehensive, but in the course time, of she perceived a change in attitude:

> It's really just been a case of them always being there in the first year or so, and you could call and say 'can I speak to (name of person)?' and he or she would be there and would tell you how to do things in layman's terms. People are busy, I know that, but . . . I phoned them, e-mailed them and even sent them letters but never got any reply, so I don't know about the support any more. I think we just do things by ourselves now.
> (Interview June 1997)

While Sun itself were not partners in the Cable-School project, (donating equipment and training to Glen Academy before the school became involved in Cable-School) the perception that there was a change in attitude of those located within industry appears to be a common theme within the Cable-School project.[5]

In the first months of 1995 CableCo,[6] the company originally canvassed to undertake the connection from Glen to SuperJANET, concluded that they could not donate the connection to the school, and offered an alternative arrangement. Barry, technology manager at CableCo describes the early developments around what was to become the Cable-School:

> . . . We spoke to the school and said, 'look, private circuits are our bread and butter and we wouldn't feel very comfortable about giving you this connection free of charge. But how would you like to get involved with us with this new technology brought by modem?' They said yes, they would be interested in doing that. So the upshot was that we eventually got delivery,

that was around March/April '95; when it was (finally) working, it was December.

(...)

(S)o we gave the school the (connection) and they carried on quite happily for about 6 months before anything else began to happen.

(Interview 28 August 1997)

The connection to Glen Academy was initiated by the school as opposed to the cable company. That is to say, the school wanted connection to the Internet and canvassed a number of Internet Service Providers (ISPs) with regard to the provision of the system. This is interesting in that, as the project developed, the ISP CableCo canvassed a number of schools to become involved in the project. However, as Barry has pointed out, the service that Glen Academy wanted was not something that CableCo felt able to donate in the same way that Sun had done. Rather, the service could only be obtained through participation in a trial of cable modems initiated by CableCo.

The connection between Glen Academy and Super JANET was the only one of its type until other schools began to ask about the service and were canvassed by CableCo to take part in the trial of cable modems. Glen Academy had requested a connection to SuperJANET as a part of their school computing policy. CableCo had been unable to donate a connection to the school but undertook to provide one on the condition that the school took part in the trial of cable modems. The constituency for *what was to become the Cable-School* started with Glen Academy and spread through CableCo's cable modem trial to other schools, *resulting* in the initiation of the Cable-School project. The demand for the service was initiated by one school and, as the potential user constituency enlarged, the Cable-School project was established by CableCo.

Organisational Framework in CableCo and Its Impact on Cable-School
Before discussing in more detail the establishment of the Cable-School as a service, it is important to outline some of the developments within CableCo that affected the place of network services within their overall strategy. Firstly, the growth of publicity about the internet around the time that the connection was established meant that it was difficult for anybody not to know at least something about the internet. Of course, schools at this time had become more 'IT aware', assisted in part by government policy. Thus, teachers (especially teachers of computing) were perhaps even more aware than others of the pedagogic potential provided in and through the internet. It is notable that two of the schools visited were relatively new[7] and had

been provided with a computer network infrastructure. The physical equipment of the schools together with the growth of the internet meant there was a momentum towards the provision of networked ICTs in educational contexts. In the current study this was to take place through what would become the Cable-School project.

To sum up: this awareness of the importance and potential of networked ICTs within education had an impact on CableCo in that they began to implement a co-ordinated national strategy for network communications. The internet was taken up as an area for development within CableCo, leading to the establishment of a multimedia group that established and tried out a cable internet service in mid-1996. Becoming involved in CableCo's trial of cable modems was the only way that schools with little financial resource to spend on even basic equipment could take part in what was regarded as the ICT revolution. As one of the teachers involved in the original trial notes, the high cost of buying a connection to the North British Technology University[8] and SuperJANET was prohibitively expensive:

> It was a thousand pounds a year for the connection to Super JANET and then another four hundred on top of that for their services. So that's when we got hooked up with CableCo.
> (Interview, June 1997)

Barry notes that during the time that the company had initiated their strategy, other factors outwith the purview outside the range of the of the project had an impact on it. The main development that Barry identifies is the re-organisation of local government. This took place because of the policies of the then Conservative government, whose avowed aim was to 'rationalise' the structures of local administration[9] so that there would be a single tier responsible for all local government activities. This was important for CableCo in that they aimed to provide network services to the newly established local government bodies, and saw their work in networking schools as a way of announcing their interest in and capability of providing similar services to local government. Barry describes this as follows:

> This being '96, there were a few other things on the horizon, one of which was the imminent reorganisation of local government, so the last, the dying months of the M Region, you know, *we were talking to various people in M Region about education because it was under their remit and what we decided was that we would develop a trial that could maybe act as model for*

delivering this service on a wider basis. With the reorganisation of local government we saw an opportunity to provide an administrative network as well. Although the word intranet had started to be bandied around we didn't really think of it in those terms because it wasn't a true intranet (. . .) but essentially (. . .) it adds up to an intranet (. . .) *so we started to think in terms of providing an administrative network, or promoting this as an option to use it as an administrative network and we started to think about adding some value to the internet experience* because again it's one of these things, I suppose because the internet has really kind of come to the fore all in the past 3 or 4 years

(. . .)

(It was) partly serendipity in that the timing was good, with the councils' reorganising, otherwise it might not have come immediately to mind that we should be including that in the promotion to the councils. I mean, until the council has actually deployed Cable-School; Cable-School is nothing more than the promotional literature that I put together a year ago. So, in that respect, it's words more than actions, and it's as much down to the council to make use of this. *You could argue 'what's a telephone line?': It' merely copper wire?, it's once you actually start using that telephone line to sell that it becomes a business tool, or to talk to your relatives then it becomes a sort of, I don't know whether that is entertainment or what! You know, so it's more putting spin on something that is there anyway.*
(Interview 28 August 1997 modified. My italics/emphasis.)

I take this account of the development of Cable-School as an adequate basis for explicating CableCo's aims since I have no other account upon which to rely – this is not the result of problems in the research process but because the interviewee was responsible for the development of the project in the organisation. While the project might have looked different to teachers and to others outside of CableCo, this definition was used to bring Cable-School into being. However, as we shall see later, the view of Cable-School that teachers had was very different, but that is a matter of empirical evidence and not sociological scepticism.[10]

CableCo developed the Cable-School project as a means of *inter alia* 'proving' the concept of networked communications to the local councils within the area to be served. As I have noted, the concept of connecting schools to the internet came, at least in part, from the initial request of Glen Academy to be connected. This concept was taken up by CableCo and developed (based on the trial of cable modems) into Cable-School. This is not to say that the service was itself a marketing strategy *ab origine*, but became so as a result of two trends. Firstly, the interest of other schools in the connection. Secondly, the recognition by CableCo that the internet was a growth area (especially in terms of connecting the more lucrative re-organised local councils by way of cable-based intranets). These two trends seem to have run parallel or to have elaborated each other, leading to the establishment of the Cable-School as a part of CableCo's strategy. From the interviews, it appears that schools did not uniformly seek out CableCo as a service provider, but became involved in the Cable-School project as a part of the constituency for the cable modem trial. The internet, as I have said, was regarded as an increasingly important pedagogic tool. A web connection signified that the school was a ratified participant in the ICT firmament. With school 'performance' being assessed[11] and placed in 'league tables' (with consequences for funding and student numbers) it was important to be a 'player' in the area of new ICT's in education.

Development of the Cable-School

Having given a 'prehistory' of the Cable-School and an outline of its import within CableCo, I will discuss the development of the service in more detail.

Barry describes the development of the service thus:

> . . . (W)e were looking at ways of adding value and one of the things that we decided to do was to engage NBET to develop a website for the Cable-School and to create, or to bring together, a set of tools that would allow teachers to create curriculum materials and homework exercises and so forth, and put them on-line (. . .). We invited all the schools where we wanted to try out the service and NBET invited another couple, so a total of seven schools were involved. While NBET were developing the website and working out what should be included in the suite of tools, I was working on a strategy for marketing the service to schools.

As can be seen above, once it was established that there was a user constituency for the project, some schools were invited by CableCo and others by NBET. CableCo initiated further work on the Cable-School, contracting NBET to write a corpus of web-based worksheets for the schools to use. NBET was also contracted to host the initial website for the project – it was envisaged that this would move to CableCo in time, but this apparently did not take place.[12]

From a request by one school for connection to SuperJANET, through trials of a cable modem, the service had developed into a project involving seven schools. In addition to this, the network was regarded by CableCo as a proving ground for their network systems – forming a component of their marketing strategy to local government in a bid to provide network connection across the newly reorganised North British City Council (see Barry's comments, above).

Cable-School Web Provision

NBET involved a Professor of educational technology from a South-eastern English University in the early stages of the project. His concern, as seen by one teacher, was to address the architecture of the web pages so as to make them accessible to the users, who were, on the whole, neophytes. According to one teacher, the original design conceptualised the Cable-School in the following manner:

> You go in and there's all the departments and the teachers and the staff room, and if you want to go into, lets say, geography, then you click on that and you're in and you can get into the teacher's materials in the filing cabinet by clicking. So it was a very nice idea, and it seemed to work well in principle. *Now the thing was that we didn't see him again, and we were left very much to get on with it by ourselves and with [the cable company]. So we developed the system in concert with NBET and got things to the state you see them now, but then things started to fall by the wayside a bit.*
> (Interview, June 1997. My italics)

Multiple Constituencies and/as Marketing Strategy

In this section I want to move from a description of the system to an explication of the dynamics of its development. I will provide an analysis of the manner in which a number of separate but cognate constituencies were built up as part of a marketing strategy for Cable-School.[13] It is within these multiple cognate constituencies that we can find some of the social learning issues central to the paper, and also a source of fundamental problems. My argument is that the two may well be linked.

There are a number of different constituencies that the system has been required to address. Taking the northern British City Council, for example, one finds that the Cable-School was articulated as a demonstration of a concept, namely the possibility of a distributed network communications system. Obviously, the system was shown in operation in schools and sold as a system to connect schools – in that sense it is cognate with the articulation available to schools – but it was also part of CableCo's marketing strategy.

Further, if we refer to the web page, it is notable that there are a number of different constituencies addressed within the one area: parents, students, teachers and so on. Each is apparently open to all other groups – there are no passwords required, for example. Just as teachers can access the web to place worksheets onto the site, so parents can access sites dealing with their child's school (all the schools in the project have web sites of varying quality), and students can access the system to work on assignments and to do homework.

Marketing the System

Among some of the teachers I spoke with there was a feeling of cynicism regarding the ways in which the Cable-School had been 'sold'. The perception was that it was more a marketing ploy aimed at getting parents to invest in the cable services provided by CableCo as opposed to a pedagogic tool *per se*. As one teacher said:

> I think that CableCo, when they sell cable, are well aware that they can sell it to the lower C's and people who watch a lot of television, that's the easy part. The problem is the B's and A's, and that's where the homework thing comes in – it's a money-making thing.[14]

In short, the Cable-School was sold to domestic customers as *another* reason for having cable in the home: as a part of a marketing strategy. Teachers felt that this conflicted with their understanding of what the system should be. Coupled with their perception that there was no attempt to provide the various kinds of support[15] promised to the schools, this led to a degree of cynicism. From the teacher's viewpoint, as the perceived marketing strategy within the cable company moved on, the need to sell the educational benefits of the system to consumers *qua* parents was dropped – leaving the Cable-School, as constituted in the existing constituency of school users, to fend for itself. Cable-School's foundational and main user constituency – teachers – felt that they had been left to use the system without the support (especially technical) of CableCo just as the system was reaching a critical juncture. While we cannot say with any certitude that it is possible that with the promised support Cable-School would have developed in a different manner, it seems likely that with a teacher-

CableCo forum in place, Cable-School would have the potential to realise the teacher's ambitions for the project (ambitions that, as I have noted, they felt had been set aside in the marketing strategy).

Of course, the parents were only one group of customers within the system and thus within the cable company's marketing strategy. The local council too were a part of the system, engaging in it with a view to placing the system within all the schools in the city. However, their contribution was at a level of tacit acknowledgement and acceptance of the system as an experiment, without a commitment to funding or purchase. The cable company was also involved in tendering for other network provision[16] within the council, and one might regard the Cable-School as a 'value added' component of this bidding process.

The council was certainly more involved in the other side of the case, the provision of equipment. In one school I visited, over one hundred Power Macintosh computers had been purchased and installed on a network across the school. Investment in the 'hardware' within the area is significant, and although the school mentioned above is a somewhat special case, being new and built with networking capability, it is not untypical. Other, older, schools visited also possessed a significant number of machines.[17] One teacher in the City Academy, an example of this latter type of school noted:

> We have a computer in most classrooms – most people, when they get here and see this set-up, they just drool. All this [the computers] means that teachers can use them within the framework of lessons in the classroom.

The provision of training did not match the provision of equipment. One teacher said that while there was a lot of equipment ('we were *showered* with the machines') there was very little training, and that this was because:

> There are very few photo opportunities in giving out training, you can't show people coming in and shaking hands and handing over training like you can machines.

Thus it was up to the principal teachers in computing to teach their colleagues how to use the system. It was also up to them to come to terms with the implications of the web for teaching practice.[18] There is great competition for teachers' time, and since there were no funds for teachers to attend training sessions it fell mainly to the computing teachers to show their colleagues how to do the basics. Staff were often left to work through problems themselves or in groups after initial training. Teachers had to be shown how to use both web publishing tools and e-mail. The latter was important since e-mail was the main system used by the by teachers outside of the computing faculty and of others associated with the development of Cable-School. A teacher in New School, which was built with network capacity commented:

> 'We said, "we'll show you the system and how to use it, not attachments and preferences and all that, just the basics, and then you can go on and play with it yourselves", and honestly, within minutes there were hundreds of messages on the server, now some of them were total rubbish, but they were there and people were using the system, that's the main thing. Now (. . .) we couldn't live without it.'

I must say here that this is one (informal) mode of social learning that is a key to the adoption of the system within the schools. The system as a whole includes a great deal more than e-mail and the capability to send mail with attachments – yet it is here that people start to use it. Another user constituency, if you will, is established around the possibility and potential of using e-mail to communicate with one's colleagues both within and outside the schools. A local concentration on training teachers to use a part of the system – albeit informally – constitutes social learning in that a realisation of the potential of the system develops and, from there teachers can go on to explore other components such as the web or FTP. As an *ab initio* step this use of e-mail is significant social learning–– it is learning how to use a potentially complex array of technologies and interfaces to undertake a task in common with others. In other words, it is the learning and integration of the potential of a technology in a particular setting *for* a particular task (or tasks). The obverse of this is that the tasks themselves have to be identified as those 'ready' and appropriate for technological innovation.

To conclude this section, we can see that there are multiple actors within the system, each having their own purposes and means of realising them. Some of the aims and methods overlap, but others do not – leaving what we might think of as a residue of dissimilar aims to be dealt with, in many cases by the teachers. It would be wrong to impute motives to any group within the Cable-School project, but clearly there are different user constituencies the project has to serve in some way: the schools; the local council; CableCo; parents-*qua*-parents and parents as potential consumers of CableCo's products. In the above we have seen the ways in which the service was developed in co-operation with schools and, as it was implemented, how it was developed by and in schools. We have seen that the local council reorganisation created a new *potential* constituency and that CableCo oriented to Cable-School as a means of demonstrating the concept and the utility of cable-based networked communications within an organisational framework. We have also seen how the system was oriented as a marketing resource by CableCo to address parents as consumers of ICTs through the development of educational uses for the technologies. There was a stress on the development of user constituencies and marketing constituencies that did not centre on the original core concept of the project devised by New School in co-operation with CableCo. Somewhere within the multiple constituencies of Cable School there was a residue of dissimilar aims that had to be managed in some way. The growing 'interpretive flexibility' of the system by CableCo was something teachers began to feel uncomfortable with since the revised vision moved away from that which had been evolved in co-operation with teachers.

In addition, teachers began to feel that there were problems with the reliability of the system. *This is a central question in the use of the system.* In suggesting that teachers use the web in the classroom, the system has to be robust enough to be relied upon. As one of the main informants pointed out, there has to be a reliable connection for use with students since they will rapidly become disruptive if the system does not work. He likened the students to a 'big stew pan boiling away, simmering under there, you know, and if the network goes down it's going to be hard to contain that. If the server goes down do you have another lesson planned? No, well then there's a problem' (interview 16/12/97). Thus teachers are reluctant to use the web in classroom situations because of the problems of controlling students should something go wrong. A teacher from Glen Academy pointed out that the problem of reliability was significant in recruiting new teachers to use the web (and thus expanding the user base of the Cable-School). A technology with a reputation for unreliability would not be adopted for the reasons mentioned above. While it was fine to use the web outside of the classroom, it was simply not robust or reliable enough to use in lessons. Having given some idea of the problems of the system, we can describe the ways it was used in schools and discuss some of the solutions that evolved from the experience of Cable-School in use.

The System in the Schools

Within the schools, we can see the growth of problems with the system and the emergence of *local* solutions as processes of social learning. Having all the equipment and network connections together with the content of the Cable-School was part of an ongoing project. The aim of the Cable-School was to provide a basis for collaboration within and between schools, notably at the level of circulating worksheets via the web. However, the majority of the respondents regarded the materials provided on the web as poor and not suited to the work that they were doing with students. It is notable that while the worksheets were notionally generated by NBET, a number were written by employees of the cable company.[19] However, teachers were not simply 'consumers' of the worksheets – there was an expectation in the project that teachers would also provide worksheets as a part of their involvement with the project. Notably, teachers did not receive payment or other credit for providing these worksheets and the lack of incentives might be one reason for the amount of teacher generated content.[20] Regarding the provision of content by teachers, a member of one organisation connected with Cable-School noted:

'That was something that didn't go down that well with the teachers, (it) didn't go as we hoped it would. We didn't get the response from teachers that we were looking for, and basically we set up what you see on the web pages in-house, and that's it. There's nothing else we're going to add to the site, the ball's really back in CableCo's park. It's up to them now'. (Interview April 30 1997).

Teachers were expected to produce worksheets for placement on the web but that in the majority of cases this did not occur. Among reasons cited were: demands on time, differences in syllabus between schools and the apparent inability of teachers to communicate with each other on this topic.

There were meetings about Cable-School, but these were largely attended by senior staff in the schools, often at head or deputy-head level, and not by the teachers using the system. The meetings that did exist were used for the management of the system as an experiment (albeit one formulated largely by public relations as opposed to pedagogic concerns) by CableCo. The senior teaching staff was largely peripheral and the meetings were not a forum for the exchange of ideas among teachers. One member of staff told me that it was rare to be invited along to meetings by senior staff, and rarer still to see fellow teachers of equivalent status there.

To sum up, we are left with a system that has a more or less static content and little if any communication between teachers below senior management level. It is therefore perhaps not surprising that the system became the focus of innovation initiated by individual teachers, usually in isolation. It is to this that I now turn.

Innovating – The Social Learning of Independence

The majority of teachers that I spoke to, have now come to regard the Cable-School as *something that there is no need to consult*[21] when planning courses, lectures and the like. School computing infrastructure and the web connection meant that evolving local Intranets was comparatively simple. Materials were taken from the web and placed on local servers for use within departments. In other schools, the solution has been to maintain lists of URLs that are accessible by students either in class or in their own time, usually in the school library. The majority of teachers still do not use the system at all, save for e-mail and the like. Teachers are not, in general, conservative in terms of the teaching methods and technologies that they use. Indeed, teaching has been an area where a great deal of innovation in both technology and content has taken place over the last twenty years. Therefore, it is important that readers do not take away from this chapter the idea that the reason that Cable-School did not work was due to the inherent conservatism of teachers. The teachers with whom the Cable-School project was discussed were in general enthusiastic about the potential of ICTs and keen to discuss ways of integrating them into their pedagogic practice. For example, one senior teacher noted that she felt that the Internet could be used to provide students with self-directed learning packages that they could use both at home and at school. She felt that these would not only improve learning but also have a positive effect on students' self-esteem. Further, she saw that the potential of CD-ROM for education was significant in that it offered interactivity and a less 'dry' and enhanced way of obtaining information.[22] This is not an isolated case; the majority of teachers with whom I spoke were enthusiastic about the potential of ICTs for education.

This raises a central question: why did Cable-School encounter such problems? The Cable-School appears to be regarded as problematic by several of the teachers that I spoke with. It has been under-utilised by the majority of its user constituency. Those who do use it have tended to employ the equipment – the cable modems – to generate their own web-based teaching resources for their schools as opposed to using Cable-School to share these among schools. In short, materials found on the web have been integrated into pedagogic practice. 'Found' materials are used in preference to those generated by colleagues within the Cable-School project. One teacher had used the system to trawl through educational publishers' sites looking for examples of worksheets that she would examine before committing the school to purchase of the packages *in toto*.

Evangelism and Local Expertise

The potential of the system as it was originally envisaged has led some teachers, usually those who teach computing, to become entrepreneurs or evangelists. They showed colleagues how materials from the web could be included in their lessons and worksheets, collected lists of URLs and downloaded them, suggested multimedia for the library and so on. These teachers are in the 'front line' insofar as it is to them that their colleagues turn for advice and for resources.

These innovative teachers have become the focus of informal social learning about the use of web technologies in the schools, with no extra time or funding. During visits to the schools, the researchers were present in the offices and classrooms of the local experts when other members of staff arrived to discuss potential sites and applications as well as problems.[23] The move to employ some of the components of the Cable-School system has been extended within the majority of schools that employ other more basic network resources, notably e-mail, within their systems. In this section of the report it is perhaps useful to comment on the adoption and use of these 'banal' technologies as modes of social learning. Put simply, as the Cable-School has become problematic in the ways described above, teachers have learned how to employ the resources that were in place selectively to undertake both the tasks that Cable-School was intended to carry out and to develop novel uses of the technologies.

In short, there has been a learning of independence in that technologies have been used in new ways and for novel purposes. E-mail is used to communicate within the school and, to a lesser extent, outside. School web servers hold caches of pages for local use as opposed to being a gateway to a 'dedicated' service provided by Cable-School. Teachers use the multimedia capabilities of the computers in their classrooms to integrate CD-ROM based materials into lessons. There has been a move by staff to provide CD-ROMs and locally cached web pages in school libraries for use outside of lessons. Obviously, some of this would have happened irrespective of the Cable-School project; yet the role of Cable-School cannot be overlooked in providing a putative infrastructure both in terms of the technology provided and the underlying concepts used. Just as Cable-School was initiated out of a growing understanding and willingness to engage with the potential of ICTs, Cable-School itself provided teachers with the equipment *and the conceptual resources* to introduce materials from new ICTs into their pedagogic practice.

The Social Learning of Independence: An Example

> When the server went down a few weeks ago, pretty soon people were knocking on my door saying, (that) 'the e-mail (is) down, what do we do'. I said 'I'm trying to fix it', and they were really stuck, (asking) 'how do we communicate?' So I (said) 'think back to how you did it before, you sent a (child) round to all the classrooms with a note'. 'Oh yes' they said, but really we couldn't work now without it. (There are) some things that are on e-mail that you wouldn't say to people's faces, and I say to them (holds hand out as if reading) 'you would not say this to their faces would you', but (that is) what's different about e-mail, and it's a real part of how we work now.

From the quotation above, it is obvious that e-mail has become a central communicative resource for teachers within the system. Within the schools that I visited, e-mail has become the main mode of communication between (and in some cases *within*) departments. In one school, a new senior teacher contrasted the predominance of face-to-face communication in his previous school to the use of e-mail. He suggested that e-mail enabled him to communicate quickly and effectively with colleagues and that the medium allowed room for humour and efficient contact. He liked being able to communicate quickly, without having to send notes or to walk across the school. He stated that he would still visit people 'when it was appropriate, to have a cup of coffee', and that he did not feel e-mail eliminated or attenuated human contact. Summing up, the staff member noted that he did not know how he could live without e-mail now. The point of this example – doubtless repeated in other schools and organisations – is to draw attention to the ways that new methods of communication are integrated into the practices of the school, and the ways that these can be used as media for social learning.

E-mail as a communicative medium did not present significant barriers to use. In particular, unlike the Cable-School system, it did not presume any significant change in the pedagogic practice of teachers within the schools. The e-mail system allowed teachers to swap site recommendations and to discuss improvements to the system with colleagues. It also enabled the development of a more informal communicative culture within the school. Within the private environment afforded by e-mail, teachers could talk about topics that had previously been difficult to discuss, such as normative issues, social events and the like.

Thus, one area where some learning has taken place is the use of e-mail connections between staff. As can be seen above, there is a reliance on e-mail as a communication tool within the school. One teacher pointed out that his colleagues rely on the e-mail system where they had previously obtained most of their information in the general staff room. He noted that before the introduction of e-mail it was possible for teachers to 'learn all that they need to about what's going on' by spending a break-time in the staff room. With e-mail, the majority of the teachers now spend their breaks with colleagues in the same discipline in 'staff bases' – rooms where teachers can keep their books and files, and where there is access to telephones and e-mail. We might speculate on the implications of this self-imposed segregation for the development of the Cable-School and for pedagogic practice in the wider sense, yet anecdotally there is a perception that e-mail is central to the life of the school (at least for teachers).[24]

There is also a perception that e-mail is the way in which the majority of teachers will become enfranchised by technology. A computing teacher – regarded as a local evangelist and expert in her school – noted that her colleagues were used to e-mail and realised that they could not 'break' the computers or do any harm by sending e-mail messages. From this, their confidence improved, and it was through this that they saw the potentialities[25] of the web and other ICTs. Although this process was not without problems, as one teacher pointed out:

> I think the technology still gets in the way, I mean to get to share it with other schools, well there's only two or three in the Glen Region context who are closely associated (. . .) and there's only one other school with an internal e-mail network, I mean you have to have that to find out how easy it is to communicate electronically (. . .) and that it doesn't get in the way. (. . .) Sometimes it's quite difficult to get people to see the advantages of it, (the majority of the schools in Glen Region are cabled up, but) there's not enough of an advantage in it (for some of them).
> (Interview, New School 16/12/97.)

To reiterate, social learning took place in the use of e-mail as a way of accessing the potential of the infrastructure that was employed by Cable-

School. Through e-mail, never central to the Cable-School project, teachers became enfranchised and their confidence in exploring the possibilities of ICTs grew. In the schools visited during the SLIM research e-mail was pivotal in stimulating awareness of and access to new ICTs. CableSchool was not the only way in which teachers came to engage with ICTs, but in this research it was the main way. Returning to the theme of the social learning of independence, it is notable that as the Cable-School project became more problematic, new ways were found to employ the infrastructure left in place – hence the notion of *learning* independence. Schools became users of infrastructure and not participants in the Cable-School project. In the case of e-mail, this had the result of enfranchising teachers who had not previously engaged with Cable-School (and those who had found it difficult to use). It is interesting that such a mundane technology can both signify the adoption of an independent engagement with ICT's and enable teachers to become enfranchised.[26]

The End of Cable-School

Cable-School provided the information infrastructure, but its success would have depended on a change in the practices of teachers, in particular in making their teaching documents visible to other schools on the system. There was no incentive system or collective culture (either established or emergent) established to motivate such a shift. Though teachers did not invest in the Cable-School in the way planned, they did show in their practice how the technological infrastructure supplied could be adapted to their purposes – for example as a means of access to web-based teaching aids.

One of the main reasons for not sharing materials, quoted by a number of informants, was the question of audience. Sharing a document meant taking a risk with one's personal and professional reputation – in short the document could mean that the teacher lost face by sending a poor worksheet to peers.[27] What could count as a poor worksheet was not known because the teachers did not know the standards of the peers with whom they were sharing information.[28] There was, therefore, a risk involved in sending documents to the Cable-School that one would be revealed among one's peers as less competent, losing 'face' among an important community that has nothing more on which to judge one.

CableCo's manager, Barry, noted this as a problem within the Cable-School system:

> Two things about teachers: one is that they don't like to be taught, they prefer to be given information and then make what they will from it themselves, they don't like classrooms, albeit that they stand in front of one all day. And the second thing is (. . .) not quite copyright, but people are protective about their own materials (. . .) from two points of view. One is they don't necessarily want other people who are lazy, as they see it, using their materials and not giving anything in return. And secondly, they don't wish to be criticised by their peers, so if they put up a piece of material and other people say 'this is crap'; then that goes a long way to denting a teacher's ego. So those two issues may count against us (i.e. the Cable-School project, RS) in the long term.
> (Interview 28 August 1997)

In addition, there was also the problem of standards – no agreement was made on the way in which pages should be placed on the web. Documents were placed onto the Cable-School server in a variety of formats such as HTML, Claris Works and Adobe PDF format. This led to a problem in sharing the documents – some were readable by all, others by only one or two members of the Cable-School. One respondent noted that the problem with HTML documents was that they took time to place on the web and that one had to learn to use HTML for what would be 'essentially a paper document' (paraphrase of interview with New School Teacher, 16/12/97). As one teacher pointed out:

> It's going to be on paper and there's no need to use HTML for it, you can use Claris Works to deal with that and to make that appear on paper, and there's no need for anything else. (T)hat's something that got in the way of communicating it back and forth, an artificial barrier. The technology got in the way of what was quite a good idea. I think it could have been done, but there were problems.
> (New School Teacher, 16/12/97)

To sum up, there was no communication between the teachers at the interpersonal level, where they could discuss the Cable-School and get to know and to trust each other so that they could share documents. The initiators of the Cable-School had presumed that the system would be the basis for interactions, and that a community would arise naturally from these interactions.[29] There was no attention to the perceptions of the teachers regarding the sharing of materials and the potential for risk to personal and professional reputations. A teacher from New School pointed out that within the framework of the 'Higher Still' programme a number of meetings had suggested suitable web sites for classroom use. He noted that these were also discussed in magazines aimed at teachers. Added to this, the technology for submitting documents was not stipulated – again we must assume that the initiators of the project imagined that a *de facto* standard would arise naturally. However, with the lack of communication between teachers, this did not occur, and documents were placed onto the web in a number of incommensurable formats.

I spoke above of the learning of independence: given the presence of the technology, in the majority of schools some other way was found to achieve some of the aims of the Cable-School. As I have said, this was achieved at a local level – each school adopting its own solution with the technology available. In all this, they retained the idea that the web was a unique pedagogic tool, it was just the manner of use that changed. The majority of learning was based around the computing staff – they became informal resources – when the envisaged use of the Cable-School failed to develop and sought solutions to areas that the Cable-School did not address.

A number of teachers with whom I discussed the Cable-School in the above research were contacted again after the school vacation – what follows is a summary of the conversations and work that I undertook to follow the progress of the Cable-School.

> I haven't looked at the pages, I don't even know if the website that NBET were hosting still exists. Something like that has got to be kept alive and fairly dynamic if we could just be bothered to go back and run some stuff to tail it off.

Cable-School is now seen as being 'dead in the water' by those who were involved in it at the school level. The demise of Cable-School can be traced to two trends: firstly, as noted above, there was a growing discontent with the idea of the Cable-School – teachers were concerned that the ideas of document sharing and a common forum for educators were not working in practice. If one examines the Cable-School website, it is notable that the majority of the pages are the work of CableCo employees (notably Barry) and not the teachers themselves. As I noted in the above, there was a feeling that the connection to the web was the most important thing and that the accompanying package – the Cable-School itself – was of secondary importance.

The second point leading to the demise of the Cable-School is located within CableCo itself. From conversations with Barry I found that the company was involved in a round of redundancies and an extensive restructuring program. This had effects on the Cable-School as well as other areas. The principal member of staff responsible for the Cable-School project, Barry, left the company in late 1997 along with a number of other personnel. While there was a perception among teachers that Cable-School was not well managed before that time, after Barry's departure the perception was that *there was no direction at all* to the project.

Organisationally, CableCo gave the users no other contacts within the company (save for the people who logged faults: 'your fault has been noted and that's all we got' [Teacher, interviewed 16/12/97]). The same teacher relates the story of a visit from a CableCo manager based in London: he notes that the word of this visit spread through the school and there were a number of people who wanted to discuss the situation with the manager when he visited. There is a degree of cynicism regarding the expansion of Cable-School through the UK. All this has led *inter alia* to a more acute sense of abandonment among the teachers. Teachers learn to become independent web users and content generators while still using the technological infrastructure of Cable-School.

Interpretive Flexibility: A Case of Cable-Schools?

I have said that Cable School failed: it has been suggested (Bijker, personal communication) that this is not the case. Certainly teachers used the system enthusiastically after the demise of the first Cable-School – notably the email – but the point is that *the project-as-a-whole* failed in its own terms. This is why I speak of the social learning of independence. Teachers *did* use the system, but not in the manner intended. Cable-school as a *gestalt* of content and infrastructure failed, that much is certain from the above. Yet, as Bijker points out, the teachers were enthusiastic users of email and the like. Can we then say that Cable-School failed *per se*?

In this section of the chapter I want to examine the possibility that there is not one Cable-School but several. This possibility is opened up by the notion of interpretive flexibility (IF). IF is used within the social constructivist analysis of technology to suggest that:

technological artifacts are culturally constructed and interpreted; in other words, the interpretive flexibility of an artifact must be shown. By this we mean not only that there is flexibility in how people think of or interpret artifacts but also that there is flexibility in how artifacts are *designed*. There is not just one possible way or one best way of designing an artifact. (Pinch and Bijker 1987, p. 40)

From an IF viewpoint, there are at least two Cable-Schools: the first is that built by CableCo while the second is that used by the teachers. This does not mean, however, that we can save Cable-School from the flames and call it a success. In the terms envisaged by the developers, whatever degree of IF one employs, Cable-School failed. However, if we take the system that the teachers salvaged – for the sake of convenience let us call it Cable-School v2 – there *was* something that can be called a success. The manner in which teachers used the email system and created their own web caches illustrates the success of Cable-School v2.

The original cable-school falls away while the infrastructure is used to develop, through the social learning of independence, Cable-School v2. IF enables us to see this process and to argue that the falling away of the original Cable-School was the effect of teachers' learning how to design flexibly using the components of Cable-School. To be sure, technology develops in unforeseen ways: the case of Cable-School and Cable-School v2 shows this process.

Conclusions

Separating the Social and the Technical

The first point is the question of computer mediated interaction against interaction in groups and the impact that this has for setting up a network such as the Cable-School. This goes to the heart of the possible divide between the social and the technical. We must assess the impact of keeping the two areas separate or, perhaps, of presuming that the social will inevitably follow the lead of the technical. The Cable-School was started as a technological initiative for schools to use the web and to share information. However, there was no accompanying idea of setting out the ground rules for sharing information within a community – indeed there was no community established outwith that on the web. As one teacher noted, the Cable-School 'went too far, too deeply, too quickly' – ignoring the importance of establishing a social context in which users could know others with whom they were to share information.

It would seem that Cable-School as a project has not been greatly successful – indeed one might assert that it has 'failed' in terms of its public goals. However, in itself, that is not really of interest to us – what is of interest, and of significance is the *manner* in which it has failed. Cable-School was a technology-led project concerned with the development of infrastructure as opposed to social networks. This is not intended to be a criticism of the project *per se* since CableCo is not in the business of building social movements. There is a need for these groups to be integrated into the project: social interaction does not grow up around technology as a matter of course, there is a need for it to be promoted actively, especially in the lives of busy people such as teachers. When one considers the lives of teachers, Cable-School is just one more meeting to go to among many – there is a need to integrate the activity within the school day and to make participation meaningful in career terms.

Just as there is a need to integrate the networks into school life, the content of Cable-School also needs integration in the classroom. I have shown how the system was regarded as relatively 'thin' in terms of content: at a classroom level this makes the product virtually useless. It is not surprising that teachers regarded the system as peripheral: what Cable-School did was done already by books and other teaching materials to which teachers were used. Why, then, should they use a technology that required further training and which provided little or nothing more than extant materials?

Further, consider the potential for problems in teaching if the network fails during a lesson: we have seen that teachers regard the classroom situation as a 'stew pan' ready to boil over. The point is that Cable-School was not robust enough for teachers to rely on. This is not a critique of Cable-School alone, one could find examples of networked ICTs elsewhere that are simply not robust enough to be used in dependably in classrooms. We can say the same about other media – video programming may well fail to function properly, viewgraphs may also fail for some reason. The point is that technology is 'fragile', it involves a risk. This being the case, there has to be some unique reason for using the medium.[30] Taken together with questions of content, teachers saw no decisive reason to use Cable-School in the manner in which it was established. Regarding the use of technology in unanticipated ways, the local caching of relevant web pages[31] was one possible solution: with local caches teachers could rely on relevant content of the quality required being available as they needed it.[32] Cable-School was used for its infrastructure and not as a repository of content *per se*.

The central problem of Cable-School was its failure to be integrated as a whole into the fabric of pedagogic practice. In the above, I have attempted to provide some reasons for this and to suggest some ways in which teachers 'worked around' these, using the technology in unanticipated ways to achieve pedagogic aims. In sum, Cable-School was not robust enough in terms of technology or content, and it made a fatal presumption that social interaction would grow inevitably around a technological infrastructure to sustain the project. Again I stress that Cable-School is not alone in making this presumption, and as a final component of the paper I turn to another development that appears to be following the same trajectory: the UK 'National Grid for Learning' initiative.

Notes

1   In all, three tape-recorded interviews were made together with five other interviews in which written notes were taken. The two teachers whose comments are presented here discussed the project with us over a period of one year - for various reasons (especially pressures of time within the rubric of the high school year) other teachers were consulted less often (and in one case I was told that, on discussing the dynamics of the system, that 'really, I don't use it any more - it's peripheral to my work as a teacher' [hand-written notes of telephone conversation, April 1998]).

2   This is not to say that we wanted to 'play off' the accounts in a 'he said - she said' manner; rather the aim was to explore each in its own context and not to undercut or ironicise these commentaries.

3   In the current UK situation, there is a market for education - parental choice regarding schools was a key feature of the Conservative administration's education policy. Schools can, to a degree, select the students they take - equally students (or more correctly their parents) can select schools to which they wish to apply (although this is regulated by geographical location and school numbers).

4   The successor to the original *Joint Academic Network*. For a summary of the system, see: http://www.bus.ed.ac.uk/janet.html

5   Of course, it should be noted that I have only the comments of teachers involved - there may be 'good organisational reasons' for the perceived change in attitude. I should also note that since the interview on which these comments were based took place, Sun has been actively involved in the UK Net Year Project which aims to assist UK schools to connect to the 'National Grid for Learning' introduced by the Labor administration (see http://www.uknetyear.org).

6   CableCo is the local cable network provider - a division of a larger North American corporation, it is responsible for cable-based provision (TV, internet and telephony) within the East of Scotland.

7   i.e. built or substantially refurbished within the last five or so years.

8   North British Technology university is also situated in North British City. From this interview it appears that there were a number of potential universities available to undertake the connection to SuperJANET -however the original candidate was the University of North Britain (see above).

9   For example, the North British City area had the Lowlands Regional Council (referred to as Lowland Region), and the North British City Council. The re-organisation of local government meant that the responsibilities of the two councils were amalgamated into the North British City Council. Areas such as highways, information technology, education and so on were brought together within the one administrative body.

10   In other words the account given here serves to orient us to the service as it was planned and not as it was experienced by users.

11   Criteria such as examination results, attendance, facilities and the like are features of this assessment process. The importance of the process should not be underestimated - 'league tables' are published in both local and national newspapers, and featured in other media; schools perceived as 'doing badly' are often the subject of so-called 'hit squads' that take over management of schools to effect improvements. As we shall see, this is important in any consideration of the development of projects such as Cable-School, notably the UK government's 'National Grid for Learning'.

12   Since the initiation of the Cable-School project, the education research group has become involved in the 'Cyberschools' initiative which aims to get all Scottish schools online.

13   In no sense is this to critique the concept of a marketing strategy *per se* or in this case - to be sure, such a strategy is required. Rather the aim here is to explicate the strategy as it is sociologically interesting and as it impacts on issue of social learning both within CableCo and the schools it served.

14   By A, B, C, the teacher addresses social class of potential users: A being the upper class, and C lower middle class. The point here is that teachers are somewhat cynical vis-à-vis the pedagogic importance of the Cable-School as compared to its use as a marketing strategy to obtain coverage in homes not traditionally large consumers of CableCo's products and services.

15   Especially at the level of technical support and in terms of the meetings established for teachers and CableCo staff to discuss Cable-School.

16   Providing the city Council with a new internal network - including connections to the City Education Department

17   While the majority of the schools visited were of modern design, incorporating space for network cables etc. in their design, others were located in older, more traditional buildings. In the former network capability was a part of the fabric of the building and 'there' whatever use was made of it; in the latter, the infrastructure had to be accommodated into the schools' fabric and could be seen as more deliberate. For example, in the older schools cables often only went to areas such as the computer block; other areas had to come to these parts of the school to use the system. It would thus be interesting to examine how the spatial arrangements of network connections have an impact on the use of the system in the schools studied.

18   In addition to all the other activities that teachers undertake during and after school time.

19   Other worksheets were placed onto the system by various people in an incomplete state. Some of these have not been completed over one year after they were placed on the server.

20   This is not to imply that teachers looked for rewards - rather we can speculate that the implementation of some remunerative scheme (either financial or in terms of career structure) might be a consideration for future projects - see my discussion of the National Grid for Learning, below.

21   A recent reading of the mailings to the system showed that only three teachers regularly posted messages. From research we know that even these three had evolved methods of coping outside the system. It appears that email is used to maintain a presence within the cable supplier - perhaps in the hope of maintaining the cable modem connection.

22   Extracted from interview notes (SM/G/26-6-97).

23   Of course, they do not always turn to these teachers for any problem. An informal network of teachers has evolved within each subject area (and between subject areas) to whom the teachers can turn with problems. Many of these teachers learned to solve problems in practice, but an equal number had originally sought solutions from the computing staff.

24   One good illustration of the importance of email is to be found in the example given in previous reports of what happened when the system crashed. A teacher in Glen Academy related the problems teachers had in communicating through the school, suggesting that teachers should remember that it was still possible to send a student around the school with a note.

25   And, in problems with crashing, the pitfalls of reliance on such technologies.

26   While it is not a recipe for enfranchisement, the use of banal (and perhaps robust) technologies appears to be a good place to begin. A conjecture: if Cable-School had begun with such a mundane, 'bottom up' technology might its success have been greater?

27   One teacher summarised this succinctly, saying 'well they might ask 'what is this?' and they might laugh at it. Now I'm not going to put things onto the server because they might be crap and they (other teachers) might laugh and say 'who is this guy?' You know'. (Interview 12/12/97).

28   Equally, there was a possibility (especially in a situation where schools compete in 'league tables') that a good worksheet could be used by poor teachers, raising the standard of their school without any improvement in the educators performance.

29   OG noted that he established a list server for computing teachers. He said that less than half of the teachers joined this mailing list (interview 16/12/97).

30   It is not surprising that the majority of those interviewed noted that students used CD-ROM outside lessons and within the context of the library - where supervision and advice could be given.

31   Something else that teachers had to do outside the usual activities.

32   Quality and reliability are linked here.

6 From 'Spice Girls' to Cybergirls: The Role of Multimedia in the Construction of Young Girls' Fascination for and Interest in Computers

HEGE NORDLI

Abstract

The article has a gender approach to multimedia use. The case is about why some girls use multimedia and why they actually like it. The computer-enthusiastic girls learn their skills mainly at home by using the trial-and-error strategy. The role of formal education is taken over by home learning. Different from other girls, the computer-fascinated girls attach a fun meaning to the computer. They do not look at the computer as a tool but more as a 'play pal' they can have fun with. This gives us some indication about the process of diversification of the meaning of multimedia, and of appropriation processes at school and at home. Last but not least, we learn about ways to create an interest for multimedia among girls.

Introduction: May Girls Be Configured as Computer Enthusiast?

Studies of computer users have contributed to forming the popular image of the computer dedicated, usually called 'hackers', as an all-male group with exotic features (see, e.g., Aune 1992; Turkle 1984, 1996; Håpnes 1996; Nissen 1996). They tend to have computers as their main, or even only, life interest; they work extremely long hours and spend nights in front of a screen, and are not particularly interested in 'normal' social activities. For such reasons, hackers are interesting to study, and we probably know more about boys' and men's relationship to computers than we do about the way girls and women think and act in relation to these machines.

Even if there has been a sustained interest in women and computing, a dominant concern of these studies has been the assumption that women do not like to use computers. Moreover, female users are seen as not having the same kind of intimate and compelling relationship with the machine sometimes found among men. In fact, women are portrayed as instrumental. They perceive the computer as a tool, rather than as a friend (see, e.g., Rasmussen & Håpnes 1991).

It seems reasonable to assume that the interest in computers as a school subject and a potential vocational area is related to computer enthusiasm, although we should not assume that enthusiasm or strong dedication is a prerequisite for engagement with computers. While male hackers are not representative of male computer users, the study of their culture may teach us important lessons about male relationships with computers. Similarly, the existence of female computer enthusiasts could be seen as an indication of a growing interest in computers among girls. Moreover, the features of their enthusiasm might tell us about what aspects of computers that are interesting to girls as well as providing a basis to analyse in greater detail the gendering of computer fascination. The latter term refers to the possibility of gender differences in terms of styles of using computers as well as the way that different aspects of computer fascination may be understood by the actors themselves in terms of 'masculinity' and 'femininity', and attributed to male or female practices or cultural expressions. Our main hypothesis is that the current transformation of personal computers into multimedia machines with Internet access makes computers more fascinating to girls and facilitates the development of feminine styles of use.

In the last few years, there has been a public concern in Norway about the need to increase girls' interest in computers. Particularly, the multimedia turn with the introduction of the Internet, cd-roms, and e-mail, has meant that information and communication technologies (ICTs) have been heralded as an obligatory condition for future success in the labour market. Since the number of females studying computer science or working in the computer industry has long been low in Norway, there was good reason to worry. Even worse, a couple of years ago the 'alarm' was sounded because the amount of women studying computing was even decreasing.

Norwegian education authorities have been very much concerned with girls' lack of interest in computers,[1] but their strategies have mainly been aimed at a general strengthening of the role of computers in primary and secondary schools. As is argued by Aune and Sørensen (this volume, chapter 8), the Norwegian education authorities may be seen to be involved in a full-scale experiment to promote ICT skills and competence through schools, even if the policy instruments that are employed are rather general in nature. The effort to encourage girls to become interested in ICT, multimedia and computers may be interpreted as a part of that experiment, conducted through general encouragement to schools and teachers to take the problem seriously and also through specific development projects at selected schools.

The study will not be concerned with the educational politics in particular, but look at whether any of these moves can be said to have had an effect on the girls' enthusiasm for computers. For a more detailed description of the development of the education politics in Norway, read Aune and Sørensen, chapter 8 in this volume.

In this chapter we will examine the effects on this experiment by studying a selected group of girls that were, in fact, enthusiastic and fascinated by personal computers. In this way, we will provide an in-depth view of some features of this fascination as well as providing information about what kind of initiatives/efforts (if any) strengthen the girls' interest in the use of ICTs. In particular, to evaluate the national full-scale experiment, we will analyse whether the schools are doing anything that evokes interest among girls, and if so, what? Is their fascination with ICT a result of educational strategies, or is it an outcome of other influences? This will be considered as a possible instance of learning by regulation, to learn from efforts to configure and shape a particular instance of socio-technical relations (Sørensen 1996).

The paper uses empirical material from the study 'Communication and information technology – new possibilities for girls?'[2] The total data-material consists of observation and in-depth interviews with 41 girls at the age of 14, 15 and 16 at five Norwegian schools. Here I am concentrating only on the girls whom I characterise as computer-fascinated.[3] These informants were chosen according to three criteria. First of all they had to be computer enthusiast. This means that they displayed a definite positive attitude towards, and a clear interest in the use of computers. Secondly, they had to have computing skills. I did not expect them to be experts, but to have greater skills than girls in general at that age. Thirdly, they should use computers on a regular basis. These selection criteria mean, of course, that the informants are atypical and do not represent Norwegian girls in general.

Gender and ICT: Differences and Differentiations

Computer-use statistics of Norwegian pupils show that boys make the majority of those using computers actively in and outside school (Sjøberg 1985; SSB 1995). We find the same trend in higher education in Norway. The relative share of female master-students at the Department of computer science at the University of Oslo in 96/97 was only 6 % (Stuedahl 1997). However, from 1997 the trend seems to have turned and progressively more women start to study computer science. The autumn 1997 the percentage of women studying computing at the Norwegian University of Science and Technology had increased to 37%.

As already mentioned, much of the research on the use of ICT has focused on hackers. Sherry Turkle, one of the pioneers in the field, argues in *The Second Self* that hackers have a fear of relationships with people and therefore have relationships with machines instead (Turkle 1984). The computer becomes a partner that offers a particularly seductive refuge to someone who is having trouble dealing with people. She found that many hackers first sought out such a refuge during early adolescence, when other people, their feelings and demands seemed particularly frightening. They found an escape in the computer and never moved beyond it. The hacker culture is held together by mutual tolerance and respect for radical individualism. Turkle (1984) sees the hacker as a personality who is fascinated by the possibilities of control in computer technology. They have a culture of mastery and individualism. Above all, she found that hackers loved the machine for itself. In this study she describes a universal hacker culture.

As a contrast, Tove Håpnes (1996) found in her study of Norwegian hackers that they did not consider their relationship to their machine to be personal or close. The hackers she studied had domesticated computers as a tool for work. They developed and shaped a style of work and manners that contained elements of competition as well as collaboration. The culture she described, was individualistic and collective, with elements of competition and collaboration. Play and entertainment went hand in hand with work and utility. Håpnes' hackers talked about winning and mastery, but also about the importance of being artistic and interactive. In comparison with

Turkle's MIT hackers, Håpnes found the Norwegian hacker culture less extreme and more heterogeneous. Moreover, it allowed members to model different masculinities through accepting a variety of personal qualities.

Turkle (1984) has also put forward two influential arguments about the gendering of computer use. First, there is the assertion that one may identify two ideal types of programming that she calls hard and soft mastery. Hard mastery is a rational, step-by-step, pre-planned programming strategy, while soft mastery is more of an artistic and interactive, trial-and-error type of approach. The former is preferred by males, but not all, while the latter is preferred by females, but not all.

The second argument is that women's relationship to computers is hampered by what Turkle (1988) calls 'the fear of the intimate machine'. In the computer culture, she argues, it is perceived as natural to have an 'intimate relationship' with the computer. However, women feel that intimate relationships are for humans and not for machines, and therefore they turn away from computing. The argument has been contested, for example, by Bente Rasmussen and Tove Håpnes (1991). It was the culture around the machine that pushed the girls away, not the machine in itself. It was some boys' dominating behaviour around the machine that contributed most to creating the insecurity that the girls felt towards the machine. The girls began to believe that there was something important they did not know, and they began to feel insecure in relation to the boys, the ones that supposedly knew what they did not.

In her recent book, *Life on The Screen. Identity in the Age of the Internet*, Turkle (1996) argues that the culture around computers is being transformed and in some sense trivialised. The previous influence of 'hobbyist' PC users who felt that they needed to understand how the machine functioned, is diminishing. The computer culture is, according to Turkle (1996), close to the point where full membership does not require programming skills, but is accorded to people who use software out of a box.

Turkle (1996) argues that the computer culture has changed from a culture of calculation to a culture of simulation. The fascination of computers used to be tied to the seduction of programming. Today, it is, according to Turkle, tied to the seduction of the interface. She claims that the lessons of computing today have little to do with calculation and rules; instead they concern simulation, navigation, and interaction. Turkle (1996, p. 19) also claims that 'programming is no longer cut and dried, but it is elusive'. It seems as if programming knowledge is no longer as important as before. Turkle has found that it is no longer so important to know what is happening beneath the surface of the machine, but to be able to move between easy recognisable icons on the surface.

The social image of the computer is, according to Turkle (1996), far more complex than before. It now evokes both physical isolation and intense interaction with other people. Multimedia personal computers have become the tools we use to write, to design, to play with ideas, shapes and images, to create video sequences and musical effects, to create interactive novels and graphical images. This means that the new machines have led to development of a new set of intellectual and emotional associations. The culture of personal computing now makes room for ways of knowing that are dependent on the 'concrete' manipulation of virtual paintbrushes and paints, virtual pens and paper.

Thus, we face a new terrain of computer use and possibly also a new configuration of computer users. This means that we should be careful not to invoke traditional masculine and feminine stereotypes. In fact, since technology and gender are in mutual interaction (Berg 1997; Lie 1998), we have to be open-minded about the nature of fascination with ICTs among girls/women as well as boys/men. On the one hand, however, it seems reasonable to follow Turkle's lead and look for an ICT fascination among girls that is based more on interactivity and communication than on programming. On the other, the idea of mutual shaping of gender and technology should make us sensitive to the possibility that a fascination with ICTs could be related to a different understanding of femininity. In the following, we will examine these possibilities.

The analysis of computer fascinated girls should be understood on the basis that PCs have become a standard part of the inventory of many households. Today, 39 per cent of the households in Norway have computers.[4] More than one million Norwegians have Internet access.[5] The number of pupils with Internet access at school is growing. At junior high school, the average number of pupils per computer is 11, and more than half of the computers have Internet access.[6]

The aim of the education authorities is to achieve the integration and use of ICT within a variety of subjects at school. In this manner, they also want to make girls more active. In this paper, we will look at what computer fascinated girls perceive of the role of computers at school. Do computers affect them in any way? Is it a problem for them to get access to computers? How do they characterise their relationship to the computer? Are they afraid of being absorbed? How do the girls experience the computer culture? Are they attracted to or averted by it?

The multimedia transformation of computers makes us expect a more widespread use. Do the new opportunities offered by multimedia applications make computers more attractive to girls? Do the girls become more like the boys? Or do they think that boys become more like girls in their relationship to ICTs?

In the rest of this paper, I will describe and analyse the girls' relations to computers, how they become computer-users, and how they use computers in their everyday life. The argument is structured in three parts. The first part compares the girls perceptions of themselves with some general expectations and myths about 'computer-girls' as having an untraditional, 'male' interest. In the second part, I will look at computer-fascination. What aspects of computers are attractive to the girls? In the third part, I analyse the girls' use of computers and their computer-related activities. In the conclusion, I will return to the question in the title of this paper, do the girls become 'cyber girls'?

Computer-Girls or Tomboys?

If educational strategies to create computer fascination among girls are to be effective, this would most probably be because the strategies interact with other qualities in the girls' environment or characteristics of the girls themselves. Thus, it is important to assess if there are some common features of computer fascinated girls that would make them more open to the efforts of schools. Also, they might display qualities that would marginalise them and imply that computer fascination can be achieved only at-considerable individual cost.

Previous research and the images provided by mass media cause some general expectations about 'computer-girls'. First, they are assumed to be '*tomboys*', to be more masculine than most other girls. If this were the case, computer fascination would certainly be relegated to the margins of normal social life. However, this seems not to be a relevant description. None of the computer fascinated girls appear to be tomboys. Neither their interests nor the way they look and dress is in line with such a characteristic. In fact, they appear to be normal teenage girls with an interest in fashion, music, make-up and boys.

Secondly, such girls are expected to do well or at least have an interest in mathematics. Previous research indicates a strong connection between maths skills and being interested in computers. This would also limit the potential of computer fascination. However, the data do not support this. When the girls talked about a favourite school subject, or their best school subject, there were no similarities among them. Some liked maths and science, others language and social science. There was no clear relationship between their computer fascination and favourite school subjects besides the fact that all the girls were high performers. Half of them were among the best in their class, and the others declared themselves to be above average. Consequently, it might be the case that computing is just another 'subject' that these girls are good at. It is not as simple as that, because when we look at the girls in the total material we find many high performers with little or no interest in computing (Håpnes & Rasmussen 1997).

It is known that female engineering students tend to have parents with higher education (Kvande & Rasmussen 1991). Therefore, one could expect that computer fascination among girls would have a similar explanation. However, the parents of the computer fascinated girls had very different educational background and jobs, ranging from a cleaning lady to an engineer.

What is important to notice, though, is the fact that, compared with the other girls in the larger study, the computer fascinated girls were different in their educational and vocational ambition. The less computer fascinated girls want jobs where they can help other people (Håpnes & Rasmussen 1997). The computer fascinated girls would also like to work with people, but this is not important or central when it comes to choosing a job for the future. Instead, they emphasised that the job should be exciting, challenging and well-paid. One of them said she wanted to become a career-woman without husband and children.

Finally, there is the image of the *computer-nerd* as an unsociable, unsuccessful person. Again, this does not match very well with my informants. In fact, all the girls were very social and spent much time with friends. I also observed them in relation to classmates and saw that they tended to be among the *popular* rather than the *unpopular*. Since the girls were all social, popular and accepted as girls, this might be important to their willingness to expose themselves as computer-girls. Non-nerdishness might thus be a condition of computer fascination among girls.

Thus, my informants were not a homogeneous group and did not fit with any stereotypes of computer users. This gives an optimistic basis for believing that educational strategies might be quite efficient due to the rather limited number of clear constraints or conditions of computer fascination. However, there were some other interesting similarities. First, it is interesting to notice that none of the computer fascinated girls have elder brothers. We know from the larger study that many girls seemed to suffer from the fact that their brothers tended to occupy the machine at home. Most of my informants were the eldest child. Only two of them had elder sisters, but they were not interested in computing. Thus, they did not have to fight with someone else for time in front of the computer.

The second similarity is that most of the girls got in touch with computers at an early age. Not all of them had a computer at home, but all of them remembered using a computer at their parents' workplace or at a friend's house, if they did not have one themselves. I do not mean to say that girls have to start using a computer at an early age to become interested, but early use might be one of the reasons why my informants did not seem to host a fear of the machine. Instead, they appear to feel very comfortable using computers, since they had domesticated the computer into their everyday life at an early age.

Today, all the girls, except one, have access to a computer at home. The girl that does not have a computer at home uses her uncle's machine on a regular basis. Only one of them has a computer that is exclusively hers. The others have machines that the whole family share, but most of the girls were the main users of the family machines:

> Mostly it's me. But sometimes my father does some work on it and my brother plays the boring card games. (Trude)

Although the girls used the machines at home a lot, they were not the ones to decide what machine to buy. Most of them said that their parents made the decision to buy a computer, and it was always the father who made the final decision of which brand to buy. The girls explained this by saying he was the most competent person in the family. Since some of the girls actually have computer skills comparable to that of their fathers', it is interesting to see that the girls do not influence the act of buying the home computer at all, and that none of them complain about this.

> My father suddenly came home one day with a new computer. We did not even know about it. He is probably the best qualified to assess what machine is best. It might have been him and my mother that picked it out. (Inger)

We could interpret this lack of influence as an indication that the computer fascinated girls are not recognised as really skilled by their parents, and that such recognition is not very important to them. In some sense, their interest in computers and skills in using them are not displayed publicly in a very visible manner. In fact, none of the girls read any kind of computer magazines, and they rarely talked with friends about computers.

So far, there seems to be few 'structural' prerequisites to become a computer fascinated girl besides the possibility of accessing a computer. Nor is the fascination related to marginalising social or cultural features. Thus, there should be considerable room for schools to cater an interest in ICTs also among girls. At the same time, it seems that most of the reasons of acquiring such interest are related to non-school aspects. Thus, it is important to look further into the actual activities that these girls use computers to perform. Are they created by school-like interests, or do they grow out of leisure pre-occupations?

Dimensions of Computer Fascination

To assess the impact of education policy, we need to look at the location of computer use as well as what computers are used for. If school is of any importance, it should be an arena as well as a cause of use. My informants said that they used the computer at school as well as at home. The place of most frequent use and how often they used the computer, varied among the girls. They also used the computer differently, concerning both tasks and frequency of use.

Table 6.1 gives an overview of the way the girls used computers. The girls apply the Internet for several purposes. The table distinguishes between surfing, searching and chatting. *Surfing* is when they for instance

Table 6.1   Frequency of use of different computer applications among the seven computer fascinated girls *

	Cecilie	Jorunn	Silje	Ingunn	Trude	Inger	Hedda
Word-processor	+++	+++	++	++	++	++	+++
Computer-games	+++	+++	++	++	++	+	+++
Cd-rom	+	++	++	+	++	++	+++
Surfing	+	++	+++	++	++	++	++
Searching	+	+	++	++	++	++	+++
E-mail	+++	+++	-	-	-	-	++
Chatting	-	-	++	++	++	+	+++

* '+++' means frequent use, '++' means medium use, '+' means little use and '-' means no use.

look at the home pages of pop- or movie stars like the Spice Girls. This in contrast to *searching*, where they are more focused upon collecting information to be used in schoolwork or in connection with a hobby. *Chatting* refers to their use of chat-lines. I have not differentiated between different chat-lines. A striking feature of Table 6.1 is the variation. No application is used frequently by all, while very few options are reported as non-used. Compared with the girls in the larger study, the fascinated girls stand out by their varied use.

The table also indicates that schoolwork as well as leisure interests are important aspects of computer fascination. Word processing is used substantially by all of them, and there is considerable activity with searching. This suggests that school strategies have had some influence upon the development of computer fascination.

First Time Introduction to Computers

All my informants were introduced to computers early in their childhood, between the age of four and ten. I mentioned earlier that this might have been a reason for the girls' computer fascination, but when comparing with the data from the larger study, there were non-fascinated girls that were introduced to computers at an early age as well. My informants are special through their consistent and constant interest in and fascination with computers.

The girls' first computer-experience was playing computer-games. Studies of dedicated computer-users (hackers) have found that computer-games are one of the most important inroads to boys that become hackers (see, e.g., Befring 1995). Boys start playing computer-games at an early age. In this way, they acquire some skills and an interest in computing. In the longer run, this may help to cater a growing interest and fascination and dedication. Even though my informants said they had liked to play computer-games and found them amusing, they did not become fascinated with games in the same way as some boys tend to do. They kept on playing, but games never became a major interest. Instead the girls began to use other programmes, like painting and writing.

Learning to Use the Computer

None of them did really remember how they had acquired their computing skills, but none of them had learned their basic skills at school or through any form of organised training. If they could not work things out on their own, they asked their parents for help or used a trial-and-error strategy. Here, they seem to have a lot in common with other PC users (Sørensen, Aune & Hatling 1998).

Half of the girls had computer-interested fathers who had taught their daughters how to use the computer. These fathers had acquired computing skills through education or work. Only one of the girls said that she had asked her mother. She usually needed help with the word processing program, and her mother knew a lot about this.

Two of the girls had parents with very little computing skills, so there was nobody to ask for help. Silje described her learning process in the following manner:

> I worked it out myself. It was actually quite simple, it's just like an ordinary typewriter. I learned it quickly. And there was a demo on it.

Trude told a similar story:

> Nobody at home knows more than I do anyway, so at home there is nobody I can ask for help. So I just try out different things until I get through.

These girls used the trial-and-error strategy in most cases. Silje had also used a demonstration program on the computer. She even read manuals when the trial-and-error strategy failed. The trial-and-error strategy was common and a lot used among all my informants. I will come back to this later.

We see that the home is the dominant location for the acquisition of computer skills among the computer fascinated girls. Their skills and positive attitudes were obtained before they started to use computers in class. Still, most of the girls have had some computer training at school. All of them had a positive attitude towards the use of computers in class and wished that the technology was integrated in as many subjects as possible.

Computer Confidence

There is one important exception to the above pattern of skills acquisition. Since the Internet is a new medium and some of the girls were first introduced to it at school, the girls had, in many cases, better skills than their parents. All of my informants claimed that they were as good as, or even better than, their parents in using the Internet. Often, they said, their parents, usually the father, needed to ask their daughter how to manage. In this respect, the girls were the home expert. This is likely to have given them a high degree of self-confidence.

Thus, the effect of the education authorities' strategies seems to be mixed. Generally, the strategies are not important to the fascinated girls' basic skills and interest. All of them started to learn about computers at home and in an unorganised manner. Some say they have learned some new skills at school, but the main impression is that their main learning strategy is to keep on finding out things on their own, using the trial-and-error strategy.

This is somewhat surprising, given the widespread belief that women (and by inference, girls) are afraid of computers because it is an advanced machine that they do not understand. At one of the schools we met a teacher who claimed that 'They are hiding their hands behind their backs because they are afraid to press the keys'.

Fear of the Computer

When interviewing the girls, we found that this was not true since the trial-and-error strategy was common. The girls are not afraid of pushing buttons. They know enough about computers so that they do not fear that a disaster might happen, if they push the wrong button. However, we know from the larger study that many non-fascinated girls are afraid of pushing buttons because they fear that they might delete something. Some of them have learned this fear from the teacher. But this is not something the fascinated girls fear:

> It's not that easy to delete something. And if you delete something, it's possible to get it back. It's always saved somewhere on the disc. (Trude)

The computer fascinated girls have discovered that machines give many warnings before deleting, so they did not see accidental destruction to be a problem. It is of course important that teachers and parents give children this sense of security. But the problem is that they themselves often lack sufficient computer skills to invoke such confidence.

All my informants have the idea that computers are supposed to be something anybody can handle, and they do not find them difficult to use:

> Not very difficult. It depends, sometimes when I come across something new that I haven't done before and nobody has explained it properly, it may

happen that I get into minor trouble. But basically it should be a thing everybody can handle [...] that's what's meant when it's called a *personal* computer. (Ingunn)

When interviewing the fascinated girls, I was focused on possible gender differences in the use of ICTs. The girls admitted that they more frequently associated boys than girls with computers, but still they claimed that everybody could learn to use computers. It all came to whether or not you had an interest in learning to use it. They had noticed gender differences themselves, but they had difficulty in explaining why it was so. Some of them thought attitudes were changing, and that more and more girls would start to pay attention to computers.

As previously mentioned, my informants were selected because of their computing skills. However, to my surprise, the girls did not think of themselves as clever users of ICTs. This might just be an outcome of traditional Norwegian female behaviour, 'not to brag about oneself', but none of the girls hesitated to tell me that they were high performers at school. When asked to compare their skills with girls at the same age, some of them did admit they might know a bit more:

I manage to do what I'm supposed to [...] It depends upon who I compare myself with. Four or five girls in my class are clever computer users; that's me and some of the others. That's because we have a computer at home, while they (the other girls) can only use it at school. (Jorunn)

It became clear that the girls, when asked if they were clever computer-users, immediately compared themselves to some of the boys they knew. As the girls saw it, these boys knew something they did not. They still believed that there was a kind of secret, exclusive knowledge that boys seemed to have. The computer-fascinated boys talked about things like 'Ram, Rom and Megahertz', words that did not have any meaning to the girls.

None of my informants complained about boys pushing them away from computers, as Rasmussen and Håpnes (1991) found among female computer science students. Nor did they fear having an intimate relationship with the machine as Turkle (1988) found. For example, the girls used the computer as a diary and told the computer their secrets. Some of the girls also said they saw the computer as one friend among many friends. They had not turned to the computer because they found it difficult relating to other humans. Still, there was something about computers that made the girls feel uncomfortable. They experienced a computer culture of boys talking a technical language that the girls neither knew nor understood.

Transformation of the Meaning of Computing

When the computer fascinated girls were asked about their basis for seeing someone as clever computer users, they mentioned the ability to be a fast writer and to find the right information:

> It means that you can find things fast and that you, when thinking a bit, can dig up something new, or do something new without someone else explaining what to do. And to explore things without having the fear of deleting or doing something wrong. (Ingunn)

Programming has long been considered the most important skill of computing and the aspect that could seduce users to become dedicated (Turkle 1996). Among my informants, this was an unknown skill. They did not know what it was, and nobody mentioned it as a skill. Despite this, we know that half the girls had designed their personal homepages. To do this, they need to know a kind of programming.[7] But the word 'programming' means nothing to them.

This fact makes it even harder to understand why the girls do not see themselves as clever computer users. The skills they claim necessary for being good at using a computer are skills they all possess.

As previously argued, we may see the computer as transformed from a calculation machine to a machine of communication and information. Clearly, it is the latter qualities that interest the fascinated girls, in line with the argument of Turkle. Nevertheless, when we analyse the issue more closely, there are common features as well as variation in what the girls find attractive about computers. First and foremost, all of them found the computer fascinating because there were so many possibilities. They liked the fact that there always came something new, something they did not know. The Internet with all its different areas of applications was clearly fascinating.

We should also note that the girls had little interest in penetrating beyond the surface level of the interface between themselves and the machine. This is in line with the new computational aesthetics that Turkle (1996, pp. 30-32) describes. The machine's inner body was of no interest. The girls actually said very strongly this was one part they did not want to know anything about.

Computers as a Toy

It is accepted as common knowledge, at least in Norway, that women use the computer if they find it useful. In this respect, they are instrumental. The computer is just a tool and they do not use it unless they deem it helpful. Consequently, we should expect the fascinated girls to argue in a similar way about their use of computers. In the larger study, some girls accounted in this manner. My informants spent time in front of the screen and wanted to learn more because it was fun, not because it was useful. Even though, of course, they saw that computing was a smart thing to know, their fascination for computers came from their excitement about all the things they did not know and the pleasure they got from playing with it. They regarded the computer as an advanced toy that also happened to be a useful tool (see also Gansmo 1998).

Becoming Fascinated

The small number of informants in this study does not allow for general and precise conclusions about the conditions of becoming a computer fascinated girl in Norway. However, there are some observations that are remarkable. First, all the girls were introduced to the computer at an early age through playing computer-games. Secondly, they all had good access to a computer during their childhood. They never needed to fight with elder brothers or others to get access. They have been allowed to play with it, and nobody has ever demanded that they should learn formally how to use it. The girls have regarded the computer as a toy they could have fun with.

Since the computers were introduced early as a 'natural' element in the home, the girls developed a confident relationship with the computer. The computer was never anything fearsome that they wanted to keep at a distance, but a 'toy' they wanted to and were allowed to explore. The elements of (1) early introduction, (2) using the computer for fun and (3) good access, have given the girls an environment conductive to the development of fascination.

The role of the school appears to be more limited. However, it provides some impetus to keep up interest because school work may imply an interesting use of computers. Also, school may teach them some new skills or at least introduce them to new challenges. In particular, this possibility is related to the use of the Internet. However, to better understand the anatomy of girls' fascination with computers, we need to look at their everyday use in even greater detail.

Hooked on the Net?

All of my informants knew how to use word processing, the Internet and some games. To what degree they use computers and for what purpose, varies. One of the girls, Ingunn, gives the following account of how she employs the machine:

> First of all, I use it for playing, but recently I have been drawing quite a bit with it. And I have written essays. Lately I have found a lot of information on the Internet and chatted a bit. And I have started touch-typing. I haven't got very far yet, but at least I have started. And I have played CDs on it, and used it quite a bit more than I had thought I would, found photos and picked up posters.

Ingunn is making wide use of the computer (see also table 6.1), and her account is neither instrumental nor expressive, but rather constructed in a playful sense. We heard teachers say how important it was to give the girls an impression of how *useful* it would be for them to learn to use a computer, but this may impose limitation rather than encouragement.

Computer games The fact that many boys frequently play computer-games has been a standard explanation of their dedication. An educational strategy that presupposes that girls do not want to have fun, may be a serious mistake. This is not to suggest that computers are not also used for 'serious' purposes. Such instrumentality is also evident from, e.g., Hedda's account:

> I use the computer a lot for schoolwork. I write things with it, things I'm going to hand in. And I usually load down photos from the Internet and cd-roms and put those in the text. I use the computer a lot to do such things. I do not use it a lot for games, I don't do that. And I'm on the Internet, 'cause we have Internet at home, on chatting programs. So I use the computer a lot.

It is often said that girls do not like to play computer games. This is supposed to be for boys. Playing games was, as mentioned above, the girls first computing experience.

> The first time I used a computer I played games at a girlfriend's house. (Trude)

Today, none of the informants spend much time playing games, but only one of them said she did not play games at all. The others said they played, but they were easily bored by playing the same game frequently. This might be the reason why game-playing is limited.

Also, some of the girls said they could not find interesting games:

Yes [I play], but it is difficult to find games that seem interesting.[...] I have played Super Mario and games like that, but that's just funny games. I prefer playing games where I have to think, not fighting games. (Silje)

It might look as if there is a mismatch between the games offered and the kind of games that girls find attractive. Girls do like to play games, but there are very few games made for girls. However, some had found games that they liked:

Yes, I play once in a while, but I'm not fond of those small games, games where you only go around eating strawberries or such things. I don't find that funny. I think it's funny using games that last longer, where you are supposed to find different things and get points when you do. Then you have sort of a goal. (Hedda)

Still, games are not the activity that maintains computer fascination among the girls.

Using the Computer as a Type-Writer

All my informants apply the computer as a writing tool. Often they use it for schoolwork. Some Norwegian schools allow homework to be done by computer, some do not. But even if the school does not allow word-processed papers, the girls still often use the computer to write drafts. They apply the spelling control to correct mistakes, and then they copy it out nicely by hand. However, schoolwork is hardly the only objective:

I have a computer in my room at home. If something special happens during the day I write it down. I write a lot on my computer. I practice writing. And I also spend some time drawing pictures in Paint Brush. But most of all I write, write poems and things like that. (Cecilie)

It is interesting that girls use computers to write their diaries, since this indicates that they feel comfortable telling the machine their inner thoughts and having, in that way, an intimate relationship with it.

One of the skills that the girls seem to give the highest appreciation, is the ability to write quickly. In fact, many of them practice to become fast writers. This is clearly not because they plan to become secretaries. The quote from Cecilie above show how the computer has become a way to 'textualise' her life, in the sense that she uses it to surround herself with different types of texts. This may not mean that her relationship with the computer is intimate, but perhaps that she enjoys the freedom of computer-based word processing to shape and reshape written expressions.

Internet – The Girls Favourite

Writing may be important, but when we asked the girls what they preferred to do with their machines, they all referred to the Internet! To many of them, computers were actually synonymous with the Internet. As said before, the girls' use the Internet for fun as well as serious work. The Internet is new and therefore exciting. They meet a totally unknown world, a world that seems endless.

> It's the whole thing. It's in a way a totally different world. You can meet a lot of people living in totally different places and in totally different parts of the world. It's great fun. (Cecilie)

During our first period of observation at one of the schools, we were intrigued to learn what they were actually doing. We watched six girls surfing on the net to find photos of pop or movie stars, or to find lyrics from Backstreet Boys' latest CD. To begin with, it seemed like a waste to give girls multimedia machines to do such things. The computer became just a substitute or an addition to pop magazines. But having thought about it for a while, and followed the girls during a couple of months, it became very clear that this was just the way to do it. Let the girls play and have fun:

> The first thing we looked up was some pop groups and handsome boys in Hollywood [...] To print out such photos I find amusing. (Silje)

After having used the Internet only for pleasure, the girls started to use it to collect information they could use in schoolwork. This also includes using cd-roms. Inger explained the reason for using multimedia to collect information in this manner:

The fact is that you can get information from the whole world. You are spared from having to look up in an encyclopaedia and rush around to find different things. They pop up directly. If you just write something in, it comes forth.

Internet became a substitute for the library. It was faster and more easily accessible. When they wrote essays or did a project, the girls downloaded photos and information from the net or cd-roms.

Chatting was discovered relatively late in their Internet career. Some had tried e-mail, but they were not so fond of that. Chatting on the net was the very best. Or, as Hedda put it:

I find it really funny using those chat programs. Such chatting programs make you sit on the Internet for hours, making you feel as if you haven't spent any time at all. Time passes really fast.

What the girls find fascinating about chatting is that they can talk freely and easily with people they do not know. It is a new kind of communication where they can at the same time appear in person as well as anonymously. They want to get in touch with people, some of them prefer boys, of their own age. It is not common among girls to invent a new personality, but sometimes they 'cheat' a bit:

It depends, if I talk with a boy aged 22 or so, then I do not write that I'm 15. That's not very smart. So I write that I'm about 16-17 years old. But I do not pretend being someone other than myself. (Hedda)

When they chat, they all use nicknames. They do not know why they do so, but that is just the way it is.

I don't know why. That's really no point 'cause everybody reveals his or her name anyway. (Silje)

None of the girls admit having experienced disagreeable things on the net, but they are all a bit sceptic. They know that they cannot trust people to tell the truth. They say they do not think that they would dare to meet them face to face. Some of them have friends that have found pen pals through a chat line, but only Hedda had met somebody she met on the net face to face:

Once I had an e-mail friend. He said that he lived in another city and that he was 17 years old. We were supposed to meet outside the supermarket, 'cause he was coming to my town. And then it all appeared to be two boys in my class that had been playing around with me all the time. 'Very funny'.

Hedda has been more careful since. The girls are all at a difficult age. As a teenager, it is hard to find out who you are and what you want to be. You try to discover your identity as a girl and as a person. They experienced much pressure, and having to match the ideals can be hard at times. Therefore, the chat programs function as 'free spots' for the girls. Nobody can see them, and they are judged by what they write, not on how they look. Moreover, the programs give them a very good opportunity to get to know boys, which is one of the main interests during these years. Taking these facts into consideration, it is no wonder that girls love chatting.

In comparison, it is interesting to note that Hendrik Storstein Spilker (1998) in his study of the Norwegian cd-rom, 'JenteROM' (Girls' ROM), found that it was designed with three elements that where supposed to attract young females. First, there was a diary part that invited the girls to come forward electronically with their inner thoughts. Second, the cd-rom contained links to information about trends, sports, body, health, music, environment, cooking and IT. The information was presented in words and pictures, and occasionally accompanied by sound and video clips. Third, the cd-rom tried to be useful by providing information about, as well as giving access to, the Internet. We do not know if this cd-rom was successful among girls, but from what we now know about girls' interests in computing, there seems to be a good match.

From 'Spice Girls' to Cyber Girls? Dimensions of Social Learning

This paper has given an account of some features of young teenage girls labelled as computer enthusiasts. To begin with, one should note that they appear to be quite different from the stereotype of the male hacker. They are, by and large, like most other teenage girls in terms of the way they conduct their social life, and their relationship to computers is just enthusiastic, not dedicated. They have an active and varied use of ICTs. This makes them stand out as different from other girls, but not in any radical manner. They do not construct any sub-culture, in the sense that male hackers do (Håpnes 1996).

The most obvious inference from the study is the importance of the multimedia transformation of computers. While the traditional stand-alone personal computer has a limited attraction, the addition of the Internet creates a very different situation. The Internet suddenly offers possibilities of playful activities that the girls perceive as fun. The freedom of creative writing offered by word processing is also important, but it is the Internet that is the backbone of the enthusiasm.

As mentioned in the introduction of this article there has been an effort in the Norwegian education system to increase computer skills and interest in computing. These efforts have been directed towards girls as well as boys, but girls have been given a particular focus. Judging from the accounts of the computer fascinated girls, they appreciate the efforts, but are not affected by them in any major way. The source of their enthusiasm is located in the home, rather than at school. This may appear as surprising, given the fact that these girls have a rather varied social background, but it is probably related to the fact that we are looking at a group of girls who generally do well in school.

Maybe the most striking feature of the situation is the modest role of the education system, compared to the importance of the home as a learning locality and of the cultural industry as a provider of incentives as well as occasions for learning. If we take the accounts of the computer fascinated girls seriously, they indicate a very important shift between public education and a private mixture of 'edutainment' and 'infotainment', a wielding of education, information and entertainment with which schools may find it increasingly difficult to compete.

From this point of view, the relatively successful reconfiguration of the gendering of computers we believe may be observed in Norway, is only marginally brought about through the education system. The most important factor is in the development of multimedia, in particular in the form of the Internet. This has, in a very profound manner, changed the meaning of computers and made them far more attractive to girls. One should be more careful when suggesting that the construction of girlhood has changed, since even the computer fascinated girls emphasise their gender normality. Nevertheless, there seems to be a change under way in the gender distribution of computer skills that may be more consequential.

Thus, we may be moving in a direction where the system of primary and secondary education has to compete more with other means of getting educated than in any previous historic period. It is not safe to assume that increased engagement in computers is the best way for the education system to regain its previous position. But still the school may have to consider *edutainment*, the slippery slope between education and entertainment, to attract the students' interest. As we have seen here edutainment was what had caused the girls enthusiasm for computer use. It was also through fun they had learned to use the computer in the first place and later developed their skills.

As I see it, it is important to get girls interested in and fascinated by computers. To obtain this goal, we have to exploit the attraction of playful activities. Girls should be given the chance to learn what a fantastic toy the computer is by letting them explore it. In this way, they may get to know the computer as a 'play friend' and get interested in keeping on playing with it. As with human friends this friend can grow with you, so there is no need to put the toy away as you get older. In this respect, and with reference to the concept of social learning, it is important to notice that the girls analysed in this paper acquired their computer skills mainly through learning by doing. This may also be a paradox to the education authorities.

The title of the paper asks if young females are moving from being 'Spice Girls' towards becoming Cyber Girls. This was meant to describe their career on the Internet. The girls start as 'Spice Girls', surfing for photos of handsome boys in Hollywood. On the next level they are searching for information, and end up on the last level chatting with others on the net. A 'Cyber Girl', to my mind, lives one life in the virtual world of multimedia along with a real-world life. Their virtual identities may differ from their real-life identities. As I see it, my girls are moving in this direction but are still not 'adequate' Cyber Girls. Even though I thought of this as a development from level to level, the girls have shown that it is not a matter of either-or. They start out as Spice Girls, climb to higher levels, and end up using all the levels. A Cyber Girl can still be a Spice Girl, and Spice Girls are likely to become Cyber Girls.

Notes

1   See 'IT i norsk utdanning. Årsplan 1998' (IT in Norwegian education. Plan for the year of 1998), Ministry of Education, Research, and Church Affairs, http://odin.dep.no/kuf/publ/1998/itplan.html#49.

2   The project was managed by Bente Rasmussen at NTNU (Norwegian University of Science and Technology) and Tove Håpnes, research scientist at SINTEF-IFIM. The

datas were collected by Kjersti Kvaløy, Helen Jøsok Gansmo and myself, all students of sociology at NTNU. A report with the results has been published (Håpnes & Rasmussen, 1997).

3   This article is based on my master-thesis in Sociology. In my master thesis I concentrated on the girls that where fascinated with the computer (Nordli 1998). After criteria described in this article I 'picked' out in-dept interviews with seven of the girls.

4   Numbers refered in the Norwegian computer-magazine *Komputer for alle*, 6/1998:34.

5   The information is drawn from an article at Alex skole, a part of the Norwegian newspaper Aftenposten's hompage on the 15th of August 1997 under the title '*Læring i cyberspace*'. The article was written by Morten Søby, phd-student at the Pedagogical research institute at the University of Oslo.The adress of the page was: http://www.aftenposten.no/alex/skole/d17592.html.

6   IT i skolen 1997 - SSBs tilstandsundersøkelse. ODIN, Kirke-, utdannings- og forskningsdepartementet (KUF). http://odin.dep. no/kuf/proj/it/ssb.html. SSbs Notater 97/42.

7   There is a problem in defining what should be considered using and what should be considered programming. If you use e.g. Excel and you record macros, that might be perceived as 'using' but when you look at those macros and change some things by hand, in fact you are 'programming'. It is similar with the design of homepages. You can create them with several programmes without actually writing codes, but in fact you are actually programming.

7 Distance Teaching on Bornholm

FINN HANSEN, CHRISTIAN CLAUSEN

Abstract

The case study represents an example of a top-down introduction of distance teaching as part of Danish trials with the introduction of multimedia in education. The study is concerned with the background, aim and context of the trial as well as the role and working of the technology and the organisational set-up. On the basis of an analysis of the problems met by different actors – mainly teachers and students – it is debated which kind of social learning has taken place. The background and justification for the distance learning pilot on Bornholm was recognition of the lack of suitable educational possibilities combined with the increased emigration of young students from the island of Bornholm to other parts of Denmark. The case study shows that the introduction of distance teaching on Bornholm created a working situation based on the implementation of a very inflexible video-conference system without any proactive consideration of organisational change or pedagogical development. It even proved difficult to establish the necessary resources to support the working of the technical system. The innovation process included very limited awareness or consideration of the organisational and pedagogical implications. The analysis further emphasises the asymmetrical relation between the sending and receiving institutions and the context of a centre-periphery debate on economic development and education.

Introduction

While the use of computers in education has been debated in Denmark for many years, it is only during recent years that substantial changes and experiments have been carried out. While the earlier debate could be characterised by a critical distance to the use of computers in education by most teachers, a more qualified debate on the related pedagogical problems and opportunities is now being asked for. One of the areas for development and experimentation with technology and teaching using multimedia is distance teaching, and several Danish educational institutions have already established working teaching systems. Today, government supported experiments with distance teaching are funded as part of the development programmes of the Danish Centre for Technology Supported Education (CTU).

The following case study is concerned with the social learning processes related to the conception, planning and implementation of multimedia-based distance teaching on the Danish island of Bornholm. The Bornholm case was set up as a trial on technology-supported teaching before the establishment of the CTU. Consequently, the Bornholm trial is not necessarily a typical case of the introduction and use of multimedia in education, due in part to the fact that travelling distances in Denmark are normally comparatively short. Due to government recognition of a need for economic and educational development on Bornholm, however, the island was selected as the target for the first distance teaching trial in Denmark. Furthermore, the Bornholm trial has been subject to a comprehensive evaluation project, thus providing good opportunities to study a range of relevant aspects concerning social learning in educational multimedia.

We consider the technology used in the Bornholm distance teaching trial as an example of multimedia in the sense that video representation of teaching activities is made possible with computer-based data-links (video-telephone) and control equipment. Supplementary computer-based equipment for communication between the near and distant classes, and facilities for 'looking over the shoulder' of distant students operating their PCs, were also used to some extent.

The focus of the case study is on the innovation process and the implications for social learning of the chosen top-down approach, the asymmetrical relations between the sending and receiving institutions, and the limited considerations of organisational and pedagogical aspects. Another important aspect to be considered is the political context of the centre-periphery debate at the time of the conceptualisation of the trial.

Methodology

The case is based upon an analysis of the social and educational context of the Bornholm distance teaching trial. The core actors involved in the set-up of the trial are defined and analysed, together with their diverse perspectives and the chosen technical and organisational solutions. The outcome of the experiment is analysed with respect to the institutions involved, the teachers and the students. The analysis is mainly based on empirical data collected after the termination of the first trial period by the Danish Centre for Quality Assurance and Evaluation of Higher Education during 1996, one-and-a-half years after the distance teaching started and one-and-a-half years before the end of the trial. The evaluation was commissioned by the Danish Ministry of Education. The data are collected from the following sources:

- An analysis of the organisational and technical aspects was carried out by the Danish Centre for Technology Supported Education during spring 1996. This account is based on interviews with the project managers from each of the five participating institutions as well as collected documents and the self-evaluation reports.
- An analysis of the economical implications was carried out by the Danish Ministry of Education after one-and-a-half years of distance teaching experience.
- A report containing extensive interviews carried out with the students participating in the trial represents a major source for this case study. The interviews were carried out by the Danish Centre for Quality Assurance and Evaluation of Higher Education during spring 1996. 51 students were interviewed. Each interview took 75 to 120 minutes and was carried out on the basis of a standardised question guide consisting mainly of open-ended questions. Participants were near- and distant students from the classes of autumn 1995 and spring 1996. From the most important classes (in regard to the total teaching hours and the relevance for the conclusions here), 32% of the near- and 38% of the distant students were interviewed. Less important classes were covered by a smaller proportion of interviews. The material is not representative, but it provides an insight into students' experiences with distance teaching that is sufficient for the conclusions of this case study.
- Another major source is the self-evaluation reports carried out by the teachers involved and their institutions. This report includes the

involved institutions' own accounts of the results of the trial, collected during a report in 1996.

- In addition, the broader implications and learning processes are analysed on the basis of arguments and statements from the conclusion of the consolidated evaluation report. This report is based on the above-mentioned evaluations supplemented by further visits to the different institutions by the evaluation committee and a final conference representing the various parties involved.

Even though the findings and conclusions in this case study are mainly based on reading the Danish evaluation reports, the conclusions differ as a consequence of the different research questions posed. However, our conclusions do not contradict the conclusions of the evaluation.

The case study is also part of an account of the situation of multimedia in education in Denmark, based on public reports and debate stressing the potential implications for wider social learning in multimedia. A follow-up on the broader continuation of distance teaching took place in 1997-98. Two telephone interviews concerned with the broader social learning implications were carried out in October 1998 with main actors in the Danish Ministry of Education and the Danish Centre for Technology Supported Education.

Introduction to Multimedia in Education in Denmark

The Danish Educational System

Education in Denmark, from the primary school to the university level, is mainly carried out by publicly-owned institutions. Only a varying minor part of education at primary level is carried out by private schools. Exceptions from this general rule are mainly found in the middle-range area of education. For example, many business colleges are private institutions. Primary and lower secondary school for children from 7 to 16 years old are funded and controlled by the local municipalities, secondary schools (high school) and adult education are typically funded and controlled by the county administrations, while institutions at the university level, including business schools, are state institutions. Most Danish education (public and private) is based on rules and regulations set by the

Ministry of Education, while some special education is regulated by the specific sector's administration.

There are many private schools in Denmark. They are independent and can have their own profiles. They can be regarded as alternatives to the dominant public education for social groups with specific interests that are willing to pay. But the private schools are also subject to rules and regulations and receive most of their funding from the Ministry of Education. All schools that offer officially recognised education (whether public or private) have to follow the educational programmes issued by the central level. The main differences between public and private schools depend formally on whether a representative political body or a private school board determines how to implement the rather broadly defined reading plans and how to supplement the resources that go with the educational programmes.

According to current Danish education policies, all children should have access to computers and the possibility to learn to use them, including weak or uninterested pupils who cannot or do not want to use computers at home. The aim of this democratic idea is to spread the use of computers in society and to provide equal access to computers and computer education to everyone. In contrast to the past, this means that computers should not only be available to higher level education but to all schools. In a debate report on information technology and education in 1997, the Danish Ministry of Education states that use of computers, networks, the Internet, word processing, databases etc. should have the same priority as learning to read, write and calculate. 'It is as important to be able to use the modern information technology as it is to be able to read, write and calculate' (Undervisningsministeriet 1997). As a consequence of the international and national discussion of the information society (for instance, based on the Bangemann report and the Danish: 'The Info-Society for all – the Danish Model' from 1996), the Danish government has provided access to the Internet through a national network for all schools in co-operation with locally funded systems. As a result of this model, the end-user systems in the schools are contributed by several national and local actors.

Information Technology in Danish Education

Computer-aided education has been debated in Denmark for the last 20 years. Whereas the early debate was about learning to use computers and teaching children to programme computers in BASIC, the focus has now moved towards the use of information technology as a tool in teaching and education in general. The role of computers is no longer the subject of debate but is now treated more as a means of achieving other educational goals and subjects. The content and background for the debate on computers in education have changed radically since the beginning of the 1970s. The once great debate on whether children should learn programming in BASIC is today totally outdated. And the other big debate about artificial intelligence and whether computers could take over human intellectual work such as that of teachers has also disappeared. Instead, the discussion about the Internet and multimedia is a hot topic, and the main question is whether the Internet and multimedia are a waste of time, dangerous for the individual user and/or dangerous for society. An important background for these shifts in the debate is of course the dramatic changes in computer applications since the 1970s, from simple data processing, advanced production and design systems towards complex multimedia programmes.

As PCs have become cheaper and, as a consequence of political priorities, the current situation is characterised by a common and widespread purchase and use of computers in the entire educational system. There are, however, considerable differences in coverage between municipalities ranging from 5 to 20 students per PC. While the Danish government subsidises the municipalities with 'block' funding, it is up to each municipality administration to decide how many resources will be put into the schools and for which purpose. More important than machines, however, time, technical support, education of teachers and availability of relevant software have become critical resources. Another general problem is that it is often difficult to bridge the gap between the very proactive orientation of many students and some teachers versus the more sceptical orientation of other students and the majority of teachers. In contrast to the past, only few teachers are openly critical of computers in education, but many teachers ask for a qualified debate on the use of computers in education and the related pedagogical problems and opportunities. Even though the government has launched a range of initiatives to develop software, teachers often find themselves in a situation where their only choices are between standard educational software and advanced computer games, the latter being regarded as non-serious entertainment.

A new type of initiative has been seen in the 1990s: Some institutions receive fairly advanced and expensive equipment in connection with advantageous agreements with computer companies. On the basis of such agreements, computer- and multimedia-oriented education and courses are developed. In this way, institutions seek to attract students and trainees and to market themselves as leading advanced education centres.

Resources and Projects

The discussion about resources for development of computer-aided education has aroused general controversy. Public funding in Denmark is generally moving towards more specific and limited projects and limitations of the basic funding. A general political statement from the Ministry is that the institutions should, within the existing appropriation, find resources for information technology and the use of it in courses. There is no general increase in grants to the schools directed towards information technology. On the other hand, a number of specific programmes and projects have been launched.

Report (1253) from the Danish Ministry of Education presented a model for specific initiatives such as the establishment of CTU, Denmark's National Information Centre for Technology Supported Learning (Center for Teknologistøttet Uddannelse), autumn 1995. The centre was established by the Ministry of Education as an information centre for the collection and dissemination of information about Technology Supported Learning. CTU's task is to develop the education of the future with the aid of information and communication technology. In this sense, CTU is a national service organisation that distributes a certain amount of public funding for experimental projects, provides advice for projects and educational institutions, provides education of teachers and facilitates social learning processes. The centre is mainly concerned with technology assisted teaching in adult and higher education.

Except for such classical education in computer technology as computer science, until now, there has been an incoherent variety in the courses and education offered in computer and electronic media subjects. There are differences between the primary school and higher public education that leave the primary school far behind. Other differences developed as a consequence of an uneven variety of short courses offered by private companies and the growing group of courses offered, for instance, by technical and business colleges on a commercial basis.

But also in the schools we find incoherence between the elements involved. To illustrate the tendencies, the situation can be described as follows: Most primary schools have joined the state-funded network connection to the Internet; several computers are funded by the local municipalities. The software includes standard software and a few old educational programmes. But there is no time to integrate computers in the education, no time for customising programmes for courses, no time for system support etc. A limited use of computers can also be the outcome of a combination of different factors. The schools often face a situation where the technically interested children are hacking the schools' computers with a virus, the teachers have too little time to repair or maintain the computer systems and there is no national service organisation (besides private companies).

Distance Teaching on Bornholm

The Context of the Danish Multimedia Trial on Distance Teaching on Bornholm

During the period 1994-97, the Danish Ministry of Education commissioned and supported a distance teaching trial on the Danish island of Bornholm. The funding and initiation of the trial became part of the initiative by the Danish government for a long-term effort on Bornholm to improve the economic position of the island. Bornholm is situated in the Baltic Sea and the traditional occupation of fishing had been declining for several years. Technological developments in the fishing industry as well as establishment of fishing limits had resulted in a reduced need for labour. Consequently, the relatively small and occupationally vulnerable society with its 45,000 inhabitants encountered a financial and social crisis. After several years of complaints and demands for government support for development, a broader political recognition developed of the need to create alternative employment and new types of jobs on the island.

The design of the trial was rooted in a report (Betænkning no. 1253) on technology-aided teaching from the Danish Ministry of Education, where the possibility for technology supported distance teaching was mentioned as one option among a range of opportunities. From this report, the Ministry chose the model entitled 'simultaneously distributed teaching'. The report suggested two other alternatives: 'time displaced education' and 'independent studies' (differentiated education). 'Time displaced education' refers to a situation where a lecture is recorded on video or programmed in a multimedia-based system and displayed for classes in a different time and place. 'Independent studies' refers to a model where students are connected individually to a teaching programme and can attend their lessons at a time and place according to their own wishes (typically from their homes). This is accomplished through an Internet connection and e-mail communication with the teacher. Concerning the chosen model, simultaneously distributed teaching, the 1253 report described it as a model where neither the role of the teacher nor the role of the student were expected to differ significantly from the traditional roles. This assessment turned out to have a significant influence on the technological and organisational set-up, and in the course of the pilot, it turned out to be a rather misleading conception.

The Role of the Parties Involved in the Project Set-Up

The very definition of the specific context of the trial as an integrated part of a centre-periphery political debate formed another important premise for the project set-up. Even though Denmark is a small country with a relatively homogenous distribution of income and living standards, recurrent political debates deal with the unequal possibilities for maintaining and developing educational, economic and technological development in certain regions when compared to the perceived administrative centre of the Copenhagen area. These political themes have influenced governmental decisions concerned with transport infrastructure, the location of educational institutions, as well as other measures concerned with technological and economic development in a region. In the case of Bornholm, several possibilities for regional development were discussed, among these the possibilities for utilising information technologies to bridge the geographical distances and connect Bornholm more closely to technological and economic development processes in other areas. These ideas included projects for combining social experiments with information technology and the promotion of social learning processes. However, the Bornholm distance teaching trial did not become related to this broader debate. Instead, a quite narrow development model was adopted where qualification was seen as the primary prerequisite for business development.

Despite several years when there were no sound political initiatives to support the island, the political package for special economic development measures for Bornholm and the general political situation did not allow for a long planning phase and a more true consideration of the project. Contrary to the aim of a long-term development of the island, the project on distance teaching was planned quickly in order to keep up with the pace of the financial programme.

The County of Bornholm had, in connection with the economic development programme, developed a rather elaborate strategy for regional development that included a vision of a 'European mini-university of Bornholm' based on collaboration with a Danish university on the mainland. This, together with local research initiatives, was supposed to create the possibility for attracting students from other parts of the Baltic Region. The Ministry of Education, together with the other major actors in the realisation of the financial package for Bornholm (Ministry of Research and Ministry of Trade and Industry), found these visions too ambitious. The realisation of the more elaborate vision was dropped when the County was confronted with the plans for a distance teaching trial and realised that it did not have the resources to further develop its own vision.

In regard to the regional development perspective, the pilot became part of an 'educational push' strategy in which educating people on the island in business economics and computer science was intended to support the business community and a general economic development. Besides the economically oriented aim of developing the qualification base in this respect, the trial also aimed at offering the students the choice of staying on the island during their education. For only one single and minor subject (a course in religion) did a Bornholm institution become the sender for a recipient in Aalborg (adult education course in religion). Thus, the possibility for developing the educational capacity on the island as a means of attracting students was not pursued either. Hence, Bornholm only had the role of supplying the receiving institutions for the trial. This was a critical decision since the receiving institutions had no innovative role in the trial: The sending institutions had all the economic incentives and the learning prospects related to the trial, since the distant students, in every respect, became enrolled in their teaching programmes. The role of the receiving institutions was to supply the building facilities and some technical support in order to house the distant students. The imbalances in the educational resources at the outset became, in this sense, reflected in a centralised model for collaboration and were further enhanced instead of counterbalanced. Already at this stage, it became obvious that the more visionary perspectives of regional development were displaced by a more traditional economically oriented educational perspective. This is also reflected in the later formal evaluation of the trial by the Ministry, in which the analysis of economic aspects was given special attention.

The Danish Technological Institute (DTI) was selected by the Ministry as project co-ordinator for the Bornholm trial. DTI is an independent, but government supported, non-profit institution working to support Danish companies as well as society at large in the transfer, development, uptake and use of technology. A department of DTI was one of the Danish pioneers in technology supported learning and the use of video in education. Later, the expertise of DTI was incorporated in the establishment of CTU, Denmark's National Information Centre for Technology Supported Learning. DTI prepared the project. A board headed by the Ministry and including representatives from the participating institutions was set up in order to control the pilot.

The time sequence for the project From its conception in 1993, the project developed in the following steps.

June 1993:	Report from the Ministry of Education No. 1253 on Technology Supported Teaching (Distance teaching) was launched.
25.6 1993:	The Ministry of Education and the county authority for Bornholm agree on the trial project in distance teaching.
14.9 1993:	The county authority for Bornholm decides which education is relevant for the project and formulates some wishes for technology.
14.10 1993:	Internal meeting in the Ministry of Education determines that the starting point shall be video telephones (video link) with traditional class teaching. The county authority for Bornholm asks for other data-communication facilities (computer conference facilities) to supplement the video link.
3.11 1993:	Meeting with agreement on which institutions should participate. The subject is not yet determined. It is decided to use an external project manager.
31.1 1994:	The Danish Technological Institute (DTI) delivers the last project plan, which describes the purpose and goal, organisation and activities.
27.4 1994:	The preparation project is finished.
Apr. 94 - Jan. 95:	Pilot phase.
Summer 94:	Installation of equipment in institutions.
Autumn 94:	Distance teaching starts as experiment.
Jan. 95 - Jun. 97:	Trial project with distance teaching.

Dec. 95:   Evaluation of the project starts.
             Contract signed between Ministry of Education and
             sending institutions primarily concerned with economic
             conditions for the trial.

The courses involved   There were 5 colleges and education centres
involved, which, in the educational year 1995/96, offered the following
courses:

Recipient: Bornholm Business College
Sender: Lyngby Education Centre (near Copenhagen)
Subject: Computer science course
Duration of education: 2.25 years
Recipient: Bornholm Business College
Sender: Copenhagen Business School
Subject: Management accounting (as a whole part of an education as
well as single subject courses) offered as a distance course in the
1995/96 educational year
Duration of the education: 2 or 3 years

Recipient: Bornholm Adult Education Centre
Sender: Aalborg Adult Education Centre
Subject: Single subjects (Russian, philosophy and religion) offered as
distance courses at Adult Education and Higher Preparatory
Examination level in 1995/96 educational year
Duration of the Adult Education courses in philosophy: 80 lessons
Duration of the Higher Preparation Examination course in Russian:
224 lessons

Recipient: Aalborg Adult Education Centre
Sender: Bornholm Adult Education Centre
Subject: Religion offered as distance courses in Adult Education in
1995/96 educational year
Duration of the Adult Education courses in religion: 80 lessons

The Technical and Organisational Solutions

The choice of technology was made early in the project by the Danish
Ministry of Education and before the educational institutions were
involved. At this stage, the economic considerations of the Ministry of

Education as well as the logic of the institutional set-up for educational planning played a decisive role for the experiment. The basic idea of the Ministry was to implement distance teaching within the ordinary system of education. An alternative strategy to the described implementation oriented model could be to set up a more open space for technical and pedagogical experiments, but this opportunity was not considered by the Ministry. The Ministry decided to fund only the extra equipment and transmission costs needed for the trial, while the involved educational institutions were to fund their expenses for teachers, students and technical support from ordinary budgets. Ordinary budgets meant for some institutions a negotiated rate per student (taximeter system), and in other cases a negotiated sum for the whole education administered by the county. This meant that the Ministry selected the technology and let the local institutions decide on the resources allocated for the implementation.

The technological concept was based on establishing video-links (such as video telephone) between the near and the distant classrooms. From the outset, it was believed that a virtual classroom could be established by inserting a video-link between two already existing classrooms, manned by the existing teaching, administrative and technical support staff. The other part of the idea was that the receiving institution should be able to host courses for the sending institution without having a teacher present. In addition, the courses were to be carried out under normal circumstances (as opposed to an experimental situation). Accordingly, the students could easily transfer to other institutions without any crucial change in their study situation. Viewed in this way, technology was simply seen as a substitute for a teacher at the receiving institution.

A somewhat different perspective was pursued by the educational institutions. Already before the first experiences with the video-link system, it became clear to f the participating institutions that the virtual classroom as a bridge between the sending and the receiving institution could not be established within the framework of the video-link system alone. A letter from the County of Bornholm to the Ministry of Education states: 'The social room shall encompass both classes. The students are, in principle, going to have the same opportunities to see, hear, participate and be seen and heard as if they were in the same room. The possibility for informal talk across the borderlines of the near and distant classes should be present before and after the teaching sessions' (letter from County of Bornholm 1993; Evalueringscentret, 1996a, p. 67).

The video-link system that was installed was perceived by the teachers as originally developed to work as a video-conference facility or for linking working groups over distances. As a distance teaching facility, it was not seen as a working technology. In the self-evaluation reports, teachers typically reflect over the adopted technology as follows: 'At a meeting, only one person speaks at a time and only few persons are considered to speak. In teaching situations according to the "Danish model", which are based on dialogue between the teacher and the students as well as between the students, all students are expected to be heard.' A common experience of all the classes was that the systems offered were not able to facilitate this situation. This led to the demand for better microphone facilities and better facilities for operating and directing cameras. In order to provide a better basis for social interaction and inter-activity between the two parts of the intended virtual classrooms, a common working space or electronic blackboard and computer-based conference facilities were wanted. Consequently, the involved institutions demanded additional computer-based communication for the video-link system. In order to allow for a more interactive and individual teaching situation, a PC-based Lotus Notes system was suggested by the educational institutions, but it was not implemented during the trial period.

Why was this adjustment on the technical side not accomplished? There is no simple explanation of this narrowing of the pilot experiments. The official explanation in the evaluation report is that the project organisation was waiting for the installation of a common communication network to cover the whole educational sector. But this network was not established during the trial period. The limited perspective, scope and selection of technology pursued by the Ministry are another explanation. Accordingly, the Ministry would not fund additional expenses going beyond the original set-up but left this to the local institutions. The local institutions on their side had different perspectives on the trial. The sending institutions (as in the case of Lyngby Education Centre) saw the trial as a strategic possibility to gain experience in the distance teaching area and viewed distance teaching as a new business field. They were willing to invest resources in the experiment and allot PCs as well as technical support to the experimental (sending) class. On the other hand, the receiving institutions (for example, the Bornholm Business College) were not prepared to channel PC resources to the receiving class at the expense of other manned classes. While the sending institutions put extra resources into teaching, technical support and the setting up of dedicated classrooms (with special light facilities, sound regulation, Power-Point facilities for overheads etc.), the receiving institutions had difficulty in reserving a dedicated classroom facility. At one of the Bornholm institutions

(Bornholm Adult Education Centre), the students had to unpack the video equipment before every distance teaching session, because they had to share the classroom with other classes. An important mechanism behind this asymmetrical situation can be explained by the fact that all the income from educating students goes to the sending institutions. Whether the receiving institutions are compensated depends on agreements. In the case of Bornholm Business College versus Lyngby Education Centre, this was agreed upon informally resulting in economic compensation to Bornholm Business College for some of the expenses for hosting the distance classes. The economic relations between Bornholm Adult Education Centre and Aalborg Adult Education Centre were concluded in a formal agreement between the respective county administrations.

In addition to this asymmetrical approach, investment of local resources in the trial was generally hindered because the signing of the contract was significantly delayed. The contract explains the mutual responsibilities (especially financial) of the involved parties. The budget for the trial on the part of the Danish Ministry of Education mounted to 4.5 Mill DKR (600 KECU) of which 100,000 DKR was to cover expenses of the local institutions (200,000 for Bornholm Business College). Besides these extra amounts for the trial, financial resources were available from the ordinary taximeter funding of each educated student and class according to the general funding of education in Denmark. The local institutions also provided extra funding from their own budgets. The private Lyngby Education Centre made important financial contributions in order to develop their own teaching facilities, seeing it as an investment. But as it turned out, the County of Bornholm did not support the experiments financially at their institution, the Bornholm Adult Education Centre. This had been expected due to their original positive attitude, but such a contribution was not specified in the contract. The County may not have seen this trial as the opening of a new market for education that called for investments.

Technical set-up in the classrooms A typical technical set-up would consist of three ISDN online data-links connecting the two classrooms with two-way video and sound communication. In both the transmitting and the receiving classrooms, two TV monitors in each classroom transmit what is happening in the other classroom. One camera in the transmitting classroom is dedicated to transmission from the 'blue'-board. Another camera can be controlled via a key-pad by the teacher (original solution) or also by the near and distant students (later solution). A camera for documents as well as fax, telephone, video and sound recorder is also available.

Especially for teaching in computer science, Lyngby Education Centre installed additional facilities for PC view and Power-Point presentation in the transmitting classroom and an additional data-link for 'looking over the shoulder facility' used for instructing distance exercises on computers.

Teaching Basically, distance teaching followed the same pedagogical forms as traditional classroom teaching. As one teacher reported: 'We said that we should carry on as if the near and distant students were in the same classroom, only separated by a wall of glass.' The activities consist of teacher presentations, dialogue with students, exercises. Distance teaching would be more programmed (story-boards describing the specific use of the equipment) and less spontaneous.

The Distance Teaching Situation and the Problem-Solving Effort

A range of technical and organisational problems surfaced during the trial, and most of the extra resources devoted to the project from the participating institutions went to 'fire-fighting' these technical problems. The main attention was devoted to make the video-technique and the data-transmission work. The teaching situations were frequently disrupted by signal fall-outs, and there were unsolved problems with the sound reproduction which sometimes made communication between the delivering and the receiving classrooms very difficult. The project managers reported that the institutions at the outset had no experience with the new equipment and data transmissions. Teachers and students had to develop trouble-shooting skills in order to maintain classes in the evenings and after ordinary working hours, when computer technicians were not available. Emergency procedures had to be developed for calling assistance, and a mobile telephone was installed in the classes. Also the suppliers of the video systems had limited capacity to solve problems, since they had no prior experience in the use of their systems in classroom teaching situations. The supplier of data transmission capacity (ISDN connection) experienced problems in maintaining the kind of stable connection required by online distance teaching. As it turned out, the ISDN supplier admitted that fall-outs were much more critical with video signal transfer in an online teaching situation than with ordinary data transmission. Furthermore, the scarce data transmission capacity in Jutland caused by changing and re-routing the ISDN net was temporarily (during

1995-96) directed towards other customers by the Danish telecom-munication company, TeleDanmark. This deficiency led to formal complaints from one of the video-link suppliers, but was only admitted by TeleDanmark after the end of the first trial period. In this regard, the evaluation report states that alternative data-communication channels should be investigated in the future.

Due to these problems, only a minor effort (if any at all) was made to develop the teaching organisation and practice. But it would be a misjudgement to say that this was a direct effect of the technical problems. There are no indications that any of the involved parties really recognised the magnitude of the pedagogical development problems related to distance teaching. As a representative from the Danish Ministry of Education put it in retrospect: 'We did not want to put extra burdens on the teachers, as they had enough to do with making the system work' (interview, Oct. 98). The project organisation's major attention and effort was dedicated to negotiation of an agreement between the Ministry of Education and the educational institutions regarding resources, which for unknown reasons took much longer than expected. The educational institutions negotiated agreements with unions at the local level without any problems.

Implications for Teachers and Students

The role of the teachers changed in distance teaching but not as a consequence of experiments with new forms of teaching or new teaching materials. It changed as a consequence of practices developed in response to problems of teaching in a presumably virtual classroom established with video-link technology within traditional practice and pedagogical framework. The media did not work as simple dissemination of the teacher's actions. It was not a simple transfer of picture and sound as if the students were present in the same room.

The teachers experienced this as an increased workload. As a result of maintaining the existing organisation, the sending institutions imposed more work upon the teachers. Even where additional technical support was available, the teachers had to take on the task of technical trouble-shooting and use more time for preparation. The intensity of the teaching situation was increased: 'One problem is that the teaching systems are only geared to operate on the basis of a factor compensating for time used for preparation. Here, it would be fairer to speak of a compensation for technology, competence or strain, or something like that. It resembles a situation where you listen to the radio, watch television, read the newspaper and have a conversation at the same time as you try to repair the doorbell. After 5-6 hours you are tired' (teacher at Lyngby Education Centre, author's translation; CTU 1996, p. 18).

A more positive account of the same problem by a teacher at Adult Education Centre Aalborg: 'Of course, it takes more time to teach classes that are physically separated (...). Another reason why one can not accomplish as much as normally is found in the new demands on the way that you ought to plan your teaching, if you want to facilitate dialogue and interaction. When you teach with a video-conference system, you have to break up your lessons into shorter sequences. I find demands on the teacher for increased differentiation of the teaching positive, both concerning language, content and form' (teacher at Adult Education Centre Aalborg, authors translation, CTU 1996, p. 18).

Teachers also experienced difficulties in establishing contact and getting feedback from individual students in the distant classes. A differentiation has to be made between different modes of teaching. In the case of the Copenhagen Business School, the teacher held his lecture in front of a relatively large audience. Here, the situation of the distant student could be compared to (and might be better than) a student sitting in the back of the sending classroom. But, in the case of an interactive teaching situation in small classes (the most common teaching form in Denmark), the trial shows, according to the educational institutions, that the pedagogical forms are put under pressure. The evaluation report (Evalueringscentret 1996a) points to the tendency that technology accentuates the difference between good and poor education (pedagogy). The best teachers and the best students will benefit. For this reason, a certain selection of students has taken place which took their motivation and other prerequisites into account before they were admitted to the distance teaching courses. Such a selection would normally not take place in the Danish teaching system as long as the student has the formal qualifications.

The distant students were generally satisfied with receiving teaching in a course that otherwise might not be offered on the island, and they found that, in this sense, distance teaching had worked. But many of the students felt that their learning was less effective than through ordinary teaching. The students' experiences related to different problems. First, they had to involve themselves in trouble-shooting and problem-solving in order to get the technical equipment to work. All the students expressed disappointment that often the technology did not work. As a few of the students remarked after the pilot: 'By participating in this pilot we have learned to take a critical stance toward technology and the introduction of technology.' Secondly, the students experienced that the teachers had not changed their teaching and pedagogical routines in comparison to existing courses. Thirdly, they experienced a range of difficulties in establishing a social space that could support the learning situation and encompass both the near and distant classes. The distant students felt they had to be extra active and very eager in order to be heard by the teacher and by the near students. Several students felt that their group was a third wheel and described the students in their near class as their enemies. Fourth, all the distance students had a series of critical comments about the lack of facilities in the receiving classrooms, such as light, sound etc.

A common experience for the near and distant students and the teachers was that a teaching situation based on discussion that involved the teacher and students from both classes as well as development of social relations between the classes had to be abandoned. Common excursions or visits have only rarely taken place. Many students found social relations to be important in themselves and for the effectiveness of their learning. They missed opportunities for conversation and dialogue 'across the waters' in the teaching situation, which they felt often made them passive. This was especially the case when the number of students in the distant class was small.

The distant students were deprived of some of their freedom to shift attention (from teacher to blackboard, overhead, oral presentation, watching other students etc.). Hence, the demands on both teacher and students became greater compared to teaching where all are present in the same room and can control their attention in a common space. The distributed picture and sound (one camera permanently on the 'blue'-board, the other camera available for either the teacher or the class or focused on a few students or a single student) is the focus of attention but is not always relevant for every student in the actual situation. In order to cope with all these difficulties and agree on the selection of channels and focus, the distant students had to discipline themselves. Spontaneous behaviour was almost impossible. This experience is reflected in the formal evaluation, where the panel suggests a contract with the students regarding discipline, their own activity, rules for conversation and examination. The distance students should have the opportunity to clarify individual matters of dispute. This should also be related to the fact that the situation is new and unknown for all involved actors. The limited value of traditional norms and rules of how to behave makes it necessary for teachers and students to develop new social skills in the social situation of distance teaching.

Lessons Learned

Theoretical Approach

During and after the closing of the Bornholm trial in distance teaching, different elements and forms of social learning have taken place, even though they are of a rather limited and controlled nature. We see social learning as a concept for characterising forms of feedback in socio-technical change processes. In the following analysis, different perspectives will be used as a means to highlight the most relevant socio-technical change processes of the case. These perspectives and concepts are based on Van Lieshout, Bijker and Egyedi (this volume, chapter 3). They also serve to extract lessons of social learning.

We see appropriation as a process in which technology is very much taken for granted by the actors, and the socio-technical change is limited in scope to minor adjustments of the technical aspects and/or seemingly necessary adjustments of the social aspects. The question of appropriation is very much linked to the question of whether a social system adopts a technology or not.

Configuration is here seen as a question of to what extent the users (students, teachers, support staff and administration) or the technical aspects have been shaped (or actors roles have changed) during the trial process. Such a shaping process can often take place as an interaction between the users and suppliers of technology.

By translation we mean whether wider perspectives and interests regarding distance teaching have changed during the process. This would often be the outcome of true negotiations about the meaning and use of technology, where the involved actors change their perspectives and make a shift in viewpoint or expressed interests.

The implications for social learning processes and the lessons learned can be expected to vary according to different potentials for feed-back or improvement as integrated elements of the socio-technical change processes.

Appropriation of Distance Teaching

The Bornholm trial has shown that distance teaching can be accomplished, either in a situation of one-way presentation for large classes or in an interactive teaching situation for very small classes. A formal appropriation is accomplished, in the sense that the Danish Ministry has decided to fund courses established on the basis of distance teaching in line with other courses. But the trial also shows that distance teaching is not economically feasible in Denmark, since the investment cost is higher than the reduced costs incurred by saving a teacher at the receiving institution. If a teacher cannot be found in the local area and the course will not be offered in the normal way, displaced teaching carried out by another institution (sending out a teacher) will be cheaper than distance teaching. However, such an economic analysis is of course quite sensitive to inputs concerning the cost and pay-off rates of the equipment.

The technical solutions based on the inflexible video-link system, together with the project set-up, created a very narrow experimental situation that closely followed established institutional and economic frameworks that did not facilitate innovations. If the proposal of some of the users (the local institutions) to supplement the video-link system with a more interactive PC and data-communication network had been pursued, it is quite possible that better results could have been obtained. Minor innovations by the users were accomplished in the operation of the equipment and the layout and regulation of sound and light in the classrooms. Also, the teachers gained experience and made recommendations concerning the preparation of classes and the modulisation of presentations. But, all in all, these 'innovations' can only be regarded as adjustments in using the video-equipment in a distant teaching situation.

The implication for social learning in multimedia is that an approach in which a specific technology is pushed forward can lead to user appropriation of the technology by just adjusting to and solving the immediate technological problems. But the immediate implication of this was a working system that seriously hampered the learning situation for the students involved and caused extra workloads for the teachers. The case clearly shows that the idea of implementing distance teaching technology without considering the changed role of the users (students, teachers, technical support), pedagogical questions and even adjustments in the institutional framework for planning and funding the teaching, seriously hampers the possibilities for furthering multimedia development in education. A sustainable situation for distance teaching in classrooms in Denmark was not tested or established.

Configurations: New Roles for Teacher and Student

The basic trial set-up and context, including an asymmetrical relationship between sending and receiving institutions combined with the economic orientation of the involved ministries, have prevented adaptation of the technology so that innovative processes could involve technical and pedagogical improvements. Users (distant students) can, after the trial and as a result of the trial, be identified as disciplined students eager to take a course in a peripheral area and accept the inconveniences of not being able to take part in discussions and social relations as part of the teaching situation. Teachers have become configured in a role with extra workloads in which a multiplicity of technical skills and pedagogical variation have to be exercised. The users (mainly students and teachers) and their classroom and inter-classroom interaction have been configured as figures that fill out gaps and connect the loose ends of the technical system. This means that the pedagogical solutions and the social interaction have been hampered in comparison with the traditional one-teacher one-class on-site system.

Translation: New Perspectives for the Classroom?

Two different visions for establishing distance teaching in remote localities were in opposition from the beginning of the trial. One vision was centred around a teacher-saving solution that should make it possible to offer courses that were not economically feasible on a traditional basis. Reasons for this could be teacher shortage, few students etc. The Danish Ministry of Education advocated this opportunity with the idea that distance teaching could be accomplished with video-link technology without changing organisation, pedagogical methods etc. Supported by the actual political opportunity and the time shortage, the Ministry gained support for the idea among the receiving and sending institutions and the local authority for the receiving institutions (County of Bornholm), since these actors could not find support for their alternative vision. The alternative vision was based on the idea of establishing a virtual classroom where interaction could flow unhindered across spatial and social distances between teachers and near as well as distant students. The virtual classroom could even be a stepping stone to a broader development, in which the County of Bornholm would attract students and become a centre for (distance) learning in the Baltic Region. The County of Bornholm tried to convince the Danish Ministry of Education of the feasibility of this idea but failed. Faced with the proposal by the Ministry of Education for a distance teaching trial, the County accepted this as a possibility. However, at the same time, they lost their own initiative and had to accept that the Bornholm institutions ended up a receiving and asymmetrical role.

Differences in Social Learning

A certain change of perspective on distance teaching has actually taken place when viewed over a longer time span than the immediate trial. During the trial, the transmitting institutions developed their expertise in using video-link as well as PCs in the teaching situation, while the receiving institutions learned almost nothing. Parallel with the trial on distance teaching, parts of the educational system (including the sending institutions) have learned the lesson that individual home-delivered interactive education based on the Internet connection could be the answer to the limited supply and demand for classroom teaching. The authorities and institutions responsible for planning educational systems have thus concluded that distance teaching is only one possible and expensive solution to specific centre-periphery problems. All in all, this points to a future situation in which distance teaching will be individual and not class based. Actually, many business colleges already have established a network among institutions serving several hundred students. If this situation continues, the economically oriented vision of the Danish Ministry of Education has not helped either to establish class-based distance teaching or support for developing the prospects for an education-based development on Bornholm. If a class-based distance teaching concept is to be developed, it seems that the virtual classroom has to be developed in time-displaced settings, such as network groups, e-mail communication and Internet-based meeting places. The common social space that the students wanted will be very difficult to combine with this 'individual collectivity'. In this broader view, the perspective on distance teaching changed primarily as a consequence of social learning processes related to the wider socio-technical context.

The lesson for the social learning processes closely related to the trial would be that the Bornholm trial was too strongly governed by the social learning mode of control (van Lieshout, Bijker & Egyedi, this volume, chapter 3). This implies a basically economically oriented approach imposed by the Danish Ministry of Education in combination with the restricting modes of the rules and regulations of the traditional educational system. Against this, the experimental situation was very narrow, limiting the mode of experimentation to an almost non-existing possibility.

Conclusion

As an example of the introduction of multimedia technology into the Danish educational system, we have described the case of a distance teaching trial. The case study represents an example of a top-down introduction of distance teaching on the island of Bornholm.

The case study shows that distance teaching only came to function as a result of a long and troublesome problem-solving process pursued by teachers, students and the limited technical staff of the educational centres involved. A major explanation for this is the early adoption or choice of an inflexible video-conference based system without any proactive consideration of organisational change or pedagogical development. Another important and related aspect was a project set-up characterised by a top-down approach in which the strong educational system administered by the Ministry of Education decided which scope, teaching model and technology should be implemented. This top-down approach with its very limited awareness or consideration of the organisational and pedagogical implications can be explained against the background of an asymmetrical relation between the sending and receiving institutions and the context of a centre-periphery debate.

One implication for social learning in multimedia is that such an approach can lead to user appropriation of the technology on the basis of a very limited understanding after adjusting to and solving the immediate technological problems. The immediate implication of this was a working system that hampered the learning situation for the students involved instead of offering new pedagogical opportunities and caused extra workloads for the teachers. Social learning in the configurational sense has also taken place. However, the users (mainly students and teachers) and their classroom and inter-classroom interaction have been configured as the means of filling gaps and connecting the loose ends of the technical system. This means that the pedagogical solutions and the social interaction have been hampered in comparison with the traditional one-teacher one-class on-site system.

Seen in a longer perspective, a translation of perspectives on distance teaching has taken place. The authorities and institutions responsible for the planning of educational systems have learned the lesson and conclude that distance teaching is only a possible solution to specific centre-periphery problems. Parts of the educational system have drawn the conclusion that individual home-delivered interactive education based on an Internet connection should be the answer to limited supply and demand for classroom teaching. In this sense, it is quite possible that the trial in the long term will turn out to be most beneficial for a new commercially based expansive strategy for teaching development in public and private schools for adult education.

The basic idea of giving the island of Bornholm an educational push cannot be said to have been fulfilled, only because there was no investigation of which competence was actually needed in order to promote business development on the island. Other projects in the financial aid package for Bornholm encompassed a much broader development perspective for the use of new technology (Jæger & Storgaard 1997), but there was no collaboration between the different initiatives. The centre-periphery debate seemingly lost its momentum during the course of the trial.

The broader debate on pedagogical issues and questions related to technology and multimedia-supported education wished for by teachers and the general public does not seem to have been the outcome either.

8 Teaching Transformed? The Appropriation of Multimedia in Education: The Case of Norway

MARGRETHE AUNE, KNUT H. SØRENSEN

Abstract

In this contribution, the learning economy of the Norwegian Education system is explored, in relation to the integration of computers and multimedia. With the concepts of domestication and social learning as analytical tools, the authors discuss how ICT is perceived and integrated into different localities of the education system. The focus is upon scenarios as well as the practices of ICT in teaching.

The authors show that there is a considerable flexibility in the understanding of the opportunities of ICT in education. The view that is represented in planning documents from the Ministry of Church, Education and Research (KUF) is rather conservative. ICT competence is presented as a necessary skill, thus the goal is to develop such competence, primarily in relation to word-processing, spreadsheets and the Internet. The number of computers available at each school becomes a major concern, together with the challenge to provide teachers with elementary computer skills.

The conservative scenario does however, not dominate every level of the educational system. We find schools and teachers domesticating ICT in completely different manners. Here, ICT is first and foremost perceived as a reform tool to improve teaching in general. However, the differences between schools are considerable. The 'social innovations' at the practical educational level, are is highly dependent on 'resource' persons/ICT enthusiasts. To learn from these practices there also has to be effective local learning economies that enables contact within each school and between different schools.

The Importance of Computers: To Have or Have Not?

Since the late sixties, computer skills have been seen as an important resource in the labour market. To qualify for the use of this new technology stood out as a major challenge to the educational system. In the last decade, the computer and its qualities has become more and more important in the discourse about schooling and training. The provision of computer skills has become an education policy requirement. The current uses of personal computers as gateways to explore the potentials of multimedia technologies has reinforced this view, while at the same time radicalised the potential of this technology to provide a basis for a transformation of teaching.

Compared to previous machines, like typewriters, gramophones, tape recorders or television sets, the personal computer with multimedia capabilities displays some important similarities. It is commonly found in many households, even if it seldom appears as an education tool. Skills required to use it are more commonly developed at home than in schools. Also, the educational potential seems much greater in theory than what is realised in practice.

Of course, the uptake of multimedia in education belongs to a well-known set of problems related to social shaping of technology and the introduction of new artefacts in society (Williams & Edge 1996). We know that technologies often diffuse slowly, that critical decisions about social configuration have to be made, and that user constituencies may need to be persuaded to find a new technology beneficial. However, compared to mainstream technology studies (Bijker, Hughes & Pinch 1987; Latour 1987, Bijker & Law 1992), a study of multimedia in education offers a very interesting opportunity to analyse how technology is integrated into a large, mainly public, social system. It is a way of providing better insight in the way that technologies are appropriated in complex, multi-layered social institutions, in particular about the construction of new practices in relation to conventional ways of acting and arguing.

Consequently, this paper is an effort to explore some strategies aimed at integrating multimedia personal computers in the educational system. This integration may be perceived as an effort 'from above' to *regulate* the role of multimedia in the education system. This refers to the need to construct aims, strategies, standards and practices that put this new technology to use, not only as an educational tool but just as much as a needed skill. Thus, here, regulation refers to public sector efforts to influence, facilitate, standardise and/or restrict the use of multimedia. In principle, the multimedia challenge to the education system is to initiate use, provide machines as well as software, and above all to stimulate discoveries of new multimedia-based teaching and learning practices. This could be seen as an issue of shaping and implementing policy 'top-down', but also as constructing a system of social learning to cater policy needs.

However, we do not think that this is a sufficient perspective because it places too much emphasis on the constituency of policy makers in education. In line with the approach of the Social learning in multimedia-project, we will focus on broader processes of social learning, in particular related to regulation (Sørensen 1996). Thus, we are also concerned with the way practices are constructed 'from below', thus exploring the possibilities of strategies 'bottom-up' and systems of social learning emerging among users.

Consequently, the paper is an effort to analyse the emergence and characteristics of different strategies of social learning related to multimedia in education, in view of the need to communicate insights and experience. To do this, we will examine the system as *a learning economy*. This way of thinking highlights the way that producers and users interact and exchange experiences and ideas, an interaction that may provide a basis for learning to produce as well as to use technologies more efficient and beneficial (Andersen & Lundwall 1988). The notion of producers may be less relevant to systems of education, but this way of thinking may be just as important to an analysis of interaction and learning between the different groups of actors in education: policy-makers, administrators, teachers, etc. This may mean that we find different processes of social learning in the education system, perhaps even smaller sub-sets of learning economies, for example between teachers at a given school.

We believe that such analysis may be facilitated by the use of the concept of *domestication* as a way of characterising the appropriation of technologies like multimedia (Lie & Sørensen 1996). To be put to use, multimedia needs to be domesticated at different localities of the education system. Social learning happens when the outcomes of this domestication process result in new ways of using the technology as well as when the experience is communicated. Here, we are particularly interested in the communication process and its discursive structure. Can we observe exchange of information between the actors of the system, and what kind of information is flowing?

We will emphasise that the relationship between actors and localities has to be examined. Even if there is a formally defined hierarchical relationship between them, we do not make assumptions of, e.g., the existence of efficient top-down strategies. The point is to break away from either determinist or rationalist assumption, from either the view of technology as an imperative that *will* come through or the view of technology as something implemented according to social planning.

Of course, as we shall explore in some detail, multimedia technology has been brought into national education policy discourses. However, we have to be sensitive to the possibility that this technology is introduced in an independent manner in other localities as well. Multimedia technologies have not been developed according to some overarching plan, but are in fact brought into Norway as tools that, in many respects, are ready-made. Thus, there is no need to give policy makers a priori privilege as the main shapers of multimedia in education.

Domestication implies, metaphorically, the taming of a new artefact or a new set of knowledge (Lie & Sørensen 1996). Originating from the study of the way households make sense of technologies (Silverstone & Hirsch 1992), it has been developed as a tool for analysing the production of routines as well as the meaning related to technologies in everyday life (Lie & Sørensen 1996; Sørensen, Aune & Hatling 1999). This means analysing three dimensions: the practical, the symbolic, and the cognitive. These dimensions have different implications in different localities. In the classroom or by teachers and students, we should be concerned with the ways a given technology is put to use, the related attribution of meaning, and the learning needed to achieve this.

In the context of policy making, practice is not just related to ideas about how the technology may be used. In addition, an infrastructure has to be set up, policy makers have to develop a division of labour between different sets of institutions, people, and competencies, and they have to provide guiding visions for the achievements one could expect of the new technology (Dierkes, Hoffman & Marz 1996). These are potentially important dimensions of the regulatory activities required, and thus, possibly, objects of learning by regulation (Sørensen 1996).

From this mindset, our analysis of the use of multimedia in education will be furthered by studying the following problems:

- What are the main features of the policy view of multimedia and the political tools that are applied in order to implement this technology in the Norwegian primary and secondary education system?
- What are the main features of national, regional and municipal planning regarding multimedia in primary and secondary education and of the related social experiments to explore and promote multimedia technologies?

- In particular, we are concerned with multimedia in individual schools. How do school managers and teachers engage in multimedia? How are local strategies of applying the technology constructed? To what extent and in what manner may multimedia be appropriated by individual teachers, and how do they relate to the potential of the technology in relation to teaching?

Thus, the analysis of multimedia will take us through a cross-section of the system of education. The underlying idea is that multimedia in education is used in ways that are shaped through the interaction of people and institutions at all levels in this system. We should not assume that this shaping takes place only in the Ministry, or only in the classroom. In principle, all localities may prove to be important.

In our paper, we have used the Norwegian system of education as a case. Of course, we cannot claim that Norway is in any way typical. However, that is not the point. Our main concern is to identify interesting strategies and constellation, to use them as the basis of conceptual development, rather than outlining the typical or most common strategies in this or that circumstance. Also, we want to show how the domestication of multimedia needs to be studied through a multi-local ethnography in order to map out the complex interaction of actors and institutions in the shaping of this technology. In order to do this, we have chosen to analyse different strategies that may be observed regarding multimedia in the Norwegian system of basic education.

The paper is based on analysis of relevant policy documents and interviews. 12 teachers from 9 different schools have been interviewed. This includes primary and secondary schools, covering the age group from 6 to 18.[1] Also, we have talked with two informants from the National Centre for Educational Resources.[2] A few administrators and representatives of teachers' unions have been interviewed as well.[3] Reference is made in the text to indicate the nature of the source that provides the basis of observations and arguments. Even if different sources of information have been combined, our study is of course limited by the rather small number of institutions and individuals that has been approached. Thus, we do not claim to have produced a complete study of multimedia in education even in Norway, although if we believe our observations offer some general insights into the Norwegian situation.

The reader should also note that we do not study multimedia in the form of specific, advanced experiments where interactive combinations of pictures, sounds, and texts are performed. Rather, we look at multimedia as an aspect of computers that has been added to the traditional potentials of this technology. This means that our analysis is based on an understanding of multimedia technology as something related to, and difficult to separate from, computers (Brosveet & Sørensen, 2000).

Computer Angst as a Policy Vehicle

The structure and logic of national systems of education vary. In the case of Norway, primary and secondary education is funded and managed publicly. There are only a few private schools, and the majority of them receive substantial governmental support. Thus, the management of primary and secondary education is a public responsibility. Standards are set by central government to ensure that the system of education is homogeneous. However, in practice, the system is characterised by a complicated system of division of responsibility and control between central, regional, and local government, and with considerable discretion of decision making residing with the individual school and even the individual teacher (see, e.g., Lauvdal 1994, 1996).

This means, of course, that it is difficult to change the system quickly, for example, by introducing multimedia technology into local curricula in a homogeneous manner. Central government may set certain standards as objectives, and they may even call for quite distinct didactic changes. However, the decision to buy computers resides with local authorities and the individual school. Concrete educational planning is mainly a prerogative of the individual school and teacher.

The situation presents very definite challenges of social learning. In theory, we should be facing a 'learning economy'. Since we are studying a hierarchically organised public sector with long traditions of learning by regulation, we would, in fact, expect to observe such linkages. On the other hand, there is no reason to expect that the learning economy of the education sector is well-functioning. As already indicated, the system in question is set up with considerable autonomy of the actors involved. We have a Ministry of Education, Research and Church Affairs (KUF) responsible to the Norwegian Parliament, that commands a set of regional offices of education, one in each of Norway's 18 counties. Each county has an education administration of its own, answering to the Fylkesting, and there is a similar arrangement in each of Norway's 435 municipalities. The number of schools, teachers, and classes is, of course, much too large to allow for close control by any administrative body. Thus, it is by no means obvious how this learning economy functions.

Even if the system of education is administratively segmented, there is definitely a national discourse on computers and multimedia related to the sector. This discourse is clearly shaped by the belief that information and communication technologies (ICT) is vitally important, to society and industry as well as to the individual citizen. The sector of education is supposed to help qualify young people for the labour market of the future as well as making them knowledgeable and skilful members of society.

However, politicians as well as citizens fear that the education/school system will fail to do so. One of the main diagnoses offered at the moment is related to computers and multimedia. Presently, it is a public concern that Norway may be lagging behind other countries in preparing its youth for the coming of the information society. This anxiety of falling behind, that the country may not provide sufficient skills for the 'information society' could be called computer angst because the argument very seldom is grounded in any form of analysis. Often, it is just a response to some simple and not very meaningful numerical indicators, in particular, the number of pupils per PC. The indicator does not place Norway in a particularly favourable position, compared to other countries (Sundvoll & Teigum 1997).

Thus, the Norwegian discourse on ICT in education has been focused on the physical availability of computers, rather than on multimedia content or teaching practice. This indicates a way of thinking that is influenced by technological determinism, a belief that access to ICT in itself will provide the educational value. Thus, neither policy nor plans are strikingly visionary. The general aims are quite vague, while the specific goals are mundane and down-to earth. Pupils are supposed to learn to use word processing, spreadsheets, and information data bases, supposedly the most basic computer skills required in today's workplaces. This means that ICT is perceived as an object of instrumental skills, rather than a reform tool of education.

Lately, the ability to use the Internet has been added to the list of important skills,[4] and there is an emerging awareness that ICT may become a tool to improve teaching. Still, the analysis of potential gains remains vague and the strategies to integrate multimedia in teaching are described in general terms.[5] One might be tempted to conclude that the use of computers and multimedia is perceived as so obviously necessary that – in the policy discourse – no clarification of benefits is really needed.

The concern for availability of computers, measured numerically, has been sharpened by surveys that give evidence of substantial differences between regions, and even between schools in the same municipality (Sundvoll & Teigum 1997). A particular emphasis has been placed on the fact that many pupils, but not all, have access to a PC at home, and that boys, on the average, have better access than girls. Thus, once more, there is a strong call that the Norwegian school should assume its traditional mantle as 'the great equalizer', the institution that is supposed to rectify inequalities created by differences in society. This concern for equal access to computers has meant that Norwegian policy for ICT in education is to a large extent shaped to provide for equal opportunities of skills in computers and multimedia.[6]

This does not mean that the ICT in education plans made by the Ministry neglects other issues besides equal opportunities. However, the plans suggest that the challenge of producing visions about how ICT may be used to improve teaching is left to the professionals, mainly the teachers themselves. The role of the Ministry is more often that of the overseer than the inventor or innovator. On the other hand, it is not fair to argue that ICT policy for primary and secondary education is mainly driven by computer angst. Clearly, the fear that Norwegian education may fail to provide the needed ICT training has been prominent in the debates. To the extent that politicians have become engaged in pushing for greater use of ICT and multimedia in schools, the fear of lagging behind other countries and of creating new social inequalities have provided them with their main motives. On the other hand, most politicians are basically confident that the system of education will be able to take care of the challenges. As far as we have been able to observe, there has been no great interest among politicians to try to intervene in any other way than reminding educators about the challenges. Thus, we need to study the features of this system more carefully in order to understand the way multimedia is being domesticated.

Learning Economy of Central Government: Learning by Plan and Paper

A focus on processes of social learning related to multimedia in education may be sustained through an effort to clarify what we previously called learning economies. This implies a concern for the communication of ideas and experience between different institutions and groups of actors in the system. In this section, we will look more closely at the social learning practice of the Ministry of Education and the way it communicates to schools and teachers as well as the way it is informed about current developments in practice. What are the strategies of implementing plans for ICT in education, and how are the plans evaluated?

The concern for computers in education is by no means a recent one. The Ministry of Education produced its first white paper on the topic in 1984, and this initiated the first programme to support experiments with computers in schools.[7] 1998 marked the start of the fifth consecutive ICT programme.[8] Thus, the Ministry has considerable experience in the area.

Interestingly, in the light of manifest technological changes, there has been considerable stability in the visions promoted by these five generations of plans. The computer has been envisaged mainly as an object to be mastered by pupils and students. Only recently can we observe greater concern regarding the potential of ICT as a tool to improve the quality of teaching and learning. Above all, there has been no real concern that computers might replace teachers. Computers – with or without multimedia capabilities – are constructed as tools that can open up new educational possibilities, new strategies for teaching, but the potential has been assessed conservatively. The ICT challenge, as indicated above, is seen mainly as an issue of availability of computers and the provision of simple office-type skills, with a limited potential for improving the quality of teaching. Computers are not seen as a technology that might help transform primary or secondary education in any radical way.

Thus, the five generations of ICT plans represent a steady, but small-scale effort to make some basic computer skills a part of the core curriculum. For example, the central authorities never provided extra resources for investments in PCs. These investments have been funded through the ordinary budgets. This strategy of making investments in ICT a local responsibility is clearly expressed in a talk that the present Minister of Education, Jon Lilletun, gave early in 1998:

> Regarding the issue of possible governmental programmes to stimulate investments in equipment, particularly in primary schools, it can be gathered from the documents that 'the matter is under consideration', as the saying goes. I neither can nor want to promise extra governmental funding for primary schools to buy computers. However, regardless of the outcome of the budgetary priorities, there is no advantage in waiting. My advice to schools and municipalities is therefore: Go ahead! Regardless of the size and timing of an eventual effort on the part of the Government to provide extra

incentives, it will be modest compared to the needs we perceive. The new IT-plan under consideration will also have as a premise that the owner of the school (local or regional governments, authors' comment) is responsible for providing computer equipment.[9]

This strategy indicates clearly the indirect nature of the ICT strategy. The role of the Ministry is not to implement multimedia in education, but rather to provide a discursive framework for local efforts. For example, instead of providing extra funding, the concern of the Ministry has been to establish training programmes so that teachers may learn about computers/ICT. There is also a small-scale effort aimed at providing them with proper software. Earlier, in the late 1980s and the beginning of the 1990s, the Ministry launched a major effort to develop a tailor-made system for Norwegian schools. The system, 'Winix', was later abandoned and described as a costly failure. While the nature of the failure is still debated, the Ministry has later cautiously avoided any direct involvement in software development, even if some financial support is provided for outside initiatives.[10]

In fact, the new curriculum plan for primary education, from the 1st to the 10th grade, has only passing references to information technology and multimedia, even if the technology is considered important. The matter is discussed briefly, following some short notes on traditional teaching tools and school libraries:

> The training shall contribute to pupils' development of knowledge about, insight in and attitudes towards the evolution of the information society and information technology. Pupils should acquire the ability to use electronic devices and new media critically and constructively, as practical tools in various subjects, topics and projects. Information technology should enable pupils to use domestic as well as foreign databases. Girls as well as boys should be stimulated to use information technology to counteract social and sexual bias in education.[11]

Clearly, quite traditional values and attitudes are front-stage in the curriculum plan, whereas new technologies are not.

Current plans for computers and ICT in education leave a clear impression that the Ministry's knowledge about the situation in Norwegian schools relies on rather standardised and quantitatively oriented written reports. It is regularly informed about the use of ICT in schools through large-scale national surveys (see Sundvoll & Teigum (1997) as a typical example) and annual reports from the regional offices of education.[12] They get statistical information about the stock of computers in different schools (including teachers colleges), about the number of schools, municipalities, and counties that have plans for the use of ICT in education, about the number of training courses held for teachers, and how extra money has been spent through the ICT programme. The survey also tells about the number of teachers who report that they know how to use word processors, spreadsheets, and the Internet.

This exchange of information could be interpreted as the backbone of a learning economy, but the Ministry has formatted its own social learning in a distinct way that we will term learning by plan and paper. Through its plans, the Ministry defines a set of topics and the relevant indicators. In this manner, the system of evaluation and reports that is established to feed the planning process shapes and limits the information made available to planners, and by implication to politicians. While thoroughly rational in design, the resulting system of social learning is fashioned by the concern for availability of computers and does not facilitate exchange on issues of multimedia content and education practice related to ICT.

Learning by plan and paper is a concrete instance of learning by regulation (Sørensen 1996) and is shaped by the agenda-setting role of the central authorities. In the Norwegian case, the agenda of the Ministry of education is dominated by the following items:

The need to mobilise interest and enthusiasm for ICT in the educational system. Thus, in the planning documents, we find many references to the importance of computer skills and to the importance of ICT in the future. In this kind of system, actors have to be motivated to do their part. To command, e.g., teachers is difficult and expensive.

- The need for teachers and administrators to acquire the skills required to participate in the implementation of the ICT programme. Many teachers do not know the first thing about computers.
- Political correctness plays a prominent role. The planning documents argue that the use of ICT in education should be compatible with Norwegian culture and values. In particular, equal opportunity issues are placed high on the agenda.
- It is emphasised that ICT initiatives should be compatible with traditional values of education in Norway. There should be no radical change through computers!
- Thus, the Ministry's social learning through plan and paper is shaped by the need to address the above concerns, rather than by a more open exploratory and experimental approach. In particular, the focus on

issues such as access to computers and equal opportunities has reinforced the tendency to produce mainly numerical indicators because they are well-suited for such monitoring purposes. From this perspective, the system provides a good overview, and it is made good use of in the planning documents.[13] Arguably, learning by plan and paper represents – at least in this case – a form of learning by regulation that is well adapted to the context of current Norwegian ICT and education policy.

On the other hand, such a system of learning by plan and paper appears to be ill-suited to provide knowledge about new educational practices related to ICT. Such practices are difficult to monitor and analyse on the basis of crude surveys. A clear indication of this limitation is the abstract and non-consequential descriptions of actual pedagogical achievements made by the use of ICT. We are told that it is important to teach children how to use word processors, spreadsheets, and the Internet, and it is acknowledged that the multimedia computer represents an important resource to teachers. But what is achieved through the employment of ICT remains unclear. Examples of pedagogical gains are seldom provided. In general, the information about local processes of planning, learning and implementation in municipalities and individual schools in the Ministry's planning documents is sparse.

The Ministry's ICT programme supports experiments that are evaluated, as well as research projects that focuses on particular aspects of the programme, such as equal opportunities for boys and girls (see, e.g., Håpnes & Rasmussen 1997). Through such contracts, researchers are hired to become intermediaries between the Ministry and the practising education communities. They provide supplementary information that, in principle, is a corrective to the deficiencies of learning by plan and paper described above. This may be described as another form of social learning; learning by research and evaluation.

However, if one is to judge from the planning documents of the Norwegian Ministry of education, this learning process is not so important. At least, there are few explicit references to concrete results, neither from Norwegian studies nor from international efforts. Thus, in this case, the role of researchers as intermediaries is not rectifying the above-mentioned weaknesses of learning by plan and paper. Still, the ICT plans compare favourably with the Curriculum plan[14] in terms of concrete measures and analysis of the situation. Arguably, Norway has a tradition of using lean indicators as the basis of managing the education system from above.

Detailed, qualitative information is probably perceived as relevant only to decisions made by other actors than the Ministry.

However, there is an important exception to this observation. During the early generations of the ICT programme, there used to be a unit within the Ministry that carried a special responsibility for computer in education issues. The Datasekretariatet ('The computer office') generated a lot of experiments and even started its own software development (in particular the infamous Winix initiative). While the latter initiative contributed to the closing of this office, today, many of these activities have been delegated to the National Centre for Educational Resources (NLS).

Originally, NLS was established to aid schools to find useful tools for education and training. ICT and multimedia meant a modernisation of the concerns of the institution, but its previous functions meant that NLS was already integrated in the Norwegian school system. The institution is managed by the Ministry, but since it is not part of the Ministry, it has a certain autonomy and can act on its own in developing and implementing strategies to support the use of ICT and multimedia in schools.

NLS plays an important role in the shaping and implementation of the ICT programme, partly as an institution that oversees experiments and provides support, e.g., software development, partly as an advisor to other actors in the education system, and partly as a provider of information to the Ministry.[15] Therefore, we have chosen to analyse the role of NLS in greater detail since this institution seems to be a particularly important inter-mediator. We will do this by focusing on two large-scale experiments that influence social learning of other actors in system and illustrates how the role of inter-mediator may be enacted. These experiments consist of two web services, the 'School Net' and the 'Guidance Net'.

To summarise, the domestication of multimedia through Norwegian education policy has resulted in a definition of this technology as an object of obligatory, instrumental skills, rather than as a reform tool of education. The Ministry has created an agenda where computers are focused on, and the effort to format local strategies is mainly directed towards the issues of access to computers and of providing competence to teachers. The resulting form of social learning, learning by plan and paper, provides a narrow perspective on the role of multimedia in education by focusing on crude numerical measures, rather than 'thick descriptions' of ongoing activities.

Thus, the policy of ICT and education is formatting multimedia strategies in Norwegian schools to become conservative as well as open. It is conservative in its instrumental orientation towards skills like word processing and the use of spreadsheets and the Internet. It is open in the sense that the suggestions made about the use of multimedia in education are rather loose and non-directive. Arguably, the Ministry is leaving the issue of constructing educational multimedia to local initiatives, again with NLS as a possible exception. If this is the case, we would expect to find small learning economies at individual schools, with weak links to other schools or other parts of the system of education.

National Experiments at a Meso Location: NLS and its Web Services

The Internet has interesting qualities in its ability to provide flexible information. Thus, it is well suited to be an organism of social learning, a tool that facilitates, e.g., learning by interaction. Through the establishment of its web services, NLS has been able to situate itself as an intermediary in the process of social learning about ICT in education.

To begin with, one should note that NLS has been set up to inform about, supervise and certify teaching accessories. For example, textbooks to be used in primary and secondary schools have to be approved by NLS. This means that NLS operates in several networks, such as education policy, the publishing industry, and the school system. In this respect, it is an intermediary institution with strong links to relevant actors of the education system that enables it to mediate between policy making and educational practice, between policy making and the textbook industry, and between the textbook industry and schools.

We have chosen to focus on two initiatives that highlight the intermediary role in a highly pregnant way, giving NLS a central role in the learning economy of the Norwegian education system. The first one is called the School Net. It is an Internet site for Norwegian schools provided by NLS. The target groups are teachers and other school-related professions, pupils and parents. It was 'opened' on October 15 1996. The immediate purpose was to respond to a suggestion by The Ministry of Education to establish 'electronic meeting-places'. NLS, as responsible to develop and approve teaching aids for primary and secondary schools, got the responsibility to construct this new service. NLS had been engaged with computer issues for some time and had acquired considerable expertise in this field. They constructed an Internet site that offered more than meeting-place functions. The School Net also provides information, documentation, discussion and advice on educational issues.

NLS had started to work with web technology a couple of years earlier, and they established their own homepage on the Internet in 1994. They had also been involved in the development and exchange of educational software as part of a Nordic group. This activity is still an important superstructure for the Norwegian School Net, even if the net is developing in country-specific directions. The Norwegian School Net has put a lot of effort into building resources to support the new national Curriculum Guidelines, 'L97'. Here, ideas about general education are transformed from written text into a world of electronic messages, pictures, sounds etc. It is considered important that L97 supports the abilities of pupils to manage these new complex symbolic ways of expressions.

An important function of the School Net is to support this development. NLS employees who are working with the School Net say that they want to make the access to electronic educational resources more democratic. The School Net is supposed to be a tool or a workshop for everyone. One of the goals is to be able to produce most of the content locally and in interaction with its users. In addition, useful links are to be offered. As the co-ordinator of the School Net states:

> One of our most important goals was to provide content for the schools, in keeping with the standards of the (the new reform programme) L97 (...) Nobody, when logging into the School Net, should have to be sent to another net site (...) We want our own self-produced content. It may be something that a teacher or someone else has found in the L97 (the reform programme), an exiting new way of using the net, or other information about ICT applications. We want to distribute this information ourselves.[16]

Thus, the main goal of the School Net is to be a source of quickly distributed information, relevant to schools and teachers. It also aims to be a site for the mobilisation of interest in the use of ICTs in school, a tool to develop competence in the management of electronic information and a forum for the exchange of experience and points of view. According to the director of NLS, the ideal is to combine new and old ways of developing tools for a good school, not losing sight of the merits of traditional ways of teaching.

Till now, the School Net has been developed mainly to cater for the needs of schools where the children are below 15 years of age. Their homepage[17] provides an extensive set of information on many different topics. Under the headline of educational plans, you can for example, download or order National Curriculum Guidelines (L97) for primary to lower secondary school. Further, you find documents that deal with theoretical and practical implications of these guidelines and the new educational reform ('Reform 97'), and the page has a lot of links to relevant documents and books. The user of the School Net may also find a quite pragmatic guide that is supposed to help the individual school to evaluate and select educational resources for the coming year. This is a co-operative effort of NLS and The Norwegian Publishers' Group.

Another set of items is related to teaching resources. Here is a very detailed overview of recommended books and other educational tools (software, CD-ROM) for each subject in every course offered. There are also exemplars of tools for teachers, like games or Internet addresses.

NLS has also established an initiative called the 'Guidance Net'.[18] This homepage is basically an Internet version of an existing physical guidance centre, located at NLS. It aims to provide actors within the school system with information, ideas and possibilities of consultation about ICT-related subjects. The administrator or teacher may learn about different agreements with suppliers of soft- and hardware, established by NLS, or how to make plans for the use of ICT in their institutions. Here, one can find planning documents of the Ministry of education, but also plans made by many different counties, municipalities and individual schools. The homepage also provides information about ICT projects that are carried out in other schools, on a national level or even internationally. This information is made available so that one may learn how others perform planning and projects. In addition, there is an overview over courses one may take, relevant literature and self study books. Of course, one will also find a catalogue of software made and/or distributed by NLS as well as Internet addresses where relevant software may be downloaded, educational as well as technical.

It is not clear if the two experiments have been successful, but according to the two representatives of NLS whom we interviewed in June 1998, there were on the average 1600 visitors to the 'School Net' per day. By the end of the year, the number had increased to 3,000. Regardless of the notion of success, the two experiments represent an interesting effort to use multimedia as a technology to do information brokering and thus to stimulate a particular sort of learning by interacting. While schools, teachers, or developers of multimedia products have little direct interaction, these web-sites allow a simulated contact that provides an opportunity for the exchange of experiences and information that – in principle – is very important. Through these experiments, NLS provides exactly the kind of intermediary function that should stimulate the learning economy of the education system. Arguably, the experiments support social learning that transcends the learning by plan and paper set up by the Ministry. The two web-sites work primarily as links between schools, but they have the potential to mediate ideas and experience between the policy level and the schools. Thus, the 'School Net' and the 'Guidance Net' are interesting examples of multimedia as a tool of social learning.

In our opinion, NLS and its two web-sites have not been set up as a conscious part of a learning economy of the Norwegian system of education. As far as we can see, the role of such meso-level institutions is not well understood, even if they play an important part in making the system work. This exemplifies the neglect of social learning in developing policies, e.g., for ICT in education. Or rather, that the Ministry believes that new ideas may be diffused through formal training by teachers, so that exchange of ideas and experience is superfluous.

On the other hand, the kind of simulated interaction performed through NLS' web-sites is clearly affected by the formatting of the field by the Ministry. For example, the examples of plans from schools that are made accessible through the 'Guidance Net', are very much shaped by the concerns to make computers available to children and to provide standards for the integration of multimedia into the curriculum. The quite formal structure of the plans, clearly influenced by the Ministry's learning by plan and paper-discourse, is obviously a barrier to the exchange of more valuable information about concrete strategies and classroom applications. However, one may find traces of such information in some documents. Thus, the conservative formatting of multimedia policy seems to have definitive effects on the multimedia-and-computer-in-schools discourse in Norway.

While the role of NLS as an intermediary allows a shaping influence, in particular through the provision of information and the setting of standards for teaching accessories, it has to work in the policy environment formatted by the Ministry. Thus, the schools are largely left on their own in their selection of information and ideas and in their practical implementations. This means that we need to look at what schools and teachers do when they domesticate multimedia. Since the formatting from the Ministry is rather open, we should expect relatively large variations in terms of concrete practices.

This means that we expect that the learning economy related to the use of ICT in the Norwegian system of education is complex and consist of different, loosely connected processes of social learning. While the learning by plan and paper that has been set up by the Ministry may have a hegemonic position as the main supplier of information to policy-makers, this form of social learning is so weakly embedded in the local practices of schools that we have to assume that other processes of social learning are at work as well. The learning by brokering that is set up by NLS may be important, but only if is linked to local learning processes.

The Importance of Strategy: Tales of Three Schools

In this section, we will discuss the domestication of multimedia in three Norwegian schools. They have been chosen because they illuminate difference in terms of the availability of computers as well as strategies of education. However, none of them have many computers, and they do not take part in any computers-in-education experiments, even if school B is a privately owned, religiously oriented school with a particular pedagogical tradition. We will analyse three quite ordinary institutions of education in Norway to see how they translate official policy into practice, and how they react to the Ministry's formatting efforts.

School A[19] is an old upper secondary school with 55 teachers and 450 pupils. It has six computers that are available to teachers, while pupils share around 50 machines (partly with Internet access). The latter machines have been placed in special IT classrooms that are occupied by obligatory ICT teaching during most of ordinary school hours. However, in the afternoons and evenings, pupils may use these machines on their own.

Some of the teachers used the Internet and had their own e-mail addresses, but e-mail had not been established as a common communication system. Still, the school offers ICT as a subject (like all higher secondary schools), but ICT is only to a very small extent integrated in the ordinary subjects. One of our informants argues that this is an outcome of the centralised localisation of the machines. The computer rooms had to be booked a long time ahead, and there are only a few free slots. Thus, chances for 'spontaneous learning' are slim.

Our informants were not satisfied with the present situation. They argued that the financial situation of the school limited the potential possibilities. The amount of software available was too small, and there were far too few courses available to train teachers. One of them told us that he had organised some internal courses 'last year' about Word and the use of the Internet. These courses seemed to be offered by chance rather than as a consequence of planning. Neither was ICT support deemed satisfactory.

None of the informants claimed to have an overview of the ICT situation of this school. Thus, there is a theoretical possibility that this school might have had a few enthusiasts that integrate ICT in their own teaching. What seems to be a major barrier to our informants to get this overview, is the lack of lateral communication between teachers:

I would like to have an hour in the middle of the day, for co-operation-oriented meetings between teachers, where we could exchange experiences.[20]

What also seems to be missing is a systematic plan to train the staff and to provide aims and resources for the educational use of ICT in the classrooms. It seemed as if the use of ICT in teaching was delegated to the individual teacher. What you wanted to learn and how you wanted to use ICT, you had to find out for yourself.

School A has domesticated multimedia in accordance with the policy formatting in providing the obligatory ICT courses. Moreover, there was an emerging use of ICT as a tool for some teachers in preparing their teaching. The meaning attributed to computers was conservative, and the social learning strategy was quite individualised. The school did not, as far as we could see, interact with other schools, nor was there any effort to create any kind of internal learning economy among teachers.

School B[21] is a combined primary, middle and lower secondary school with 450 pupils and approximately 45 teachers. They have invested in seven multimedia machines, and the schools' policy is to make all pupils into personal-computer users. In addition to the computers, they have bought digital cameras and projectors. This interest among the teachers started when the school needed a new encyclopaedia. Instead of buying these books, they decided to buy multimedia machines and get access to the same information through CD-ROMs. In other words, they were already working with ideas and plans before they got the machines. They managed to get the equipment by writing applications to different school programmes.

The school has developed plans for integrating ICT through planned training of pupils and teachers. In seventh grade, all pupils get a basic training in how to use computers. After having tried out different approaches, teachers chose to divide pupils into three levels when training them. The Norwegian school system prides itself in a long tradition of giving every individual equal education. Dividing pupils into groups according to their computer skills breaks with this tradition. However, the rationale behind the move was simply that there were substantial differences in computer skills among the pupils. If pupils unfamiliar with computers should have a fair chance to receive proper training, they would need to start with the basics. But then the more skilled ones would get bored and disturb the others, or pressure teachers to speed up.

When pupils have the required skills, they are left to themselves to decide how much they want to use computers. The machines have been placed in a lab that is open to use whenever they need it. Pupils use the Internet and CD-ROM when collecting information in most subjects. They also use a word processing programme when they write essays or papers. Some of the language teachers also allow the pupils to use chatlines. They chat, e.g., on German chatlines when having a German lecture.

In this manner, it seems that this school has managed to integrate ICT in many subjects. They have a flexible use of the machines. Some of the machines are even made mobile by being placed on tables with castors. In this manner, they may easily be moved around when necessary.

In spite of the low number of machines, access to computers is seen as quite good. Three days a week, pupils may use the lab for three hours in the evening. They can use the Internet, CD-ROM or use the PC to write. Most of the pupils are just playing around on the Internet or chatting on MIRC, which has become very popular. They pay a small fee for every half-hour they use the Internet. There are no teachers around, but one ninth-grader is employed to be in charge.

An important key to this quite successful integration of ICT is an active and positive response from the teachers. All teachers at this school have been through several courses. As with the introductory training of pupils, they set up courses according to level of difficulty, so the participant may choose. According to our informant, this is very important. Another important factor is to keep the training close to the reality of the school:

> It is very important that training is based on practical realities. I see no use in having big courses in big halls with excellent machines. We have to relate to our everyday life. And they (the participating teachers) should have to push the same buttons in the courses as they are to push when they practice for themselves.[22]

A main feature of school B is that they have set up a local learning economy among teachers. Clearly, teachers learn from each other and exchange ideas and experiences. Some produce new ideas, some use them, and they all produce teaching. The establishment of a local learning economy means that the school has created a climate for interaction and exchange, rather than just individual problem-solving. Thus, social learning is promoted in its most basic form as collective learning by using.

Moreover, the school has developed a strategy of integrative use of ICT. Thus, their domestication of multimedia computers has produced a meaning that transcends the conservative formatting of education policy. Their computers are not just for acquiring basic computer skills, but also for exploring new options of learning, including the management of information.

School C[23] is an upper secondary school with 450 pupils and 45 teachers. This school has 44 computers for pupils' use and 8 machines for teachers' purposes. Each pupil has e-mail access, her/his own address, map for storage and a home-map. The computers are located in different places: 30 machines have been placed in a computer room, 4 machines in the library, and ten machines in a workshop-room (where there are a few scanners as well).

The teachers have 8 machines at their disposal. They are located in an office. In addition, there are a few portable machines. The intention is that there will be additional portable machines with Internet access. Like most teachers in Norway, they have only a small desk at their disposal at school. This makes portable machines a more practical tool, also for homework.

Our informant tells us that procurement of new equipment strictly follows the strategy plan of the school.[24] According to this plan, in the near future, they will establish a video-workshop and a project room with 20 machines. They also want to develop a video/sound studio and to establish an internal network. Each subject will be represented with a homepage, and the teachers can for instance present papers, tests, etc. here.

An important factor concerning the amount and the quality of the equipment is a flexible organisation. School C is not 'richer' than other schools, but investment plans can be changed and realised within a short period of time.[25] Besides, a driving force is, as for school B, one particularly interested and competent teacher and several quite interested and competent colleagues who follow the lead.

The ICT responsible teacher/enthusiast realises that the processes of educating the staff and creating interest, has to take time. They arrange some basic courses, but they also see the good effect of learning from each other, and from some of the pupils. It is important that the teacher has to be allowed work at his/her own tempo. As our informant at school B, they were in favour of offering courses at different levels and tried also to give some individual basis training.

They mean that each school has to develop a strategy plan towards the technical as well as the pedagogical. The computers have to be of a certain quality, but that is only one part of it:

> One has to use the personnel resources available (_). One way is to try to get everyone interested at the same time. Or one may differentiate. I believe that the enthusiasts should be offered good opportunities, but at the same time one has to help all the others in a way that fits their needs. We can't expect everybody to march in step and reach the same goal.[26]

According to our informants, this school has enough machines, but that is not the only key to a positive process of integration. Strategy plans, specific goals and a flexible organisation are important factors. However, they still have not reached the desired level of integration in every subject, mostly because of the above-mentioned reasons: Every teacher has to work at her/his own tempo. In addition, they complained about the level of technical support (hardware as well as software).

Like school B, school C has domesticated multimedia in a way that transcends the conservative meaning of the national plans. Also, they have developed a practice of social learning that amounts to a learning economy of interacting teachers. However, the two schools differ in the way their learning economies function. In school B, interaction is a reasonably frequent, while in school C, they are more dependent on the use of a planning document as an intermediary.

The computers-in-education discourse has been formatted to be particularly sensitive to the issue of access. The three tales narrated above indicate that availability of ICT is a more complicated phenomenon than just the number of computers per pupil and teacher. In fact, given the level of variation in Norwegian schools, these numbers seem to be much less important than politicians assume. Availability is also a question of how computers are made accessible. Locating them in one classroom has very different consequences from making them mobile or placing them in different localities within the school.

Most schools have one or more computer labs/classrooms where the ICT teaching takes place. These rooms are booked throughout most of the day. For many teachers it was a problem to have to reserve this room days ahead, in case a sudden need to use the computers arose. School B was an so called 'open school'. They had no classrooms. The computers were placed on tables with wheels and transported to wherever needed. That is perhaps the reason that they managed successfully with a low number of machines. School B illustrates clearly that the number of machines was less important than a distributed access to computers, some enthusiastic teachers with ideas and plans, and an active integration of computers in teaching.

Plans for educating teachers was nother crucial factor. In many of the schools, as exemplified by school A, this training seems to happen more by chance then through an overarching plan. Schools B and C illustrated the opposite. Here, we also saw the importance of individually adjusted computer training, as close as possible to ordinary work tasks.

As expected, we found local learning economies among teachers, systems of interaction with weak links to the administrative offices of municipalities or regions, not to mention the Ministry. Probably, this is the logical outcome of the Ministry's learning by plan-and-paper system, since this form of social learning does not cater to local information and knowledge needs.

It should be clear from the above tales that teachers have a considerable leeway in deciding how ICT should be used (or not) in the classroom. Efforts to create local learning economies may lead to the establishment of a facilitating mechanism and a resource, but not any firm structure. The plans do introduce some limitations and demands, but there is still a considerable need for the ordinary teacher to domesticate multimedia on his/her own in order to place the technology in his/her own teaching practice. Thus, we will now have a look at what happens in this area of the ICT-in-education efforts.

Teaching Transformed?

In the standard literature on technology and work, there has been the frequent assumption that new technologies are used to change the skill structure, to increase control over work, or to change the division of labour. However, few of these studies address the situation of the professional worker which is probably rather different. A rather extreme example is provided by Sætnan (1998) where it is shown how professional interests in a hospital may completely corrupt the technology and the aims of its introduction.

While teachers have less professional strength and autonomy than medical doctors, they still have considerable discretion in terms of form and content of teaching. National plans place demands on the topics to be covered, and they may also suggest didactic strategies, but these plans also offer considerable flexibility of interpretation. As we have seen, in relation to computers and multimedia, the plans are rather vague and conservative in their orientation. If multimedia is to become a reform tool in education, that will have to be the outcome of local efforts.

In our interviews with teachers, we believe we can identify three main ways of domesticating the new technology:

- The traditional teacher who continues to teach in the same way as before, with little use of ICT as an educational tool.
- The lonely innovator who is eager to put computers to use in his/her teaching, but operates mainly on his/her own.
- The supported enthusiast or the teacher who really wants to make ICT part of a modern education, who puts in a lot of effort to realise this aim throughout the whole school and not just in her/his own teaching, and who gets moral support to do so from colleagues as well as the administration.

Due to the selection of informants, we have probably missed out on a fourth type, the ones that are not very interested in using ICT in education and avoid s using the technology. Probably, this is the most common outcome of the domestication process.

Per Olsen[27] is an example of what we called the traditional teacher. He works at an upper secondary school, teaching biology and mathematics. He has a computer at home (owned by his partner), which he mostly uses for writing. Thus, he has some experience with computers. However, he does not use ICT as part of his teaching. In his case the main reason is the difficulty of getting access to machines. The computer room has to be booked in advance, and that means that teachers have to plan many days ahead:

> The rooms where the computers are placed are generally occupied by ordinary ICT classes. Thus, I cannot just bring my biology students to these rooms to work there. For some time now, we have been wishing for at least one computer in every classroom, including the biology room. Then we could search the Internet for information on subjects we are working on (...). I believe I would have used the computer a lot more in teaching if we had one available in the classroom.[28]

The problem of availability also arises in relation to his tasks outside the classroom. The informant was not comfortable with the working conditions offered by the school, where he would be sharing a few computers with many other teachers. For this reason he prefers, like many of his colleagues, to work at home. Of course, this tradition of doing all non-classroom tasks at home, makes 'spontaneous' learning and sharing of experience difficult.

This point is very much related to the idea of local learning economies. Such learning economies presuppose that interaction flow easy, a condition that is not satisfied by the long-standing tradition of teachers doing their preparation and follow-up work in the individualised space of their homes. Many of our informants emphasised this observation by reference to a form of interaction which they called the 'neighbour effect'. This made it worthwhile to create an environment that facilitated working side by side, enabling you to ask someone for advice when you run into difficulties. Combined with some introductory courses, this is viewed as an effective way of learning.

Per Olsen and the other 'traditional teachers' had not been offered much introductory training, nor stimulated to create a more collaborative working environment. They are positive to the use of ICT in education, but not at any price. Thus, the 'traditional teachers' represent a considerable resource that may be mobilised, but they will usually not take any real initiative to promote the use of multimedia.

Hans Johnsen[29] is an example of a lonely innovator. He too is a teacher at an upper secondary school, and an ICT enthusiast to the extent that he is making his own methods for the use of ICT in teaching, even if he has the same (poor) conditions as the 'traditional teacher'. The decisive difference is a genuine interest in this type of work.

He uses ICT frequently in one of his subjects (language). Moreover, Hans Johnsen's class have their own page on the net. Here, he distributes questions, essays, books to read, etc. His pupils are supposed to reply in the same manner. To manage this, Johnsen uses a lot of free time, four to five hours every evening, to work out his different pedagogical arrangements:

> The main reason is that I like to make these Internet applications (...). For instance, I may scan a piece of text (...) and I make links to different pieces of the text ... words that are difficult to understand, persons that are introduced and where I present a picture and a short biography (...). Then I work this into an analytical model and give them a lot of detailed questions. And then they have to move between Netscape and Word, and they must write down the answers.[30]

His class have access to one room with multimedia machines, but there are not enough computers so the pupils have to work together. He does not use ICT in the other subject he teaches. As he put it, it was difficult enough to get access to the computers the four hours a week that he needed for this subject. He is first and foremost interested in the pedagogical aspects of ICT in education and it frustrates him that the hardware is often the main discussion theme.

The 'lonely innovators', like Hans Johnsen, have acquired most of their skills on their own. They are active, using ICT in their own teaching, but their plans and methods are not diffused. They have no substantial impact on their colleagues due to critical deficiencies in the local learning economy. This is in contrast to the situation of the third type, the 'supported enthusiast'. Anne Petersen[31] belongs to this category. Like Hans Johnsen, she is a frequent ICT user but her conditions of work are more favourable. Anne Petersen developed her interest in ICT through her work as a teacher. Together with some colleagues, and in a school with no computer equipment, she established a successful ICT project.

The ideas behind it have met with a lot of support from the administration, and Anne Petersen has been given some of the responsibility of developing an ICT plan at the school. The plan includes pedagogical ideas, suggested courses and requests for hardware and software as well as for other multimedia equipment. It is supposed to be realised in the near future

Since Anne Petersen mainly works with pupils of 13 to16 years of age, it is very important to provide them with a basic introduction to computers and multimedia. The goal has been to make each pupil manage some simple but fundamental tasks like word-processing, scanning of pictures and text, presentations, use of CD-ROM, basic applications of the Internet such as the application of search engines, navigating the School Net, and using chatlines and e-mail.

ICT is presented as a very useful tool, but it has its limitations. In teaching situations there has to be some social interaction. Thus, Anne Petersen does not want too many computers in every class. Her main interest is the pedagogical content of ICT. That is the part she is continuously working on.

A main conclusion from this discussion is that individual domestication strategies have a crucial effect on the integration of ICT in Norwegian schools. Enthusiastic teachers are able to establish ICT as a pedagogic tool across their school, even if they lack local ICT support. They may even work in an institution with very few computers.

The enthusiastic teacher that experiences or elucidates positive feedback, like Anne Petersen, may become a driving force in the integration of ICT in a successful way. However, if local feedback is lacking or not mobilised, the enthusiastic teacher will, like Hans Johnsen, end up as a 'lonely innovator'.

In other words, ICT in education is not just a question of regulation, or a reform that can be directed from 'above'. The various individual strategies and the different local cultures in every school illustrate why the domestication of multimedia seems to be a 'learning from below' project.

The Ministry and the Classroom: Deficiencies in the Learning Economy

In this paper, we have explored the dynamics of the learning economy of the education sector in Norway in relation to teachers' use of computers and multimedia. We have analysed the domestication of ICT in different areas of this system, with the main emphasis on the Ministry, the intermediary institution set up to supervise, support and standardise textbooks and other teaching tools (NLS), individual schools and individual teachers. A major finding is the flexible understanding of what ICT represents in relation to education. Some, like the Ministry, define the technology in a quite conservative manner and see the challenges as related to the skills needed to use computers. Some schools, and in particular some teachers, have more radical ideas about ICT as a reform tool to improve teaching in general.

The learning economy of the education sector is formatted by the Ministry to establish access as the major concern of ICT in education and, in addition, to the emphasis on simple skills like word processing. The result is a system that we have called 'learning by plan and paper', a system where plans and the information provided to evaluate the plans is dominated by simple numerical indicators of access and of planning and training activities. The formatting set in motion by the Ministry means that schools and teachers are induced to be access-sensitive and quite conservative in their visions. The resulting learning economy does produce interaction, but the learning that takes place is rather limited. The Ministry gets little information about what is really happening in the classrooms, while teachers are not learning much from the output of the Ministry.

NLS has set up two experimental web-pages that modify this impression. The School Net and the Guidance Net represent a very interesting effort to stimulate the learning economy of the sector by creating more efficient links to allow a flow of information and an exchange of experience. This represents a form of social learning that we called learning by brokering. By that we mean that NLS acts as a broker to facilitate the flow of experience and ideas and thus may facilitate the establishment of a more widespread learning economy related to multimedia in education. However, these efforts are also limited by the formatting activity of the Ministry. The resulting discourse about computers and multimedia in schools, as it may be observed on the two web-sites, tends to address the same issues as those that are highlighted in the documents from the Ministry of education.

Under such conditions, and given the traditional autonomy of schools and teachers, it comes as no surprise that ICT is domesticated in very different ways in different local circumstances. Again, we may note the importance of local learning economies. Schools that are able to establish interaction between teachers and stimulate the work of ICT enthusiasts, seem to have come a long way in finding quite innovative uses of computers and multimedia. However, as we have seen, many schools have deficiencies in their learning economies. This results in a lack of interaction. Teachers, interested in ICT, work on their own, in constant risk of reinventing the wheel. And, worse still, teachers that are not very interested in the use of computers and multimedia may safely ignore the challenges.

It may be seen as ironic to state that the learning economy of the education sector is deficient. However, this is a rather precise diagnosis. There are substantial problems in creating interaction and exchange between teachers, not to mention problems between schools. The NLS initiative to set up the School Net and the Guidance Net points to the interesting potential of multimedia technologies to help overcome the lack of interaction. By using the Internet as a medium of exchange of information and experience, it is possible to improve the learning economy of the education sector considerably.

As announced in the introduction, there may be some more general lessons to be drawn. First of all, the findings from our study of multimedia in education show clearly the importance of analysing the domestication of technologies simultaneously at several locations or levels. We may not be surprised by the observation that multimedia is domesticated in different ways in different schools and by different teachers. Few would be surprised at being told that what the Ministry thinks and what is going on in the classrooms are quite different things.

On the other hand, what happens in the classrooms is not independent of the actions and beliefs of the Ministry. The conservative construction of multimedia and the establishment of a learning economy dominated by the strategy of learning by plan and paper facilitates a conservative use of multimedia by teachers as well as strategic perversions. When the policy constituency is very concerned about the ratio of pupils and computers, such ratios may very well serve as an excuse to focus on how to get more computers and to excuse the lack of integration of multimedia in teaching by referring to the bad local ratio. Thus, there is an interesting potential of interaction of strategies from 'above' and 'below' that have previously been neglected.

In particular, we should emphasise the point that regulation should not be perceived merely a type of action that limits options and raises barriers to the experimental uses of new technologies. In fact, regulation as it has been analysed in this paper, may have a very definite and productive influence on technologies. First of all, regulatory activities may push new technologies that otherwise would have been neglected. Secondly, regulation may mean the establishment of infrastructure, standards, and practices, without which the new technology would not 'work'. Thirdly, regulation may imply the promotion of certain interpretations of the technology that have considerable influence upon the way it is configured and used.

Another set of lessons is related to the concept of learning economies. Previously, this concept has been used by economists in order to understand important aspects of the context of innovation (Andersen & Lundwall 1988). We believe that we have shown that it is fruitful to analyse such learning economies in the public sector. Above all, the study of multimedia in education provides us with the insight that learning economies should be understood as potentially separated and with varying strategies for the exchange of experiences and ideas. Further research is needed to clarify how such learning economies may or may not become linked, and the translation processes involved in efforts of setting up links.

Notes

1   The interviews with the teachers were conducted at the different schools, based on an interview guide that covered various aspects of the use of computers and multimedia, including skills, practices, plans and visions. Each of the interviews lasted for appr. 3/4 - 1 hour. They were all taped and transcribed. Interview transcriptions are numbered as file #1-12. References are made to the file number. We chose originally to focus on teachers that were interested in ICT, so we have a clear bias in the interview population. This may

mean that we paint a too rosy picture of the situation in Norwegian schools. On the other hand, interviews with teachers that actually use ICT are more useful in providing information about the way computers and multimedia are applied in Norwegian classrooms when the technology is utilized. We have found it less important to describe and analyse non-users.

2   The interviews with the representatives from NLS took place in Trondheim. They were taped and transcribed as well and referred to as file #13 and 14.

3   The interview with a representative of one municipal school office is in file #15, while file #16 is an interview from one regional education office. Additional interviews with representatives of teachers' unions are found in file #17 and 18. None of these interviews were taped, but the information was written down immediately afterwards.

4   See *IT in Norwegian Education*, Ministry of Education, Research and Church Affairs, Oslo 1997 (http://odin.dep.no/kuf/publ/it-plan/eng) and *IT i norsk utdanning*, Ministry of Education, Research and Church Affairs, Oslo 1997 (http://odin.dep.no/kuf/publ/arsplan.html).

5   See also *IT i norsk utdanning. Plan for 1996-99*, Ministry of Education, Research and Church Affairs, Oslo 1996

6   See *IT in Norwegian Education*, Ministry of Education, Research and Church Affairs, Oslo 1997 (http://odin.dep.no/kuf/publ/it-plan/eng) and *IT i norsk utdanning*, Ministry of Education, Research and Church Affairs, Oslo 1997 (http://odin.dep.no/kuf/publ/arsplan.html).

7   See Stortingsmelding nr. 24 (1993-1994) Om informasjonsteknologi i utdanningen, p. 16f.

8   *IT i norsk utdanning. Årsplan for 1998*, Ministry of Education, Research, and Church Affairs ((http://odin.dep.no/kuf/publ/1998/itplan.html).

9   Jon Lilletun: Utviklingen av informasjonssamfunnet. Innlegg i Norsk Investorforums 'Utfordringer og utdanning i IT-sektoren', 2 mars 1998 (http://odin.dep.no/kuf/taler/1998/980302.html), p. 2.

10   See Stortingsmelding nr. 24 (1993-1994) Om informasjonsteknologi i utdanningen, p. 26-27.

11   *Læreplanverket for den 10-årige grunnskolen*, Ministry of Education, Research and Church Affairs, Oslo 1996, p. 78-79.

12   The annual reports of the regional offices of education from 1997 (in Norwegian) may be found at http://odin.dep.no/kuf/publ/1998/tilstand/tilstand.html.

13   See, e.g., *IT i norsk utdanning. Årsplan for 1997*, Ministry of Education, Research, and Church Affairs ((http://odin.dep.no/kuf/publ/arsplan.html). *IT i norsk utdanning. Årsplan for 1998*, Ministry of Education, Research, and Church Affairs ((http://odin.dep.no/kuf/publ/1998/itplan.html).

14   See note 11.

15   More information about NLS may be found at their home page http://www.nls.no/

16   Interview file #13, p. 6.

17   The School Net is located at http://skolenettet.nls.no/.

18   The Guidance Net is located at http://vs.nls.no/.

19   Interview files #1 and 2.

20   Interview file #1, p. 10.

21   Interview file #5.

22   Interview file #5, p. 4.

23   Interview file #6.
24   Interview file #6, p. 11.
25   Interview file #6, p. 13.
26   Interview file #6, p. 18.
27   Interview file #1.
28   Interview file #1, p. 2 and 5.
29   Interview file #8.
30   Interview file #8, p. 4.
31   Interview file #5.

9 A Project Adrift: Mechanisms of Multimedia Innofusion in Education

TINEKE M. EGYEDI

Abstract

Evaluations of multimedia projects have contributed little towards multimedia innofusion in the education sector. One plausible explanation is that most evaluations focus on the way projects are managed ('within-project-level' focus). This teaches us little about innofusion processes. It is more relevant in this respect to evaluate in what manner project-related innofusion of multimedia occurs within the institution ('at-project-level' focus).

In this chapter the 'at-project-level' focus is applied to a multimedia project in a faculty. The project drifts within the faculty. It changes meaning and locus several times until it becomes associated with a specific course. Meanwhile different actors become involved. The network of actors expands, implodes and re-emerges around a new nucleus. Most actors, notably teachers, are intermediary multimedia users and producers combined. The case illustrates that innofusion of multimedia occurs along lines of use as well as production.

Several mechanisms are noted which have propelled faculty-wide innofusion. The most salient example is the project's drifting. Usually, such a project would be criticised for lack of project control. This study concludes, however, that project control need not benefit multimedia innofusion. It may hamper innofusion.

Introduction

> I don't understand why there is so much ado about this multimedia programme.
> Do you mean that its significance is much less than all these questions suggest?
> Hm, yes, ... actually I do.

A student makes this comment during an interview. She refers to the amount of evaluation going on about the use of a hypertext programme in the course she is following. I am rounding off my third and last interview with her. Like all students, she has also been asked to keep a log and note down changes in her use of the programme during the course; and each week she and the other students score on an attitude scale. What she is unaware of, is that there is much more evaluation taking place. There are seven layers of evaluation involved in this project.

The project is one of the twelve work packages on ICT use in education which are carried out in a collaboration by four European universities. The collaboration was a European Union (EU)-funded initiative called Electronic Learning Environment for Continual Training and Research in ALMA[1] (ELECTRA). Within ELECTRA a special evaluation group compares the pilot projects at the stage of implementation. For this purpose it has developed an elaborate questionnaire with open questions (Kluge e.a. 1997), a booklet which took the managers of the pilot projects on the average eight hours to answer. To clarify some of the answers, evaluation group members have held additional interviews. The ELECTRA project management has further set out a semi-structured questionnaire, also to be answered by the managers of the pilot projects, and a list of open questions for teachers and a select number of students. The aim is to determine whether ELECTRA's policy objectives have been met. In addition, each pilot project has evaluated itself in order to determine how the project can be improved. The findings of this internal review have also been sent to the ELECTRA management and the European Commission. It is for this purpose that 'our' work package manager has developed the above-mentioned attitude scale and has asked students to keep a log. Next to the internal review, there has been an external review (Schagen 1998). The external reviewer has been invited by the EU to monitor the project's progress. Furthermore, the course that constitutes the project has been one of the education cases of a distinct EU research group: the Social Learning In Multimedia (SLIM) project. In this

SLIM context the current chapter has been written (see chapter 1, this volume). Lastly, apart from the teachers who have also evaluated the course, the faculty is interested in a general way in how to use multimedia for teaching and research. The faculty board has made an inventory of faculty members' ideas and wishes concerning ICT. See table 9.1.

Table 9.1   Evaluating parties and their interest with regard to one pilot project

Evaluating party	Purpose	Learning focus
ELECTRA Evaluation Group	To map and compare projects	Implementation of ICT in education
ELECTRA Management	To determine if ELECTRA policy aims have been met	Project management
Pilot project manager	To improve the use of ICT in course	ICT support
External reviewer (EU)	To provide feedback on the use of EU subsidy	Project development
SLIM researcher	To examine how multimedia is appropriated in education	Social learning process
Teachers in course	To improve the course	Course content
Faculty	To diffuse multimedia use within the faculty	Faculty members' multimedia needs

The student has a point, a stronger point than she realises. Although each evaluator has a different focus, the number of evaluative layers related to this one project seems absurd. But is it out of the ordinary? There are more examples of projects that have been subjected to heavy monitoring and evaluation (e.g. Rossel & Buser, this volume). The amount of evaluation that is going on is symptomatic for a more general phenomenon. It is a symptom of modern society itself, as Van Lieshout e.a. would argue, for modern society "is characterised by a permanent process of evaluation, monitoring and feedback" (see chapter 3, this volume). Evaluation and monitoring activities are a means of reflecting on and learning from developments.

What have evaluation activities brought us? Despite all efforts at European and member-state level, multimedia only slowly penetrates the classroom. There is general concern about the lack of multimedia use in the education sector. Little appears to be learnt from project evaluations, which contributes to multimedia innofusion. This is puzzling for learning from mistakes and successes would appear to be the main objective of project evaluations. Each evaluation activity presumes that there is a need to evaluate. It implies, for example, that the party who initiates the evaluation does not automatically equate project design to project control. Matters may not turn out as planned. Therefore, there is a risk of 'failure'. 'Failure' could be acceptable provided lessons are learnt. If, indeed, learning were the core aim of project evaluations, learning from 'failure' would legitimise most project outcomes. The increasing number of evaluation activities would then express that we have collectively institutionalised our doubts about, for example, rationalistic approaches to projects and decision making.

But learning does not take place in a manner which leads to multimedia innofusion in education. There are two plausible explanations. Firstly, in reality, the aim of evaluation may not be to learn from the project. It may be that evaluation and monitoring activities serve foremost as control and planning instruments. The scope of such evaluations would then have little bearing on other situations of multimedia use but the project at hand. Egyedi's discussion about verification experiments seems to support this explanation (see chapter11, this volume). The second explanation, the one explored in this chapter, is that the lessons drawn relate to what happened within the project (e.g. how to improve project management). They have no immediate bearing on the issue of multimedia innofusion. This explanation maintains that most evaluations focus on the 'within-project-level', while evaluations that focus on how the project is placed within the organisation ('at-project-level') have more immediate relevance for innofusion matters. Multimedia projects take place within an institutional setting. It is likely that if there is any diffusion of multimedia uses it starts within the institution. Of interest is then what mechanisms drive institutional multimedia innofusion. These mechanisms may well offer clues about why sector-wide multimedia innofusion does not meet expectations. In other words, the second explanation presumes that the problem of lack of multimedia innofusion in the education sector is not that too little evaluation has taken place and that little has been learned. The problem is that the focus of evaluation has generally targeted the 'wrong' project level, and that what has been learned has little bearing on the innofusion question.

Research Approach

This study takes the above idea as a starting point. It addresses the question of in what manner project-related innofusion of multimedia occurs within the institution. In the present case, the institution is a university faculty. Of interest is, therefore, how the faculty positions the multimedia project and what its wider impact is.

The social shaping approach discussed in chapter 3 is followed. That is, prevailing notions such as 'negotiation of meanings', 'interpretative flexibility' and 'closure', as well as the less typical social shaping concepts mentioned in that chapter, such as 'appropriation', are included. The term 'appropriation' is used to indicate the institutional assimilation of multimedia. Furthermore, I will regularly use the term 'actor network'. The term stems from Callon (1986), but refers here, more loosely, to a group of people with a common interest, focus, activity, etc.[2] It can thus, for example, be used to designate all faculty members. Faculty membership is a formal, institutionalised kind of membership and refers to a stable actor network. More volatile and unstable is the actor network of, for example, those who define the project or who are involved in different multimedia activities. As I will illustrate, changes in the project's actor network and in networks of multimedia users indicate changes in the state of innofusion throughout the faculty.

Methodology

This chapter is based on twelve informal, exploratory interviews (i.e. with the project manager, two teachers, a multimedia lab staff member, and a member of the ELECTRA project management) and on two structured interviews with the project manager. The latter I held in my capacity as a member of the ELECTRA evaluation group.[3] I further examined project documents[4] and the project's Website in order to gain insight into project developments. I used the results of two studies on multimedia use in the faculty,[5] and screened the minutes of meetings of a faculty department[6] that cover the year 1996 and the first half of 1997 to determine the degree to which multimedia use had penetrated the faculty.

Faculty Setting

The multimedia project takes place in the faculty of Arts and Culture of the Maastricht University. It is a young, rapidly growing faculty. It is a matrix organisation. Members from different faculty departments cooperate in cross-departmental programmes called *tracks*. One new master track, which plays a role in the next sections, is that of Visual Culture (VC). This track started in August 1997.

When the project starts, few faculty members have experience in using multimedia. Computers are mainly used for word processing. Faculty members are making the switch from a DOS-oriented to a Windows environment, which is recognised by the management as a good reason to replace old computers by more powerful ones. The use of multimedia in education is new for the majority of students, teachers and researchers. But they are eager to learn more about it when asked. Some faculty members e-mail and some occasionally use the Internet. The Web is a relatively new phenomenon. The faculty encourages its members to make their own Web pages.

The initial objective of the project, the Interactive MultiMedia In Culture and Science (IMMICS) project, has a broad scope. It is "to develop a learning environment which is fully integrated with multimedia information, and which, at the same time, offers an opportunity to study the impact of interactive multimedia as a study object in the programme of the Faculty of Arts & Culture" (IMMICS 1996). The promise of faculty-wide innofusion of multimedia is launched.

Project Adrift

The project starts in a rather mundane manner, gains momentum, branches off, implodes and resurrects in more modest and focused versions. This process is described below as a history of project activities. An interpretation in terms of redefinition of the project's meaning concludes the section.

The extra ELECTRA pilot project The first impetus for the project comes from elsewhere. In 1994 the education department of the Maastricht University has a rough idea for an ICT project for which it seeks partners. The department finds them within the regional network of cooperation that already exists between a German university, two Belgian universities and the Maastricht University. The universities set up what is to become the ELECTRA project. It is to consist of several pilot projects on ICT in education. Within the Maastricht University additional pilots are sought to join in, and the Faculty of Arts and Culture is approached to develop such a project.

Vehicle for multimedia diffusion in the faculty A few technology-minded teachers and administrators in the faculty take up the idea. They invite teachers to deliver project proposals. One of them is selected for ELECTRA, namely IMMICS. From 1995 to 1996 a teacher is appointed part-time to coordinate and disseminate ideas about the project. The project has a faculty-wide scope (i.e. Cultural Science in the acronym of IMMICS). Meetings and presentations are organised to create support for and discuss ideas on the integration of multimedia within the curriculum and uses for research. Two workshops are held for teachers, one on the design and production of multimedia, the other on the search and creation of Web-sites. A limited number of demonstrations and small-scale educational experiments take place. External expertise is called in to support some of these activities. Plans are developed to install a multimedia lab and a database with visual material. The material is to be supplied by teachers and students. Two students are employed to make a start on the database. The last faculty-wide meeting that is organised takes place in February 1997. On that occasion the state of affairs of IMMICS is presented in combination with a number of other multimedia-related activities. The development of the multimedia skills of teachers and the requirements for the multimedia lab are discussed. See Box 9.1, which illustrates the faculty-wide scope of IMMICS activities. It shows that during this period IMMICS comprised, among other activities, of *four courses.*

Course of the Visual Culture track Most of the necessary funds for the project, that is, for appointing the staff of the multimedia lab and for the equipment, are obtained in 1996. In the same year ideas about a new Visual Culture (VC) track are elaborated. It is to start the following year. Discussions that take place mid-1996 show that these two initiatives (IMMICS and VC) are becoming intertwined. Partly this is because one of the VC courses has been selected to serve as the ELECTRA pilot. Also, the integration of new media in IMMICS partly underpins the ambitions of the

---

Box 9.1   Traces of the project's redefinition on the Web

Most public activities concerning IMMICS have left textual traces on the Web. An examination of the Web during the final stages of the 'IMMICS course' (January 1988) gives an idea about changes in the scope of the project and the people involved in the period 1996-1997. It contains a number of surprises.

- In the Action Plan disseminated in July 1996 the intention is to keep close contact with other ELECTRA work packages, the IMMICS steering committee and the Visual Culture steering committee, and to disseminate information on the project faculty-wide. Point of departure is the faculty. IMMICS, as a work package of the *ELECTRA* project, is described in the same way if one starts the Web search from the ELECTRA-environment. However, when searching for comparable information from the University's Web environment, the emphasis in IMMICS is on the Visual Culture programme (28 October 1996). It seems as if either interpretative closure has not yet taken place on the meaning of IMMICS; or, if done on purpose, that the desire for inclusion of outsiders leads to different ways of addressing 'surfing' audiences.
- Starting out from the University's Web environment, the IMMICS entrance screen consists of a logo and the first project manager's e-mail address. This situates the overall design of the linked – IMMICS related – information in time, that is, before the change of 'leadership' in February 1997. It suggests that the time for extrovert activity has since then come to a halt.
- The information linked to the IMMICS homepage refers to an array of multimedia-related activities in the faculty, next to 'IMMICS the course' documents (Action Plan II and User Requirements). Apart from the latter, the agenda of a public presentation of faculty-wide multimedia activities is announced for February the 5th 1997; an IMMICS Internet Pilot is described which pertains to an inventory of web-sites relevant to the faculty (and to VC in particular); the SLIM research proposal on IMMICS is presented (namely as dealing with multimedia in Culture & Science programmes); and lastly, three other courses are linked to the IMMICS homepage, one containing text-based student papers resulting from a European distance-learning project, and two Visual Culture courses (electronic course books with many images included, one of which also with student papers).

---

new track. Furthermore, the ELECTRA management exerts pressure to focus the IMMICS project on a course and not on the whole faculty, which further highlights the VC context of the course. Despite the fact that the project's narrower scope is noticed and commented upon, the faculty context recedes into the background. IMMICS becomes the VC course.

Appendix to the multimedia lab Early in 1997 a manager is appointed to build up the multimedia lab. He starts from scratch together with a newly appointed staff member. The new manager is brought in from outside the faculty. He is asked to coordinate the IMMICS project and accepts. Meanwhile, the IMMICS project has entered the implementation stage. It is a period of seclusion. The contacts of the new project manager are largely restricted to his immediate colleague in the lab and to the teachers directly involved with the Visual Culture course on which the project focuses. The course content is developed. An electronic course book is made, course material is gathered, equipment is purchased and the student work area is furnished. The first time the course is held is also, formally, the demonstration phase of the project.

In the same period, word gets around in the faculty that the staff of the multimedia lab is willing to help out teachers and researchers with practical computer problems. The staff's daily work increasingly positions them as the help-desk of the faculty.[7] Through such contacts, individual faculty members notice the progress in the set-up of the lab.

Reviewing the foregoing, the project's meaning is continuously redefined and shifts locus within the faculty. It starts as just one more pilot project for ELECTRA; next, it is positioned as a vehicle for faculty-wide multimedia diffusion; then, it acquires the more narrow meaning of a course in the Visual Culture track; it ends up, for the time being, as one of the activities that take place in the multimedia lab. The project's initial objective is not specific. Its interpretative flexibility triggers ideas for multimedia use. The project serves as an umbrella for new initiatives, which are the first signs of faculty-wide innofusion. As such, the project's interpretative flexibility works as a stimulus for multimedia innofusion. Subsequent drifting of the project does not occur arbitrarily. It is the outcome of consecutive meaningful negotiation within the faculty. The project is deployed to give expression to the prominent role which multimedia is to play in the new Visual Culture track, and to secure initial facilities for the multimedia lab (personnel, equipment, and visual database). That is, the concrete focus of the VC track and the multimedia lab build-up determine its meaning. They are the crystallisation points for multimedia activities in the course of the project. The new multimedia lab and its staff symbolise the 'material' crystallisation point, while the Visual Culture course represents the educational crystallisation point. They focus the development of multimedia uses. But there are more innofusion mechanisms at work than the activities triggered by the project's interpretative flexibility and the direction provided by consecutive crystallisation points.

Actor Networks and Meaning Brokers

As the previous section illustrates, the project is very malleable. This turns out to be an advantage for the diffusion of multimedia uses. For while the project changes locus, meaning and scope within the faculty, different actors become involved in multimedia. Each redefinition of the project addresses and involves a specific set of actors at the matching phase of the project. Below, I give an account of the main changes in the actor network. Three phases are distinguished: a phase of growth, a phase of implosion, and a phase of re-emergence. Next, the role of the project manager in the actor network is discussed.

Actor Network Expands, Implodes and Re-Emerges

The real trigger for faculty-wide activity on multimedia is the availability of funding, and a few individual forerunners who are adept at some multimedia uses and have a drive to 'evangelise' (see also Slack, this volume). This initial process is supported by a 'technology push' policy at faculty level. Faculty policy on multimedia is implicitly coupled to IMMICS developments. The project offers the means to explore the usability of multimedia for the support of research and teaching. The first project manager and coordinator, a teacher, plays a crucial role in building up the actor network. The network grows. Some actors contribute actively. Others are passively aware of project-related activities. An IMMICS supervision group is installed. The steering committee of the Visual Culture track is closely involved in the project developments. Actors outside the faculty are called in for advice. Experts from the Open University are asked to write a report on the uses of multimedia in education and ventilate their ideas (see e.g. Weges & Wessels 1997). They organise a few demonstrations. The university computing centre installs a server for the project and organises multimedia workshops for teachers. When the project enters the stage of implementation, the style of project management takes on a new shape. It becomes concrete. The time schedule of the course and of ELECTRA have to be met. At that stage, the project management is handed over to a new person, a system developer (an art historian). The number of actors involved dwindles. Those who were passively aware of IMMICS lose track of developments. The meetings of the IMMICS supervision group stop. What is left, are infrequent informal contacts between the four people immediately involved and a few interested colleagues, some of whom participate in the Visual Culture track. The project's network implodes, and comes to consist of those who have a task in developing the course and its multimedia context. However, while the project's significance as a faculty-wide project, and then as a VC course fades, multimedia developments around the lab become more salient. A new actor network emerges around the locus of the multimedia lab and the activities of the two staff members. The number of contacts that evolve from their informal help-desk activities increases.

Meaning Brokers

The project manager is, in a certain sense, the project's ambassador within the faculty. He plays a key role in how the project is defined and who is addressed. In the initial stage of the project, faculty members associate the project with the first project manager, 'Mr. IMMICS'. He is recognizable as the one who is responsible. This works as a mechanism of diffusion for what he stands for. When his successor takes over, the 'Mr. IMMICS' effect is lost. The latter has the extra handicap that his office is located next to the multimedia lab. This positions him as a technical expert and outside the natural habitat of teachers.

Both project managers are meaning brokers. But they mediate a different meaning of IMMICS and to different audiences. The first project manager mediates between the project and the faculty. He positions IMMICS as a vehicle for discussing multimedia uses faculty-wide, and is supported therein by the faculty board. The second project manager, forced by the circumstances, primarily re-positions IMMICS as an ELECTRA project and mainly mediates between IMMICS actors and the ELECTRA management.

The role of the project manager is an important one. In his capacity he formally carries the responsibility for the project's progress. But can we go so far as to say that he has the power to determine the degree of multimedia innofusion in the faculty? Callon (1986) notes that some actors occupy pivotal positions in actor networks. They have a disproportionate influence on what happens. Where all the significant changes in the network are handled through these central actors they are called obligatory points of passage. In our faculty the project managers are very important facilitators. But the relations among colleagues are not such that the project managers can determine the degree of multimedia innofusion in the faculty. The importance of the voluntary cooperation of teachers in developing multimedia uses is essential for the diffusion of practices and ideas. Persuasion rather than extorted cooperation is the means by which the project managers proceed – and cannot but proceed because they have no means to do otherwise.

Intermediary Users and Producers

Innovation and diffusion of multimedia cannot be attributed to separate phases of technology development, or to specific loci and actors (see chapter 3, this volume). As a consequence, a strict separation between producers (locus of innovation) and users (locus of diffusion) is also questionable. Den Hertog & Van der Wee (1982) point out that there is differentiation among users. Three of the four categories they distinguish are relevant here. For example, the teachers who develop the course and integrate multimedia use within the course design are intermediate users of multimedia, or *functional users* in the terminology of Den Hertog & Van der Wee.[8] They select the multimedia that are of interest and re-create a situation of multimedia use for students. They are therefore producers of multimedia uses, and sometimes also content providers (e.g. references to information sources, visual material). From this perspective, they are not the primary end-user (i.e. the *operational user*, who works with the system); the students are.[9] Shifting perspective, teachers can be end-users too. The first project manager, for example, addresses them as end-users when he encourages them to use information services such as CD-ROMs, and multimedia software to develop teaching material. The second project manager, another intermediary, is consumer, user and also producer. In his capacity of system developer of the course, he purchases a hypertext programme from the software producer. As a staff member of the lab he produces multimedia uses. The faculty board creates opportunities to experiment with multimedia uses. It is a co-producer of social learning. (Den Hertog & Van der Wee call those who ultimately decide about the project, i.e. top management of the organisation, the *policy-making user*.) But in return the faculty board expects the project to have a spin-off from which the faculty as a whole benefits, and thus also the board itself.

The foregoing illustrates that a clear distinction between users and producers cannot be made. Most actors are intermediary users *and* producers. Analyses of appropriation and diffusion mechanisms cannot, therefore, focus on the actor network as a user-producer network without specifying from which perspective actors are examined. The dominant, economic outlook on multimedia innofusion in terms of a market of producers and users (i.e. consumer-purchasers) obscures the importance of *localised multimedia use and production*. The adaptation and redesign of multimedia to local circumstances are vital for the education sector. Local multimedia production may consist of developing additional software but more influential is that a context is created for local multimedia use. This I refer to as the production of multimedia *use*. In respect to the impact of the project on faculty-wide multimedia use, it is therefore of interest that the innofusion process develops along the lines of multimedia use and production of multimedia uses. The theoretical underpinning of innofusion studies needs to be revised accordingly.

Innofusion of Multimedia

The term *innofusion* acquires added significance in the light of the dual user-producer role of most actors. In the previous sections I described that the project does lead to faculty-wide multimedia innofusion. In this section I will try to pinpoint the moments and situations that triggered the process.

Reviewing the project from start to finish, three specific events raised the general awareness and/or induced activity on multimedia uses. The first was the call-for-tenders procedure. The IMMICS proposal was selected among various proposals. By asking for several proposals, the involvement of a wider group of teachers was secured. Several teachers started thinking about how to use multimedia for their courses. Some of the proposals that were rejected were implemented anyway, outside the formal context of 'a project'. The second event served foremost to raise the awareness of the faculty's policy makers. Concerned was the installment of the first project manager (coordinator), an organisational matter which required the support of the policy-making forum. The third event was the presentation day that was organised for the faculty. The presentation started off with the state-of-affairs of the IMMICS project. But a number of other faculty initiatives on multimedia were also discussed and demonstrated. It was a straightforward attempt to spread multimedia use.

In view of the narrow meaning of the project in its final stage, and the implosion of its actor network, one would expect it to have had little impact on the faculty. Indeed, those immediately involved in the course expected a modest impact because the use of hypertext in the course was too specific for wider use. The use of multimedia in a course about multimedia was primarily of interest to the Visual Culture track of which it was part. An interview round, held soon after the course takes place, confirms that foremost the members of the VC track were informed about the course and its content.[10] Not the faculty as a whole, but this track adopted the project. For the faculty time appears to have stood still since IMMICS' meaning became that of a Visual Culture track activity. The course itself, therefore, contributed little to the diffusion of ideas among teachers and researchers.

But the multimedia facilities, which had to be installed for the course, were the start of a separate trajectory: the build-up of the multimedia lab. The lab was a 'reusable' spin-off of the course. It developed into an informal locus of innofusion. It was one of the two calculated side effects of the pilot project. It promises to lead to a steady stream of multimedia activities faculty-wide. The second planned side effect of the course was the database with digitised visual material. The material gathered prior to and during the course served as a first input for the visual database.[11] The database will facilitate the search for and processing of visual material for both research and teaching purposes faculty-wide.

There were also unplanned side effects. As a result of early project activities, most faculty courses now have a website. The electronic course book for IMMICS was, in retrospect, one of the first in a series. On the side, the staff of the multimedia lab also offered support for the development of electronic course books for other courses.

We saw earlier that faculty-wide innofusion was part of the initial project objective ('within-project-level'), whereas this element lost significance in the last stage of the project. Faculty-wide innofusion became an 'at-project-level' side effect. The multimedia lab and the visual database, in particular, signaled the start of long-term activities and implied more widespread future use of multimedia. Thus, the temporary project, which was initially triggered by external factors, was flanked by two long-term initiatives (internally triggered). Its initial broad focus, the process of drifting and the side effects, rather than the course itself, appear to have created conditions for faculty-wide innofusion of multimedia uses.

Conclusion and Discussion

This chapter examined in what manner project-related innofusion of multimedia occurred within a faculty. The idea was that mechanisms of multimedia innofusion within an institution might teach us something about what could work for the education sector at large. The case illustrates how a project may change locus, meaning, and scope. The project on hand drifted within the faculty. During this process, different actors became involved in multimedia. Next to the two project managers, who were influential as meaning brokers, teachers were important intermediaries for multimedia innofusion. They were users of multimedia as well as producers of multimedia use (e.g. producers of electronic course books). The material crystallisation point (multimedia lab) and the educational crystallisation point (VC track), and the clear interest of the latter in the former, focused developments. A number of specific events and side activities of the project, notably the build-up of the multimedia lab and the visual database, triggered intra-institutional innofusion. The impact of these two sidelines ultimately overshadowed the significance of the course. In the final stage of the project, innofusion was less overt, more informal, and less orchestrated. It depended more on individual initiatives, but it still took place.

The case study points out several mechanisms of innofusion that also have relevance for a sector level approach. For example, the case shows that innofusion develops along the lines of multimedia use and the production of multimedia uses. It highlights the point that innofusion policy in the field of education should take into account the role of intermediaries (i.e. actors who combine user and producer roles), teachers in particular. Another example is the call-for-tenders procedure. It created a basis for innofusion within the faculty. This procedure is common practice for EU projects. The problem with the EU procedure is that evaluation criteria focus on meeting fixed 'within-project' aims and on the transfer of project results at this level. This is not the right approach to achieve sector-wide innofusion. The case pleads for not too strict project evaluation criteria. The drifting of the project turned out to be an advantage. Interpretative flexibility allowed teachers to apply multimedia to suit their own needs. If the above case had been judged according to the usual criteria, the conclusion would have been that the project remained unfocused for too long and that the transferability of project outcomes (i.e. the course) was low. The course itself hardly led to innofusion of multimedia within the faculty. However, analysed on the 'at-project' level, the project was a success. It was a success in terms of faculty-wide innofusion, largely because the rules for 'proper' project management were broken. In order to encourage multimedia use sector wide, policy should also adopt the 'at-project' level focus.

Notes

1   ALMA stands for the co-operation between the universities of Aachen, Diepenbeek, Liege, and Maastricht.

2   In Callon's version technical artefacts too are part of the actor network. My use of the term resembles that of Mulder, who applies it to technology and speaks of the "ensemble of relationships, which serve the objective of developing, maintaining and applying a new technology." (K.F. Mulder 1992, p.21)

3   The ELECTRA evaluation group developed the open questionnaire (Kluge e.a.). I was further co-developer of the semi-structured questionnaire for the ELECTRA project management, mentioned in section 1.

4   I.e. formal project documents, a colleague's private notes of project meetings that took place in 1996 and early 1997, and letters addressed to the project manager.

5   The first study (Van Lente & van 't Klooster 1997) is based on 20 interviews with faculty members late 1996. The second study was carried out in January 1998 by Henk van Renssen and led to an internal report (24 interviews). He was so gracious to include some of my questions about faculty member awareness of the IMMICS project in his interviews.

6   I.e. the department of Technology and Society Studies.

7   For the faculty, the multimedia lab represents a transition from external technical support (university computing centre) to in-house ICT support and development. It signifies an influx of expertise and tools, which facilitates a smoother operation of faculty-wide ICT use.

8   Functional users manage the area that is subject to automation. They are experts on content-related and organisational aspects in the area under review.

9   More precise, the students who follow the course are users as well as hypermedia document producers. The visual material, which they gather and use in their documents, is to be used for building up the visual database.

10   Salient too are the persistent association of IMMICS with the former project manager, and the absence of references to the course.

11   The external reviewer of this ELECTRA pilot project (see section 1) assigns an important role to the visual database. In his view IMMICS consists of two sub-projects: a course and the visual database. This emphasis of the latter is not in agreement with the way the faculty members (have) interpret(ed) IMMICS.

10 Telepoly: The Risk of Creating High-End Expectations

PIERRE ROSSEL, MARTINE BUSER

Abstract

Telepoly is a broadband real-time tele-teaching system, set up by the two Swiss Federal Institutes of Technology, Zürich and Lausanne, together with the Swiss Centre for Scientific Computing in Manno, to distribute higher education curricula components.

Three years of experiment and in-depth evaluation of this system have led a variety of actors to perceive its educational potential and limits, within the perspective of their specific academic or technical roles. The lessons learnt differ between each site and each set of actors. They are a dynamic part of a wider public debate on how best to use NICT-related educational tools and build the necessary R&D steps to do so, in a variety of organisations in Switzerland.

Introduction

Over the last three years, technologies supporting educational processes have undoubtedly become a major concern at national science and education policy level in Switzerland. Up until 1995, this was not the case. In a moment of economic crisis, and with clear encouragement from Parliament (the Swiss National Council), the Council of the Federal Institutes of Technologies, (the CEPF) comprising the ETH in Zürich, EPFL in Lausanne[1] and four other minor federal research institutions, conceived the idea of exploring how distance teaching technologies could contribute to saving costs. In a previous experiment, which was part of a European programme called BETEUS, experience had been gained on the use of an end-to-end ATM technology. As a result, the new project was to use this technology to transmit lectures and seminars from Zürich to

Lausanne, or vice versa. The aim was to investigate the potential of synchronous, fully interactive multimedia tele-teaching through large, bandwidth, digital audio/video transmissions over public telecommunication lines using the digital transmission protocol ATM. It was a means to explore, in various educational situations, both the feasibility and profitability of such a design. This is how, in 1995, the Telepoly concept was launched.

Methodology

This case study is based upon the findings of a two-year research programme. The EPFL's vice-presidency asked for it in order to evaluate the potential and future uses of this new way of teaching. The object was not only to report on pedagogical issues but also to assess the use of techniques, the costs, the collaboration and compatibility between the three locations and, finally, to identify the niches where Telepoly would be an added value in comparison with other distance teaching scenarios in Switzerland, Europe and the United States. It was based on document analysis, key actor interviews and substantial participant observation. As the project is an ongoing process, the goals and means to reach them have changed according to the success or failure of the different phases. The evaluation progress allowed us to trace these changes and to give an account of it.

The case study as we present it here, covers a wide range of issues. The aim is to show the specific involvement of various actors and the way they have, in a series of steps, co-produced a learning process. Mapping user-producer networks, in a complex situation like the Telepoly experiment, reveals the endeavours of the various actors involved. As we will see, the status and roles played by the various actors are subject to interpretations and do not always match the institutional planning (the findings that are reported in the case study and the actor-network mapping chart).

Finally we will reconsider some key aspects of multimedia use and learning in education, in particular in higher-education institutions, as well as their link with both private and public sectors.

Telepoly in the Swiss Field of Tele-Teaching

This overview of multimedia systems in education in Switzerland is aimed at describing efforts and contexts at various levels which may have played a role in the construction of education-related technology projects over the last five years. This framework is necessary to understand the emergence of an experiment like Telepoly and its possible future.

At that time, only specialised centres at the University of Geneva, the Swiss Federal Institute of Technology, Lausanne, and a few private firms in Zürich, Neuchâtel and Geneva had designed stand-alone educational supports, mainly in CD-ROM form. In addition, some limited trials had been carried out in Videotext applications in certain professional schools. This dispersed and little-known activity was not particularly innovative, but nevertheless expressed the high level of development in both hardware and software attained by public and private sectors in Switzerland. In 1995, the country was already among those with the highest density of PC ownership, and corporate culture in the various dimensions of computer applications was certainly representative of the most privileged countries in Europe.

Key initiatives came from the top and were implemented as tentative objectives on the part of the highest science and education authorities of the Swiss Confederation. The first arena where major issues concerning education-related technologies were discussed was the CUS (Commission of the Swiss Universities), in which a special subcommittee was set up to explore this domain. This CUS subcommittee worked between 1995 and 1997 to promote strategic recommendations for education-related technologies in Swiss higher educational institutions. It received a great deal of attention, but little financial support.

In 1997, the CUS decided to fund the setting-up of a national Web site for new information technologies related to educational goals. This site, which aims at being a platform for information and exchange, intended to identify all active groups in this field in Switzerland and provide them, if possible, with the necessary logistic support. Up to now, some 50 projects have been registered, from universities and the Swiss Federal Institutes of Technology. Topics and applications are quite diverse. Some are just courses, others full educational environments. The EPFL, with 14 projects, seems to be the most active higher educational institution in the country at the moment. But this inventory may well be incomplete, and much more will probably appear on the site in the near future. Nevertheless, as things stand, it provides a comprehensive overview of what is happening in education-related technologies in Switzerland.

To promote the transition of higher educational institutions to the information society, the CUS proposes the creation of a «Swiss Virtual Campus». This is partly a question of encouraging higher educational institutions to rethink certain courses, making them more available in electronic form, and partly of facilitating access to these courses for students from other schools through the creation of a credit system which guarantees their quality. It may be assumed that transmission on a national scale of courses produced in different schools will favour the specialisation and competencies of each.

A final remark on the current situation: various attempts are being made to develop distance teaching and Internet-based applications at lower levels of the educational system, even in primary schools,[2] but so far, no co-ordinated approach to that aspect of education-related technologies is apparent on a national scale.

All these constitute the national environment of the Telepoly case study.

The Case Study: Telepoly

Let us remember that the experiment was primarily aimed at benefiting from an already mastered technology. This in order to produce some economy of scale in teaching costs, by sharing expertise and competence between Zürich and Lausanne. Three phases were planned. Each aimed at covering one level of the educational curriculum, starting with postgraduate studies, continuing with 2nd-cycle studies (years 3 and 4 of the engineering diploma course) and, ideally, finishing with 1st-cycle studies (years 1 and 2 of the engineering diploma course, with general education in maths and physics. Since October 1996, CSCS/SCSC Manno (the Swiss Center for Scientific Computing) in the Italian-speaking part of Switzerland, is also part of the Telepoly concept. The CSCS is part of ETH Zürich; transmissions with Manno are limited to post-graduate studies and conferences dealing with computing science.

In both institutes, the directorate asked for an evaluation of the project. In Zürich, the Didaktikzentrum, was appointed to do so at the beginning of Autumn 1995. One of the main activities of this Centre for didactic is to build a Swiss network, including Telepoly activity, called NET (Network in Educational Technologies). This NET aims at regrouping efforts, promoting exchanges in educational technologies, and drawing the attention of various actors, public and private, to the development of such technologies. In Lausanne, six months later, ESST (Swiss subsidiary of the European Inter-University Association on Society, Science and Technology) was chosen to carry out the evaluation. ESST-EPFL thus conducted a two-year evaluation of Telepoly, culminating in the presentation of a final report and key recommendations for the future of the experiment in February 1998. The Didaktikzentrum and ESST have been working in collaboration: Zürich concentrated more on pedagogical aspects and Lausanne has focused more on the technical and strategic dimensions.

As for the schedule and definition of objectives and their modification (and with it, change in actors involved), the scenario for the experiment was designed by high-level academic authorities of both EPFs and the funding body, the CEPF. At this point it may be useful to recall that there is competition between the two institutes, Lausanne, a French-speaking town, being the 'young small sister' with a less prestigious past than Zürich, a German-speaking city. The former developed a slight inferiority complex, sometimes reinforced by the latter's attitude. Most of the classical departments such as mathematics or physics are present in both schools, but most of the teaching is given in a totally autonomous way. There is no co-ordination regarding the content of courses. Collaboration between the two institutions for lectures is rather seldom and not institutionalised, except for some studies in specific domains (such as 3-D imaging); those concern just a few students. Usually these exchanges are based on professors' personal contacts.

As for the technical aspects, we should specify that Telepoly is at the same time:

- a distance teaching concept;
- a technology (the ATM protocol), as a basis for an open multimedia platform with development potential;
- a TV- like set of cameras, videos and microphones;
- an arrangement between two, and later three, partner institutions (ETH, EPFL and CSCS/SCSC Manno), also including a fourth party which provides the ATM line (OFI, via Swisscom);
- an infrastructure, a tool and know-how linked with the use of technologies and a double, or even triple, team for implementation, one on each side of the line;
- a three-phase experimentation set up.

The 32-Mbit/s[3] ATM line used for transmission was opened by the Federal Office for Computing Systems (Office Fédéral de l'Informatique-OFI) in agreement with the institutes of technologies which helped to install it. Swisscom, the former telecommunication part of the Swiss PTT, is now managing the line. For transmission, request for use must be made on each occasion a few days before the teacher's performance. The lecture in the form of image and speech, thanks to a mobile camera and portable microphone, is broadcast from a "real" to a virtual site (the two EPFs can play either of these roles). With the bandwidth available, "television broadcast" quality can be guaranteed. The associated documents (particularly transparencies formerly used with projector) are transmitted via the Internet, the telephone being used to deal with real-time breakdowns. Different screens allow students from real and virtual sites and the teacher to follow what is happening on both sides of the configuration, as shown in the diagram on page 212.

In both classrooms, technical devices – cell stack, racks – used for the transmission are hidden in a trolley. What is visible for the people sitting in the 'real' classroom are the cameras, TV sets, microphones, the large screen and the computer connected to the Internet. In the virtual site, two TV sets and a large screen transmit the different views of the classroom: the audience, lecturer, and documents. A microphone is available for contact with the lecturer. Usually, the large screen is used to present documents. The channels are usually set for the whole transmission, each TV or screen is dedicated to one view. During the lessons all changes regarding content are very difficult to make. The lecturer can do this on the computer but it takes time, especially for the people in the real class, or he writes on the blackboard, which does not provide a satisfactory image quality through the video stream. Considering the screen size, location of cameras and seating of students, it is very difficult to recognise anyone except the lecturer. However, in Manno, an editing table allows switching from one channel to the other, in real time, with a different view of what is emphasised at will. This helps to avoid boredom and is easy to manage, even for unskilled users. In Zürich and Lausanne such a device is not present in the Telepoly settings. The cameras, except the one which can automatically follow the teacher, are fixed and do not permit modification of either focus or contrast of the picture. It is important to point out that, although the computers and audio settings are high-tech, the configuration used for the video is of rather mundane quality and does not allow good video processing. As a solution to this lack of flexibility, one of the

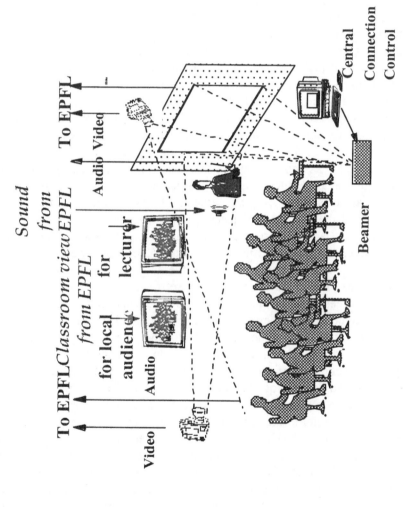

Figure 10.1   Telepoly scenario according to TIK, ETHZ

technicians involved has proposed that he be trained in editing and broadcasting. This proposal has been refused as being too expensive by the EPFL. To summarise: the quality of computing transmission is extremely good, the quality of picture composition and content rather poor.

After an eighteen-month trial period, during which all equipment had to be reinstalled and tested before every distance teaching session, a security-protected and permanently equipped classroom has been installed at the EPFL since February 1997. A similar classroom became available in mid-1998 at the ETH. Manno is also equipped.

The initial project consisted of testing the validity and effectiveness of Telepoly in three institutional contexts: "3rd-cycle" post diploma curricula (Phase I during the first semester 1995-96), a "2nd-cycle" course (Phase II during the summer semester 1996) and a basic "1st cycle" course (Phase III initially planned for autumn 1996). All phases were top-down requests. To date, the first two phases have been carried out. Phase III as originally planned, was cancelled. The latter concerned education, with no specific interest in computing networks on the part of course participants and teachers, whilst phase I and the major part of phase II concerned students and teachers involved in this specific domain.

In the course of the experiment, an important shift in objectives and actor position took place. In the beginning, the aim was to test the overall feasibility of using the ATM technology for academic diffusion and explore, at the level of the two Federal Institutes of Technology, how much economy of scale could be achieved. A subsidiary issue was to identify what significance such a system would have at the pedagogical level. The first goal was established at the top of the hierarchy by the financing body, the CEPF. Little by little, however, the front-line operators of the programme formulated their own objectives: mastering a new know-how, in order, subsequently, to offer it as a standard service to a variety of academic actors in a diversity of forms. In addition, the evaluator, ESST-EPFL, suggested a new question: what was the relative significance and future promise of Telepoly as compared with other distance teaching concepts, and therefore, with other budgetary priorities? As so many tele-teaching initiatives surged (numerous Professors in various departments),[4] the EPFL executive body wanted to co-ordinate these efforts by setting up a specific committee: the EPFL Multimedia commission. It was also a means of establishing rules and channelling all local efforts. However, whereas previously, the small committee which supervised Telepoly activity was headed by a Professor who was an ATM specialist, the new Multimedia Commission is led by a Professor who is a specialist in computer-aided education. He has certain reservations as to the value of the Telepoly approach to distance teaching. His own experience lies notably in stand-alone systems, Internet-oriented knowledge diffusion. He pressured for the evaluation to be a wider reflection on the meaning of Telepoly, beyond mere technical feasibility. The evaluation took place accordingly. In addition ESST complied the issues raised of what to do with the system and how much financial attention it should be given, and included budgetary estimates for various scenarios.

This experiment also raised the question of the transition from the experimental phases to the setting-up of a tele-teaching service within the school. Those in charge of BETEUS and Telepoly seemed to have lost interest in the product as soon as it became potentially part of a service. Not only because the technical challenge was over but also because they no longer thought that end-to-end ATM networks would develop strongly. The SIC (Service informatique central/Scientific Computing Services) had neither the power nor the money to increase transmission quality. Moreover, there was no longer anyone to promote and defend the project within the EPFL. For some time, technicians had expected the evaluating bodies to assume this role vis-à-vis the decision-makers. This happened in Zürich where the Didaktikzentrum, thanks to the NET and also its relationship with the Centre for continuing education, was able to promote Telepoly and use it as a tool for its own experiments. This was not possible in Lausanne, and the absence of a promoting body certainly appeared to constitute a missing element in Telepoly development. This could also explain the lack of interest for the project within the school.

In summary, during the entire three-year experiment the project served to incorporate new actors and items in an increasingly wide agenda. One of the issues raised by the evaluator was: who needs Telepoly? and subsequently, how to pass from a push approach to technology and distance teaching to a customer-oriented system which could evolve according to demand? And in addition, how to develop a transitional phase towards an academic service, turning potential users into participating actors in the concept.

It now seems likely that the EPFL executive body will choose minimal financial support to maintain the ongoing experiment, without any consequent technical improvement. This corresponds to the wish to promote new forms of access to knowledge, with as little financial support as possible. This is mainly due, not to any deliberate strategy of discouragement, but to economic pressure to decrease spending in all areas of research and education.

Telepoly at the Classroom Level

Type of events and nature of requirements All the courses transmitted by Telepoly were organised by the Computer Science Department and Communication Systems Division. These departments provide teaching in computing networks. ATM is part of their standard educational programme. Thus, the students involved were not only accustomed to this kind of technology, but also very attracted to it. They were very interested in the experiment. It was a means to test in a real life situation what they were taught. Even breakdowns could be analysed as case studies.

A few conferences in fields other than computing were organised. Usually, the result of the assessment by the remote audience was not very kind in regard to the audio-video quality and lecturers' performance. This means that people less curious about these technologies were not very indulgent as far as broadcast quality was concerned. They expected a TV-like presentation in respect to conception, entertainment and sound and image pre- and post-production. The idea is that a Telepoly session resembles a television set-up, therefore the ingredients and professional skills of this field should be incorporated into the current Telepoly concept. Such an option was defined in the evaluation as the "maximum scenario", and implies a new order of magnitude in budgetary spending

Audience size is considered to affect inter-activity: it seems difficult for students to express themselves freely among more than 15 to 20 persons on each side. The more students in the rooms, the fewer possibilities for inter-activity. During Phase II teachings, there were between 40 and 50 students at the 'real' site, and 10 to 20 at the virtual one. Inter-activity, despite the lecturer's encouragement, remained very low. In the virtual site it was usually the assistant who had to answer the lecturer's comments or questions, partly because he was the one holding the microphone, but also because the students remained quiet.

The course contents influenced the development of multimedia opportunities, as video tapes or web sources are easy to introduce into the session and courses based on this kind of material are enjoyable to follow, whatever the lecturer's pedagogic abilities. On the other hand, when teaching deals with theoretical analyses and formulae which cannot be supported by examples, the quality and appeal of the lesson depend mainly on lecturers' ability to retain student attention.

The actors involved Three groups of actors are involved – technicians, lecturers and students.

Two engineers from the SIC are in charge of the system. One is a specialist in ATM connection, the other is responsible for all the technical devices in the room where Telepoly is located. They are technicians and have no competencies, at least officially, at pedagogical level. Their role is to ensure the proper functioning of the system. As part of an EPFL service, they are not in a position to give advice regarding the behaviour of the lecturer, even if they have learned much about it, but they can give tips about the use of techniques. Before each Telepoly event, a two-hour check of the whole configuration has to be carried out. During this check the technicians interact with their partner sites through Telepoly. But during lectures they use a phone line to communicate, they phone even in the case of breakdown, because cameras and microphones are then reserved to the lecturer. At the beginning of the experiment, a technician had to stay throughout the entire tele-teaching session in order to deal with technical problems. As the system became more and more stable, technicians no longer had to remain in the room. They were replaced by a young apprentice who had to call them in case of trouble. They expressed their wishes and advice on how to upgrade the system, but were not recognised as an acceptable source of opinion by decision-makers. In order to be heard, they had to follow the hierarchical channels and ask their boss, who was in charge of the whole computing service for the school, to intercede on their behalf, which he did not do.

It has been observed that lecturers who did not prepare for Telepoly – with no or only little elaboration of electronic documents, classical ex cathedra behaviour, poor understanding of multi-site situations and communication flow direction – performed miserably. This added to the feeling that intermediate users also needed to contribute to the concept. Regarding the improvement of lecturer behaviour, although many defects have been identified which could easily be corrected, no further steps have been taken to teach speakers how to perform properly within the Telepoly configuration. Amongst the lecturers, two really did make efforts to prepare their teaching. Each did so in a different way: Prof. Le Boudec, in the only second-cycle course ever given through Telepoly met the challenge perfectly. He visited the virtual site to have real contact with students; he prepared his documents in electronic form for the whole course; he adapted to the particular style of communication imposed by the system, such as addressing the mobile camera, talking slowly, and thinking constantly in terms of possible interaction with the virtual classroom, visible only on a TV screen. He gave an impression of ease, which in reality concealed a huge amount of work. Prof. Thalmann, giving a post-graduate course, was less involved in behaviour control. He installed his teaching on the Internet with many hypertext links to demos, which the students could consult whenever they wanted. The result was very lively. The only criticism concerns the presentation on the Internet. It was not a text anymore with sentences logically connected, but a list of points.

The students evaluation was made via questionnaires It took place first after a month and then at the end of semester of Prof. Le Boudec's course. All students involved in the virtual site, in Zürich, were free to follow this teaching, since it was optional. As the teaching was intended for German- and French-speaking audiences, it was given in English, which presented a problem for some participants. On one occasion, Prof. Le Boudec went to Zürich to give his lecture, transforming the EPFL in Lausanne into the virtual site. The French-speaking students' evaluation of this unique event was not nearly as favourable as the German-speaking one.

Students handed in different appraisals at the beginning and end of the experiment. As they became accustomed to Telepoly, they were less tired, could concentrate more easily on the content, and felt more confident to ask questions. They appreciated the questions raised by students from the other site and regretted not seeing them on the screen but were rather glad not being able to see themselves on the TV monitors while talking. Thus, the situation was not the same for both sides,

The lecturer had to speak more slowly in order to be understood by the virtual classroom. For this reason, students in the 'real' classroom at first found it hard to remain concentrated. They waited for breaks or the end of the lecture to ask questions directly to the lecturer, feeling that broadcast time was primarily intended to the other site. The virtual site and its related constraints were nevertheless perceived by them as a minor disturbance.

At the virtual site, although audio quality was judged to be the most important factor in the transmission, students found difficult to concentrate on the screens. Two thirds of the students felt more tired than after a normal lecture. When they were willing to communicate with the teacher, they had to ask for the microphone, which left them time to reflect on the relevance of their questions. This sometimes led them to give up, involuntarily increasing the lack of spontaneity problem.

Both sides agreed that, even at the end of the experiment, greater energy was needed to follow a virtual lesson than a normal lecture.

User- Producer Network

In order to understand better the process of Telepoly experiment, we must now determine who are the users and who are the producers. We will then identify which learning processes have taken place within Telepoly context.

First we have a set of technical actors who are the physical producers of the system: the ATM cell stack supplier, local technical assistance (linked with the SIC), and the EPFL and ETHZ institutes which have researched and mastered all the knowledge necessary to understand the intricacies of the ATM technology over the last ten years. The expertise link to the digital protocol ATM comes mostly from the European project BETEUS. To some extent, it is precisely because these latter actors had acquired this specific knowledge and interest that it seemed obvious and natural for policy makers to launch the experiment. Once they had proved the technical feasibility of the system, which means two audio and video streams in a synchronous, fully interactive multimedia tele-teaching using the ATM protocol, they let the SIC take over the project. But the SIC received an unfinished concept. If the connections were good, the setting of the classroom regarding pedagogical and communicational aspects had to be adapted, tested and improved. In the SIC category, we should also distinguish managers who helped define guidelines, from front-line actors who actually configured and made the system work at classroom level, not forgetting its ATM specialist, the sole link with the Swiss PTT which provides the ATM line at national level. The ATM specialist is the only one at the EPFL to be able to detect, in case of breakdown the problem, if is comes from within the institute or along the Swisscom line and connections. Swisscom, through its testing and mastering of the ATM technology, should also be mentioned among the producing actors. It provides the external infrastructure. Finally, the firm which sold and helped install the ATM cell stacks, later bought by Swisscom, also contributed to the necessary technical knowledge.

The Telepoly experiment does not only have a technical dimension. It also has institutional and budgetary components, which partly conditioned its existence. In this respect, we can easily identify all policy makers and managing actors, starting with the CEPF, which was the most important actor for the launching of the project and the executive bodies of the Federal Institutes of Technology in both Zürich and Lausanne. In addition to these immediately involved institutional producers, there are also ESST and the Multimedia Commission (EPFL), and Didaktikzentrum and NET

(ETHZ) which helped the executive bodies identify issues, levels of performance and possible scenarios for the future. We have seen how these actors produced second step objectives, which in turn conditioned Telepoly's mode of operations (a little) and future perspectives (considerably).

The involvement of certain lecturers in preparing their electronic documents, and adapting to the particular style of communication imposed by the system makes them producers of the system in this experimental situation. On the other hand, the technology is used by teachers for the transmission of their courses, and in this sense lecturers constitute the primary user group (i.e. intermediate users) of this knowledge-delivery system. Learning acquired by each lecturer using Telepoly was, however, not systematically transformed into a collective building process. The different lecturers did not have the opportunity to share their experiment, and no one was appointed to collect their different experiences, especially because the people involved concentrate on the technical aspects and not on the pedagogical one.

The end-user, as defined by all actors on the producing side, is the student. Three phases of the design addressed starting ("1st cycle") as well as finishing ("2nd cycle"), and post-graduate students ("3rd cycle"). In the longer term, the hope was expressed that the EPFL could thus reach potential students, who today, since they work or live in a remote area, cannot benefit from EPFL academic activities. Potentially, at a second stage, enterprises could be interested in the system, especially for high-end video-conferencing and computer-supported co-operative work. But this user group was not considered during the experiment.

As far as multimedia considerations are concerned, Telepoly is multimedia in the most absolute sense: not only does it provide connectivity and inter-activity, but it uses different media simultaneously to transmit information: ATM for sound and image, the Internet for electronic documents. Yet it has never been referred to explicitly as a multimedia system, in our opinion because it is obvious and therefore implicit. The only reference to "multimedianess" is made by the the the EPFL Multimedia Commission. At the same time, the emphasis placed on connectivity and inter-activity (although the latter could be much greater than it is) gives clear indications as to what the front-line actors of Telepoly consider important to implement and develop. One key consideration of actors, critical of Telepoly (mainly competitors in the distance teaching field) and even some within Telepoly participants itself, has been the importance of turning it into a potentially asynchronous system. The idea would be to make the system capable not only of delivering real-time image and sound in a duplex manner, as until now, but also of producing reusable pedagogical material in a more network-oriented manner. And, as a matter of fact, the last main lecturer who used Telepoly in 1998 gave a course that was both real-time and Internet-based. This demonstrates the possibility of evolution for the Telepoly concept.

The Dynamics: Struggles and Negotiations

Technical and institutional goals Considering that Telepoly was designed as a spin-off of the BETEUS European research programme to prove the feasibility of ATM transmission-based teleteaching, the technical objective has been reached. Although Telepoly retained a status of experiment, there has been a transfer from the scientific to the technical domain, with the main roles shifting from developers and researchers to technical actors (SIC, as already mentioned), whose primary goal is to keep it working. The challenge was to make this ATM network operational, not to create a perfect teaching environment, nor to build a new teleteaching concept. Not much attention was paid to audio and video settings within the room, or to the kind of events which could have been transmitted.Once the experiment had proved its feasibility, the Professors involved in the building of the system, having received praise for Telepoly's success, allowed the SIC to take over. The SIC inherited an unfinished project, but without the legitimacy of an experimental trial at research level. They were unable to ask for means to improve the experimentation, as the trial was already considered as successful after the setting up of the first configuration. Upgrading, then, was not judged to be necessary. After the departure of the initial research-oriented actors, nobody was really in charge of promoting the project.

In the top-down logic of Telepoly's implementation, that goes from CUS (Conférence universitaire suisse, Commission of the Swiss Universities) to CEPF and from CEPF to EPFs, the Multimedia Commission and SIC-EPFL, the aim was that the experiment should be set up, become productive and prove, at the end of the three-year period, that it had been worthwhile. Belief in the usefulness and feasibility of the project was strong enough to start it and this remained the case throughout. The project had an implicit "push" flavour. It was based on the expectation that it would be justified by the number of users. All activities within Telepoly have reflected this optimism, smoothing out potential conflicts (see below) and creating sufficient willingness to solve problems accordingly.

However, the overall performance of the system has been moderate, as no steps were taken at the start to identify the appropriate needs and demands for such a service inside schools in terms of events and curricula (ATM-based distance teaching). Little budgetary margin remained to cover unexpected breakdowns. Bottom-up expressions of uneasiness and difficulties appeared, in both Zürich and Lausanne, most of them without answers within the time frame of the experiment.

Past and future reconfigurations of the project The only adaptation in the project planning necessary was the change in assignment of phase III, originally planned as the use of Telepoly for transmission of 1st cycle (first two years of diploma course) mathematics courses to Lausanne students, from Zürich, and in German. The academic services of both EPFs did not take kindly to Telepoly staff asking them far too late, according to them, to include such a course in the official schedule. In addition, the Mathematics Department, which was supposed to implement this course, was practically ordered to do so, and did not like that either. The lack of proper timing for the involvement of some key actors, and probably also some difficulties intrinsic to the use of Telepoly in a standard academic situation, made it impossible for the Telepoly experiment to continue as planned in its 3rd phase. Being conceived for time- and money-saving purposes, Telepoly was not really welcomed by many of the lecturers, as they feared losing their autonomy, being compared with their peers and even being replaced by a Telepoly broadcast from 'the other side', especially for the basic courses. Phase three was supposed to address young students. Using the argument of newness and instability of the system as being too hazardous for the students, the teachers rejected the idea of using the system for 1st cycle courses. It took six months to overcome this little conflict, during which Telepoly continued only in the form of a series of conferences. Finally, the experiment resumed, but with a different course and student audience, thanks to the transmission of post-graduate courses, mainly in signal-processing.

For the moment, Zürich, thanks to its NET connection, has started a new experiment with the University of Basle. Some forty students are involved on each side for a pharmacy course. Only the second semester will be transmitted via Telepoly. During the first semester the students will meet the professor in a real classroom and be trained within Telepoly system. Manno is attempting, on its part, to broadcast several courses mostly to Zürich. Only one event is planned between Lausanne and Zürich, a Communication Systems Division seminar of two hours every week.

The need to reconfigure the Telepoly set-up for future use has been identified by both Telepoly staff and the evaluator in the direction of making possible asynchronous use of teaching material linked with Telepoly (lectures, but also related electronic documents). The diversification of its assignment like transmission of scientific conferences, distance co-operative work, PhD thesis oral examinations, networking of knowledge, exercises and corrections, tele-seminars, etc., is another issue to be considered.

Struggles Competition has been a constant feature of the experiment. The evaluation itself has been the subject of a slight conflict between the Chaire de pédagogie et didactique (Institute of Pedagogy) at the EPFL and ESST-ESST, which was finally chosen, immediately adopted a Technology Assessment approach to the issue of evaluating Telepoly, rather than one which was purely didactic (this aspect was also analysed, but as one at the many components.

Other internal quarrels characterised the life of Telepoly. All other major actors of EPFL distance teaching projects rejected the Telepoly approach to teaching on the grounds of its backward "non-network-minded" philosophy, its real-time orientation, and its limited interactivity. Since Telepoly was so expensive, they questioned the very existence and usefulness of such an experiment. The ESST evaluation showed that some of these criticisms were levelled at Telepoly's original assignment and not its further potential use: for example its clear asynchronous possibilities, demonstrated by Prof. Thalmann's course on virtual reality in 1998. The whole of his course being available on the Internet in electronic form. These negative opinions were partly based on analysis of Telepoly characteristics, but also partly on prejudiced views.

Quarrels between technical actors needed to be solved: first between SIC actors and the audio-visual services of both EPFs, in which we observed a different understanding of what needed to be done; and secondly, between technical actors at the EPFL and ETH Zürich, who were partners in practice, but, in the technical progress and performance race, actually symbolic competitors. In this latter case, the language barrier did not play an important role. But the different cultural approaches to organisation and problem-solving of the French- and German-speaking parts of Switzerland were probably more problematic.

Budget negotiations The last type of struggle worth mentioning concerns budgetary claims and decisions. As for finance, it is not easy to estimate the costs of the experiment, since numerous items of expenditure are included in the ordinary functioning costs of the various institutes and services involved. The budget for the three-year period of the experiment had to be amended to allow both Lausanne and Zürich staff to operate in permanent settings (instead of reinstalling and testing all the equipment for each Telepoly session, a very time-consuming task). The global cost of the experiment, including indirect costs, for the three sites during the three years of the Telepoly experiment, thus amounts to: SFr.1,250,000. For the people involved in the process, more money was needed in order to secure the technical settings and improve the broadcast quality. For decision makers, as Telepoly was not the only teleteaching experiment to be considered, this question deserved to be looked into more deeply.

One year before the end of the experiment, the evaluator (ESST-EPFL) was requested to make a cost estimate for the continuation of Telepoly, and its evolution from experiment to a regular service to Professors and students. This specific part of the evaluation would be used as a basis for making internal decisions. In its final report, the evaluator presented three scenarios: the first one consisting in maintaining the status quo; the second one in improving the current situation, ensuring maintenance and therefore reliability; and finally, the third one in looking for innovative exploration of multimedia and interactive features of Telepoly.

For cost reasons, it seems that the minimal option will be chosen, much to the despair of the internal actors of Telepoly. Within the EPFL the belief in a promising future for ATM end-to-end transmission has also strongly decreased. However, the idea of stopping Telepoly has not been considered, as the amount of work and money already involved in the process contributes to its value. In Zürich, strong lobbying from Telepoly staff, both inside and external (NET activities, already mentioned), led to the installation of new equipment in 1997 and a permanent Telepoly room in 1998, as in Lausanne. The status quo thus seems to have been preserved. In Zürich, technical staff salaries will probably be financed in much the same way as in Lausanne. Unless there is another strong signal from the CEPF (the upper hierarchical level), the situation is likely to remain as it is. But the last line of the story has not yet been written...

Outcomes and Evaluation

The outcome of the experiment resides in its continuation and possibly extension, hopefully with new related projects. In terms of learning, it may be said that:

- technically, an interesting know-how in ATM-based visioconferencing systems has been mastered. It is part of a collective knowledge that is not likely to fade away, firmly embedded in the organisations which established Telepoly as it is;
- conceptually, Telepoly staff, the main actors involved in distance teaching issues and the EPFL executive body, with varying degrees of depth, have all acquired some understanding of what such systems can and cannot do, how they compare and can be evaluated.

Of course, important uncertainties remain in this fast-evolving domain, but a basic understanding of not only technological and pedagogical issues, but also of wider strategic aspects of distance teaching is progressively becoming part of the collective learning process at the EPFL. The actors came from different departments and services, where the evaluation has underlined some problems in communication and role distribution. The evaluation process then served to encourage dialogue and intermediate assessments between Telepoly staff members, as well as with major actors involved in distance teaching at the EPFL or ETHZ.

At strategic level, it is clear at the EPFL that the challenge regarding teleteaching resides more in the making of technical tools rather than pedagogical ones. Content and users were taken for granted. The aim of the experiment was not to develop a new kind of teaching addressing new students but to show the scientific skills of the researchers. This technology-driven development can also be seen in the lack of enthusiasm once the feasibility of the system had been proved.

Still within the realm of strategic pre-occupations, it is important to observe that in the near future, the main outcome may well consist of new projects and partnerships (domestic and foreign), as well as participation in the Classroom 2000 research project.[5] Each one of these developments could improve the original Telepoly set-up.

The major change will be the asynchronous reuse of teaching material form Telepoly transmission. There are two main possibilities: either as real-time Telepoly events, which could be recorded, archived, indexed and used by students whenever they need to. Or as the latest Telepoly course was given, with complete electronic documents support, making knowledge accessible any time, before or after the real-time event.

However, at the moment, expert opinion diverges on the future of ATM technology. The large bandwidth used is impressive, but also costly. It is no more considered as suitable for end-to-end connection, but will be rather used for backbone, and therefore unlikely to be the universal standard for telecomputing networks in the near future (the only time scale we can really foresee). This might make Telepoly either a dinosaur (the current tendency) or a candidate for pioneering practices in high-end distance teaching and collaborative work (less likely). It is still difficult to anticipate what will happen, however, and the outcome will have nothing to do with Telepoly itself, but with the strategic decisions of major players active in the area of entertainment and telecommunications.

Regarding education in Switzerland, in general terms, in two or three years, thanks to the multiplication of debates and experiments, both at national and international levels, the issues have evolved favourably, beyond naive, substitute-minded hopes. More profound and diversified solutions have been formulated in the perspective of producing networked, flexible and learning, rather than teaching, environments. Emphasis is on virtual reality, simulation and connectivity, rather than stand-alone applications: CD or DVD-ROMs are considered rather as supports to network applications. We have seen that even a real-time oriented concept like Telepoly is likely to evolve in that direction. Finally, let us stress that private-sector-based developments in education-related technologies and higher-education institution activities have apparently not yet formed a productive combination. Current trials, research and debates may soon change this situation however.

Notes

1   Two of the main actors referred to in this case study have different names in different languages. There are two Federal Institutes of Technology in Switzerland, supported by Confederation funds. One is in Zürich, the ETHZ (Eidgenossische Technische Hochchule Zürich), the other in Lausanne, the EPFL (Ecole polytechnique fédérale de Lausanne).
2   This situation is not new. Rossel and Nolde had already identified it through early but isolated experiments in 1993.
3   In fact, the real bandwidth is 155 Mbits, but only 25 + 2 are currently in use.
4   We have identified at the EPFL up to 30 individual attempts to set up an electronic course or produce CD-ROMs, and 5 major distance teaching projects characterised as bottom-up initiatives, with considerable human resources and budgetary expenditure involved.
5   Let us remember that Classroom 2000 aims at building a network and following up some promising projects in distance teaching of all kinds.

11 Diversified Hypermedia Use: An Experiment with Dis-closure

TINEKE M. EGYEDI

Abstract

In this case, a hypermedia programme is used for a new visual culture course. The course has two aims. Students are to learn how war is represented in different visual media (e.g. photography and television), and they are to learn how to do research in a non-linear way. The use of hypermedia software is a means to make explicit the process of non-linear structuring of research data. The software is new to all concerned.

Special about this course is that the two teachers treat hypermedia use as an experiment. They do not define a best practice beforehand. They seek diversified hypermedia use and therefore steer as little as possible. In this chapter I analyse their approach as an attempt to sustain and exploit the interpretative flexibility of hypermedia use. It is an attempt to postpone closure, which is a main ingredient of *diversification experiments.*

It proves difficult for teachers not to give any pointers at all for the use of hypermedia for non-linear research. They partly succeed. At times, the lack of guidance frustrates students. The students' capacities of home-computer user and experienced learner affect their hypermedia use in the course. In particular during the first weeks, these influences sometimes come into conflict with the course requirements. Some hypermedia uses are constrained by the software. In certain cases students find ways to work around these constraints. Unexpected hypermedia uses develop. Although there is no material to compare with, postponement of closure appears to encourage new uses. Furthermore, it requires frequent reflection on the use of hypermedia for non-linear research. The experiment has led to intense learning by students as well as teachers.

Introduction

In December 1997, a new course starts at the Maastricht Faculty of Arts and Culture. The course has been developed as a multimedia project that goes by the name of IMMICS. (See Egyedi, this volume, for more information about the project.) Its aim is to give students some practical experience with non-linear research. The research area is the representation of war in visual media (e.g. television, photography and CD-ROM). A hypermedia programme is used in the course as a tool for organising research findings. The tool is new to all concerned. The course is set up as an experiment in the use of hypermedia for learning research. The teachers' aim is to create the conditions in which students can develop innovative uses. Students are to learn by doing. In this manner, it is expected, unforeseen 'best practices' may sooner develop. The teachers, therefore, try to avoid giving instructions about how to use the hypermedia programme.

In this chapter I explore whether the experiment succeeds. Success is defined here as the development of unexpected hypermedia uses for non-linear research. What unexpected uses are, is for the teachers and the supporting staff to decide. Concerned are novel uses of hypermedia and novel uses of hypermedia for organising research findings. The experiment's success largely depends on whether the teachers can, indeed, create an environment that does not predefine hypermedia use.

It is uncommon for the education sector to conduct an experiment with the express purpose of stimulating innovative multimedia use. The experiment is therefore a special case of multimedia innofusion in education. In the next section this point is argued further. In this section I present my theoretical framework and introduce a few new concepts. The third section addresses the research methodology of this case study. Then I will go into features of the course, such as the curriculum to which the course belongs, pedagogical considerations and who participate in the course. Three factors in the *context of use* are examined that affect hypermedia use. One of these is the scenario of use embedded in the hypermedia software; another is the hypermedia use that is implied in the course design; and the third is the teacher's expectations of student uses. Hypermedia use in the course also depends on the *context of the user*, that is, on the student's attitude towards and experiences with computers. This is dealt with in the sixth section. Influences in the context of the user may coincide or conflict with those in the context of use. Then I examine how students handle such conflicts, and whether unexpected hypermedia uses typically emerge from conflicting influences. In the closing section I draw conclusions about the problems and the value of the experiment.

The Unpredictable User

The conceptual framework that I use to interpret this case combines insights from literature about multimedia project development with concepts from social shaping of technology approaches. The terminology used is introduced in the course of the argument. I start out with two basic concepts of social shaping. (See Van Lieshout e.a., chapter 3, this volume, for an extensive introduction.)

People may attach different meanings to a multimedia artefact. Where this occurs, *interpretative flexibility* exists in respect to that artefact. If those concerned try to negotiate a common meaning, worded in social shaping the terms, they are trying to reduce its interpretative flexibility. Where a common meaning results, this it is called *closure*. (Bijker 1995) For the moment the meaning of the artefact is stable. At this stage the number of probable uses of the multimedia artefact is narrowed down. Uses that diverge from the 'agreed' meaning become unlikely. Several parties may be involved in defining the artefact according to their own meaning and interest. One of them is the company that produces it. This party is involved at an early stage. The way it advertises its product in the market contains suggestions for use. The marketing group bases its ideas on those of the product designers. The designers of the artefact envisage certain uses. The artefact they design embeds their image of the user and of a context of use. It thus contains the designers' *script* or scenario of use (Akrich 1992). The script constrains and supports certain user behaviour. Through scripts, designers, as it were, *configure the user* (Woolgar 1991). Should the user oblige, it would lead to predictable multimedia use. But often users do not behave in ways expected by designers (e.g. Mourik, this volume). They do not primarily interpret the multimedia artefact in terms of its *context of production* (by which I refer to designer considerations and the marketed meaning). Users foremost interpret the artefact in terms of its context of use (e.g. Andriessen 1996). The *context of use* consists of the task they want to use it for, the location of use, the instructions they receive, the available technical support, etc. Besides, users have their own frame of reference for multimedia use. This I call the *context of the user*. It consists of, for example, the user's attitude towards multimedia, his or her aptitude and experience with computers at home, and his or her experience with comparable tasks. These factors affect the user's interpretation of the multimedia artefact and therefore affect his or her use of it. They may reinforce the same sort of use, but they may also conflict. It is unclear how users handle such conflicts. Are conflicting influences a source of unexpected use? In the following sections I examine whether unexpected uses can be explained as a means of reconciling conflicts within and between the context of production, the context of use and the context of the user.

User-centred approaches to multimedia development and multimedia projects are the state-of-the-art (Eurelings, this volume). Incorporating user experiences into the development and implementation process is a means to reduce the uncertain fate of an application. Instead of delivering finalised products onto the market, increasingly companies consult users beforehand through user panels, usability trials, and prototyping. To test the usability of applications and services, pilot projects and experiments are held. The term 'experiment', however, generally obscures the nature of these projects. The term implies an open-ended outcome. It suggests that those who conduct the experiment are not sure whether multimedia will be usable in its new setting. It suggests that multimedia may not be applicable in certain situations and that the user must decide whether this is the case. One would expect that, because the experiment is about determining the usability of multimedia and because information is gained whatever the outcome of the experiment, effort is made to abstain from influencing its outcome. Experimenters, one would expect, do not prescribe certain uses. But an overview of social experiments[1] with multimedia (Slack e.a. 1998) shows that they do. In these experiments and pilot projects expectations of use are fixed. The artefact is to be used as intended, which is in line with the marketed meaning. For those who conduct the experiment, the interpretative flexibility of the artefact is closed. The trial is held to demonstrate the technical feasibility of a multimedia artefact. The trial seldom fails. If the user behaves well, the multimedia artefact will prove to be technically feasible. The conclusion will be that, given the right conditions, it is worthwhile to implement the artefact elsewhere. A project like this resembles a verification process rather than an experimental process. It verifies expectations of certain multimedia uses. I therefore call such a project a *verification experiment*. By far the majority of multimedia projects are verification experiments.

Experiments with an open-ended outcome are scarce. It requires effort from those who conduct the experiment not to steer the project towards expected outcomes. Even scarcer are experiments that go one step further, and encourage exploration and seek diversification of multimedia use. These I call *diversification experiments*. They fall within the ideal-typical mode of experimentation[2] mentioned in chapter 3 (Van Lieshout e.a, this volume). In order to allow a variety of uses to emerge, those who conduct the experiment do not predefine the way the multimedia artefact is used. In so far as it lies within their power, they will try to sustain what interpretative flexibility there is with regard to the artefact in order to stimulate different uses. In other words, they will intentionally postpone closure. I use the term *dis-closure* to refer to the intentional postponement of closure. Analogous to the way closure narrows down the number of probable uses of an artefact, dis-closure facilitates the development of diverse multimedia uses. Instead of taming the unpredictable user through predefined uses, in diversification experiments the user is approached as a potential source of novelty.

I view the project described in this chapter as belonging to the category of diversification experiments. The teachers' hope that students develop unexpected hypermedia uses for non-linear research. They thereby face one important problem. In the formal classroom setting teachers are looked on as the ones who provide the answers. Their job is usually to restrict interpretative flexibility. In this course the opposite is striven for. They try not to predefine uses. They try to postpone closure. Below I will examine in what manner this is realised and to what degree dis-closure leads to the development of unexpected hypermedia uses.

Research Methodology

The case study is based on a number of sources. Before the course started I held ten open interviews with the people most closely involved in the project. I interviewed them several times to familiarise myself with the project. The interviewees were the project leader, a teacher of the course, and a multimedia lab staff member. The project leader also filled in a semi-structured questionnaire (Kluge e.a. 1997). During the course, two of my colleagues and I held a total of twenty interviews. We held four of them at the start and four at the close of the course. The interviewees were the two teachers of the course, the project leader, and a multimedia lab staff member. The other twelve interviews we held with four students. We interviewed them in the first, third and fifth week of the course.[3] The project leader selected the students. He based his selection on their different attitude towards multimedia. The four students, Annette, Marianne, Lia and Ellen, all happened to be women.[4]

Other sources are the course logs of the project leader and the four students; all the students' weekly scores on the multimedia attitude scales (eleven items, five-point scale), designed and aggregated by the project leader; project documents[5] and letters; my 'naive user' exploration of the hypermedia programme; and my personal observation of a student working with the programme.

Visual Culture course

The course is new. It is part of the Visual Culture programme for third-year students of the Faculty of Arts & Culture, University of Maastricht. Its objective is to teach students a non-linear way of doing research and, meanwhile, to increase their insight in how war is represented by visual media (film, CD-ROM, etc.). To this end a hypermedia programme is introduced. Students are to use it to structure and report on research findings in a non-linear way. The hypermedia programme is called Storyspace and can handle text and visual material. The course takes six weeks, which is the regular period for such courses within the faculty. The students work full-time. They are to work in pairs on hypermedia documents, except for the last week, during which they work individually on their final document. At the end of the course the teacher evaluates the final electronic document and the way the student argues his/her hypermedia structure. Seventeen students take part, divided into two groups. They alternately use the multimedia lab and the working-group room to work on their weekly assignments. There are two teachers, one for each group. The two-headed staff of the multimedia lab provides technical support. One of them is also the project leader.

In the faculty in which the course is situated, Problem-Based Learning (PBL) is educational policy.[6] The approach emphasises students' self-steering capacities. It is not clear yet to the faculty how new media are to be integrated within the PBL approach. In the course design no systematic attention is paid to the integration issue.[7] But elements of PBL are recognisable in the way the hypermedia programme is to be used. For example, in the course close collaboration between students is an important vehicle for learning. Each week, student pairs work on an assignment and produce a hypermedia document. They work on stand-alone computers in the multimedia lab (Macintosh platform with Internet access). The course book, available in an electronic and a paper version, contains the assignments.[8] It also lists the sources of interest (e.g. books and hyperlinks). Hypermedia use is designed to trigger reflection on the relations between research findings. The hypermedia documents are discussed in the group, which in turn results in a weekly group document. The latter document is intended as a means to structure discussions about the visual representation of war and similarities between media.

The teachers define the course as a 'usability of multimedia for learning' experiment. The field is new and there are no norms for using the hypermedia programme. Students should discover hypermedia uses by themselves. They are to develop their own norms and exemplars during the course. In keeping with the PBL approach, the two teachers do not believe in strongly pre-structuring the learning situation and lecturing students ("I will not spoon-feed students"). They intend to refrain from commenting on how students handle Storyspace and use it for research, and steer as little as possible during group gatherings. According to one teacher, it would be interesting to see that students ultimately structure their electronic documents quite differently.

Context of Hypermedia Use

In order to analyse the way hypermedia is used in the course and what uses to expect, I previously distinguished three clusters of influence: the context of production, the context of use and the context of the user. This section focuses on the context of use.

Software Design Configuring the User

The context of production refers to the way the hypermedia software used in the course has been produced. According to theory, the designers' ideas of the user and the context of use are embedded in the software. The software thus steers user behaviour and configures the user. I have not had the possibility to research the context in which the hypermedia software has been developed, instead, I infer below the manner in which the software steers uses from the way the software is advertised, from my own experiences as a 'naive user', from my observations of a student working with the programme in the fifth course week, and from an exchange by letter between the project leader and the software developers.

The hypermedia programme, *Storyspace*, was originally a hypertext programme designed for writers of fiction and non-fiction. Advertisements mention that it is useful for making field notes, writing screenplays and writing dissertations. They say that it helps writers to structure their text, 'organise facts and link ideas'. The designers claim that a new user becomes proficient in handling the programme within a week. This is not quite the case (see Box 11.1). But, indeed, one main reason to choose Storyspace instead of other hypermedia programmes for the course was that the teachers found it easy to learn. During the course students also easily learn how to handle it. They soon handle it at a level that immediately shows results.

The software designers' model writer conceptualises the structure of a text in a spatial, relational and/or hierarchical manner. The user has three alternative means to visualise text structure. The most *figurative* mode consists of lines, arrows and boxes (see Figure 11.1). The 'immediate results' referred to above relate to working with this mode. In the second mode, the *chart* mode, the user has some spatial clues about the hierarchical structure of the document. That is, he or she sees the names of primary entities, left-aligned, and lines connected to secondary entities to their right, etc. (See Figure 11.2). The third mode of visualisation is pure text with minimal spatial clues. That is, the number of left indents indicates the level at which an entity is located. This is the *outline* mode (See Figure 11.3).

The software was developed in the late 1980s. Despite upgrades, it reflects the interface concepts and technical possibilities of the 1980s. In reaction to a letter from the project leader with suggestions for improvement, the designers indicate that they follow the international guidelines for interface design.[9] So, Storyspace's interface is not open to discussion. Those students who are used to more up-to-date software experience a number of interface aspects and the absence of certain facilities as restrictive. See Box 11.1. For example, Storyspace is not 'Wysiwyg';[10] certain links between entities are not visible in the figurative mode. Its text layout facilities are limited (e.g. there are no means to enlarge and highlight text) and the software does not interoperate well with other word processors.

Figure 11.1 A Storyspace document view in figurative mode with in the foreground two opened information entities (text and photograph)

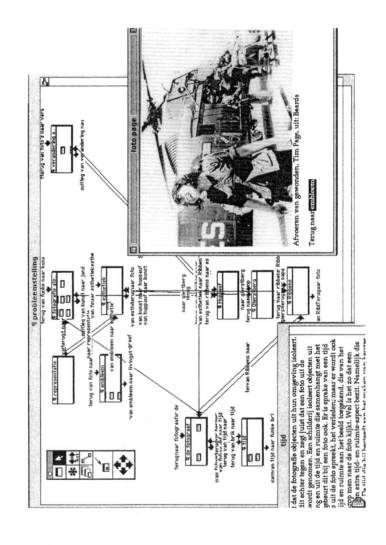

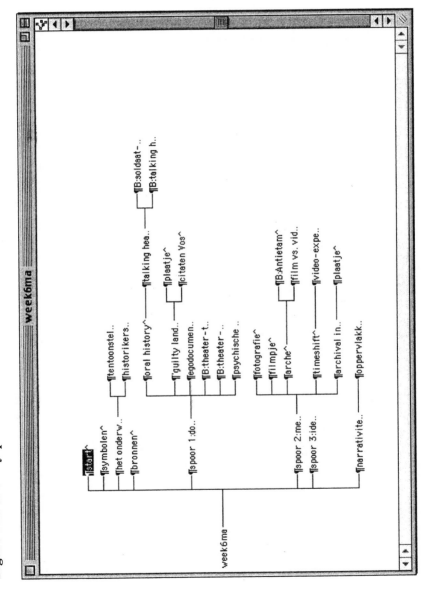

Figure 11.2 A Storyspace document view in the chart mode

Figure 11.3 A Storyspace document view in the outline mode

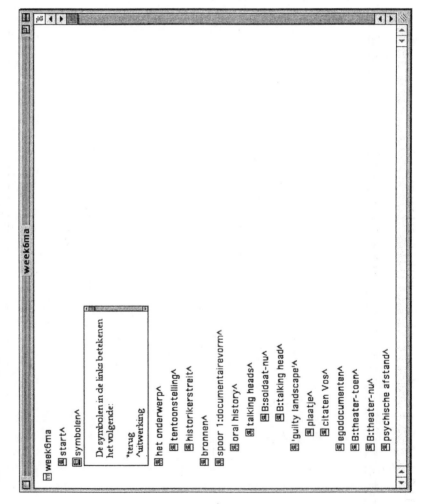

Box 11.1 My impression of a student working with Storyspace

(...) Brigitte is working in the figurative mode. She assumes that it should be possible to copy and paste part of one document structure into another. So do I, used as I am to modern software. She switches to and fro between the file she has just worked on and earlier files, which she uploads from the zip disk and closes again. While Brigitte is making attempts, I soon lose track of what is happening, mainly because I cannot determine which is the main document. Brigitte also appears to be confused. The file names on the zip disk, which partly consist of the date of file creation, are barely discriminating. I get the uncomfortable feeling that, perhaps because of my presence, Brigitte is clicking and operating Storyspace more vigorously than usual. Her pace is that of a seasoned professional. At a high speed flat, long, stringy and depressive structures originate which walk off the screen. Both she and I lose track of which file is active and what the copying of partial structures has brought about. I fear that she is saving multiple versions of these unwanted stringy structures, and is thereby replacing original (and correct) structures. But I am not sure.

After one hour of fiddling around she asks one of the staff members for advice. The answer is that it cannot be done. (...)

In short, the user can choose between three modes to visualise the structure of his or her hypertext document. Within these modes there is relatively little flexibility in use. The lack of certain facilities which the user has grown to expect in modern software, poses constraints on user behaviour.

Model of Use in the Course Design

The way Storyspace is integrated within the course is new. Using it for textual *and* visual material is innovative in itself. Using it to teach students to organise their research findings in a non-linear manner is an innovation as well. The designers of Storyspace did not specifically have an educational setting in mind when they developed it. Thus, the teachers redefine its meaning in several respects. In the course design text-oriented Storyspace is treated as a multimedia programme. Originally designed for professional writers, it is used in the course as a research tool in a learning environment. And, instead of a personal tool, it is used as a tool for direct and indirect collaboration (i.e. through use by student pairs, and through collective discussion of Storyspace documents, respectively). In other words, in theory there is the artefact as designed, namely Storyspace, and the artefact in its context of use, namely Storyspace in the course. Students do not distinguish between the two. They have no previous experience with

Storyspace. So, their first encounter with Storyspace is that in the course setting. They therefore also judge its usability and limitations in terms of the course context. The following is an account of the way Storyspace, as part of the course, constrains student uses. It is based on the experiences of the four students I interviewed (Marianne, Annette, Ellen and Lia) and on observations of the teachers and the multimedia lab staff.

Forcing and preventing operations   Students seldom integrate visual material in the hypertext document. Firstly, it is cumbersome to do so. The required additional software is located on a staff member's computer, and his assistance is needed. (In other words, the redefinition of Storyspace into a multimedia programme should have included making the software available on student computers.) Secondly, the programme's text-oriented design restricts its use as a multimedia tool. Users are restricted in where to place a picture; it is not possible to position a text next to a picture; the film fragments are often too large for Storyspace's memory; and inserting film fragments requires 'unnecessary' actions.[11] Although Storyspace is designed to structure texts, text editing can be complex. Knowledge of its peculiarities is required to trick the programme into doing what you want it to do. In order to make the document accessible to the reader (e.g. to avoid too small a window for a text entity), the user must perform a series of actions. The means to improve the document's appearance are limited (e.g. the number of colours to indicate links) or require a lot of work. The reader is often compelled to scroll through the text, something that most document designers would like to avoid.

Triggering a certain research approach   Each week the students develop a hypertext document in which they integrate their research findings. Crucial to non-linear research is how to organise their findings in a coherent structure. Students find Storyspace useful to order their thoughts and cluster pieces of information. It forces them to decide which data belong together and to distinguish core issues from elaboration. However, the programme is less suitable for developing a line of argument and presenting research findings.[12] It is not cut out for long texts. Short texts fragment information. The use of Storyspace for research purposes invites the student to postulate statements and underpin them with pieces of evidence and definitions. This leads to superficial outcomes, according to students.

The programme requires a planned research approach because, once an initial structure has been defined and a number of links between information entities have been created, it is very laborious to change them. The students' experience is that if one is not satisfied with the structure and tries to elaborate it nonetheless, such structures soon loose their transparency. As a multimedia lab staff member remarks, "If you encounter a problem while developing a document structure, it is often more effective to start anew than to try to continue with the same document." This affects the research approach. In a group discussion one student argues for defining the document structure before reading literature and gathering material, because it is easier to revise a text in a pre-structured document than to place a new entity into a developing structure. The group agrees.

The latter illustrates that the use of Storyspace for non-linear research is problematic. The programme's lack of flexibility constrains the research approach. In addition, the hypertext documents contain little visual material. The redefinition of the writer's tool into a multimedia tool for the course works only partly because Storyspace has too few means to handle visual material and because the additional software is not readily accessible to students.

Teachers Who Do Not Steer

Whether students develop unexpected hypermedia uses largely depends on whether the teachers succeed in not steering hypermedia use. But it is difficult to avoid. As one teacher remarks, the example of a hypertext structure in the course book may already have narrowed down student uses of Storyspace. The teachers try not to encourage specific uses during the weekly group discussions. They give few pointers for Storyspace use. But students 'pounce' on each slip of the tongue and are sensitive to signs of enthusiasm, despite being aware from the outset that there are no clear norms for evaluating hypertext use. The student accounts show that students distil most of the teacher's expectations.

Students discovering and developing norms In search for guidance on how to use Storyspace, the way teachers react to the work of other students is well noted. On one occasion in the second week an example appears to be set. During a Friday group discussion, Ellen notes, "There was one [hypertext structure] that was very much appreciated, and to which everyone [later] adapted their own document. Everyone thought it was clever and useful, or our teacher said so, I think. (...) A lot of attention was paid at that meeting to the fact that you should not think along linear lines and not link two entities sequentially without the possibility to [turn back]".

Some teacher norms on usage are mediated through students across the two groups. Ellen remembers that, in one of the first weeks, she and her partner sketched a hypertext structure on paper before they implemented it in the programme. They later heard from other students that "(...) it was not allowed to do so (...)". They were supposed to use the programme straightaway. It was something the other teacher had said. Using paper "(...) would be too complicated, not good, lead to too linear documents, or something in this vein."

The evaluation criteria for the final individual document are unclear, which causes general unease. Ellen consults the course book for the first time in the last course week to find out where the priority in the course lies. Annette hopes that the teacher will judge her final document on the way she has handled and structured the material, and not on the conclusions. She fears that the teacher will look at the conclusions too, although the stated course objective centres on learning how to do research and not on the research outcome. Lia mentions that the teacher's contribution to group discussions has mainly been about the course content (i.e. images of war in visual media), and that the teacher will therefore probably not pass judgement on the different uses of Storyspace. But she is annoyed and uncomfortable about not knowing by which criteria her final document will be judged. Her idea of a good document may differ from that of the teacher. Can the teacher realistically assess what is possible when using Storyspace?

Teacher norms The teachers, of course, do have ideas about how to use the programme. Norms for use crystallise during the course. One of the teachers speaks about the 'classic mistakes' which students make in using Storyspace. Students learn by making them. There are two sorts: methodological mistakes and content-based mistakes. With regard to *methodological mistakes*, some students write one long text, very much like a traditional thesis, with links to a few extra entities containing references and visual material. These students do not use Storyspace as a research experiment. Others use it primarily as a means to classify aspects of the visual medium they study. They insert the theme of the assignment as an afterthought, whilst it should have been taken as a starting point. Another methodological mistake is to ask *a priori* questions and design a structure based on these questions. Students should not try to fit the material in a pre-defined structure since this leads to bias. What students should learn is to select relevant material, paraphrase it, quote, link it to other material, and periodically summarise their findings on a higher level. They should use Storyspace as a tool for processing material. The teacher speaks of a *content-based mistake* when students use Storyspace only for text and do not include visual material. The course is about researching 'war images' and about 'visual representation'. The visual aspect of the research area should somehow be expressed in the Storyspace document. Students should relate hypermedia use, that is, the research tool, to 'visual representation of war', that is, the research content.

Right from the start the teachers advocate Storyspace as a research tool and stress that there are several ways to structure research material. It should not be used as a means of presentation. But during the course the teachers nonetheless react favourably to hypertext structures which 'look good'. As the students' work on the final document draws nearer, the dilemma between its explicit use as a research tool and the implicit presentation requirements deepens. Indeed, in the end the teachers do, as some of the students surmised, base their evaluation on presentation aspects of Storyspace too – despite earlier assertions to the contrary. The teachers use presentation aspects as indicators of the research process. They assume that the selection of material is based on certain criteria, that links between entities are intentional, and that students can therefore explain their line of reasoning by how the document looks. If students argue their document structure well, their work will be evaluated well too.

Reviewing the foregoing, the teachers do not influence the way students technically handle Storyspace but they do steer the way it is used for research, in particular during the last weeks of the course. They steer in an explicit manner when they comment on hypertext documents. Student uses are steered too by their reading of the teachers' implicit expectations, namely when students engage in a process of 'discovering the teacher's norms'.

Context of the User

Who is the user? User characteristics also influence Storyspace use during the course. The following focuses on student attitudes towards computers and how students handle computers in general. The four female students mentioned earlier, namely Lia, Ellen, Marianne and Annette, serve as cases.

Home Environment

Students use computers at home as well as at the faculty. Attitudes develop in both contexts. Looking at the home environment, three of the interviewed students hardly read computer magazines. Their family and friends do not have an active interest in computers. Nevertheless, the latter play an important role in purchasing a computer and working with it at home (e.g. solving breakdowns). The fourth student, Lia, reads her friend's magazines. Lia has the most positive attitude towards computers. She likes using it. Of the four students, Marianne has the most negative attitude towards computers. She feels aversion towards computers. Both Marianne's and Lia's attitude towards computers coincide with that of their immediate social environment at home. It reflects on their attitude towards multimedia use in the course. Lia is looking forward to the course. Marianne is not, precisely because of the use of multimedia and the fuss that is made about it. Marianne has nonetheless decided that it is 'good' for her to undergo some training in multimedia use.

Types of Home Users

How can the four students best be characterised? Aune (1996) identifies three types of home users, that is: *extenders* (who purchase and use a computer at home for their work or study), *game-players* (who use the computer as a toy) and *explorers* (who are interested in computer developments and new uses). Furthermore, home users differ in their learning strategy. There are four main strategies (Sørensen e.a. 1996): *experimentation* (overall systematic exploration of possibilities), *tinkering* (pragmatic learning by trial and error), *analysis* (starting out by seeking general knowledge), and *training* (supervised learning). Applying these categories to our students, they are primarily extenders. Ellen started out as an extender and is now an active communicator in her spare time (chat-box and e-mail); Annette is an extender and a – disappointed – (Internet) explorer; Marianne is a pure extender; and Lia started out as an extender, has become a game player, and is increasingly becoming an explorer. Only Lia is inclined to experiment. The other three students mostly tinker. All four subject themselves to learning by training within the context of the course.

Previous Experience with Computers

They choose to learn hypermedia use within a training environment, but the course provides little guidance. They therefore need to draw more heavily on other experiences, that is, on their previous learning experience and their experience with other computer uses. A salient example is the Internet. All students, even the most reticent ones, are acquainted with it. The Internet is an influential example in two ways. Firstly, it defines their expectations of hypertext. Students expect Storyspace documents to possess certain provisions, like a button in order to return to a previous link. The designer herself should define such a possibility. Secondly, the Internet offers a frame of reference for structuring documents. For example, it is customary for Internet sites to have a first page, the home page. Therefore, the students too design an introductory entity to start with, that is, an initial overview that guides the reader and to which to the reader can return.

Lack of experience with computers also affects the use of Storyspace. Most students do not own very advanced computers, nor do they generally use the computers at the university for more than text processing and communication. As a consequence, the students are not so much put out by the out-dated features of Storyspace. The lack of familiarity with advanced interface and software design is therefore an advantage. It facilitates acceptance of the hypertext programme.

Previous Educational Training

The aim of the course includes a transition in educational culture, that is, from a culture of individual products to collaborative products, from writer control to reader control, from linear to hypertext document structures, and from drawing conclusions to developing associations. The students have been trained in previous courses, for example, to write linear essays and do theory-driven research. This does not match with the manner in which Storyspace is supposed to be used, namely non-linear and material-driven. Especially in the first weeks, when in doubt about how to structure their hypertext documents, students resort to their previous training.

Conflicting Influences

The designers' scenario of Storyspace use and the model of use implied in the course design may reinforce the same sort of use. But they may also conflict and pull or push towards different directions. For example, Storyspace was developed for individual use and is not easily used for co-operative work. Most student pairs divide the research tasks and each adds to the document in turn. But it proves to be difficult to understand the additions of the partner and maintain coherence in the document. In this respect, the software design and the course design are in conflict. In the same manner the user's past educational training and her home computer use may conflict with the course design, or the course requirements themselves may counteract each other. How do students reconcile such conflicts?

Their means to resolve such conflicts are restricted. The course is tough. There is a limited amount of time in which to learn how to use Storyspace and do non-linear research, as well as gaining insight into 'visualisation of war'. The students have difficulties combining the aims of the course. Learning a new way of structuring research material competes with the aim of familiarising with ways in which war is represented in visual media. The weekly discussions about the hypertext documents and the teacher's final evaluation of the individual documents require that the documents be presentable. It invites an outcome-oriented manner of working instead of a research-process oriented approach; an emphasis on Storyspace use for others instead of for oneself; an analysis instead of a synthesis of the material found; a 'demonstrated logic' instead of an 'associative logic'. The weekly assignment, too, requires argued results ('stories') and not fragments of information. It demands a self-explanatory document structure, which guides the reader through the document. The students all have problems coping with the idea that hypertext documents have no 'starting point', and with not being allowed to tell 'a story'. They try to find a compromise between using Storyspace as a research tool (hypertext links) and the implicit request for presentation of research outcomes (guided reading) by doing both.

In previous sections a number of occurrences were mentioned that can be interpreted as conflicts between the context of the user (e.g. the student's learning history) and the context of use (e.g. course aims, user script of Storyspace). For example, although students are expected to integrate visual material in the hypertext document their past educational training, the absence of certain multimedia lab facilities and the difficulty of using the programme for this purpose leads to text documents in the first weeks of the course. Furthermore, the teachers and the programme 'conspire' against long texts. The students respond by writing short texts, but according to their own standards it makes the document content superficial. These examples illustrate that students cannot fully resolve the conflicts. They abide by the most forceful influences at certain moments in the course, but are not comfortable in doing so. Thus, their use of Storyspace remains subject to change during the course.

Unexpected Hypermedia Uses

As was explained in the introduction, the course is an experiment. Teachers try not to prescribe hypermedia use. This suggests that there is considerable room to develop new uses. For several reasons this is only partly true. Firstly, the time is very limited. Without taking into account the time needed to explore Storyspace, the course is already too ambitious. Secondly, the four interviewed students – and most of their peers – are primarily extenders. This type of home user does not match well with the explorer type of attitude, which leads to new uses. Thirdly, the teacher-student relationship inscribed in the educational setting conspires against new hypertext uses. The ultimate need to meet the teacher's evaluation criteria encourages the sounding out of expected uses rather than the exploration of new ones. Therefore, the room to explore and develop new uses exists, but is rather limited.

However, the interpretative flexibility with regard to Storyspace use is large. The students are uncertain about what is expected and what to do. They are aware that there are no strict norms for Storyspace use. Conflicting aims in the context of use signal competing meanings. Where competing meanings are at stake, no closure exists in respect to Storyspace use. This suggests that more diverse hypertext uses are likely to develop. Has this been the case? The examples below refer to uses of Storyspace, which are unexpected and strike students, teachers or the staff members of the multimedia lab as special.

A number of unexpected uses are observed. One couple wants to insert a video fragment with sound, the same fragment without sound, and the sound without the video fragment. A trick is used to achieve a 'blank' film, the third condition. Another couple attempts, in vain, to design links within a text entity. The teacher interprets this as an attempt to make the document more 'hypertextual' than Storyspace allows. A third couple inserts a picture as a back-button, a use not foreseen by the staff. A fourth couple uses an entity as a 'message window' for informal communication among themselves. This too is an example of unexpected use of Storyspace.

Lastly, there are the examples of innovative document structures that emerge when using the figurative mode of Storyspace. Symmetric structures often turn out nice and sometimes evoke figurative associations. There is one structure in which all entities are interconnected. This means that the reader can jump from each entity to all other entities. The information entities are ordered in a circle. This layout gets "Wow, that looks great!" reactions from other students. Further, Lia mentions the case of a structure in which a student couple uses the lines (links) and boxes (information entities) to draw a balance. The balance has scales hanging from both sides. A line links the two scales (boxes). They contain examples of the way war is visualised in two different media. In between these two examples and drawn as the footing of the balance, there is an entity (box), which clarifies the terms used in the two examples. The symmetry in the drawing expresses symmetry in the research content of the document.

Are conflicting influences within and between the context of use, the context of the user and the context of production a source of unexpected hypermedia use? The examples do not indicate so. Some student couples overcome the shortcomings of Storyspace (designers' model of the user) in order to insert visual material (the teachers' model of use), and do so in an unexpected way. But this does not univocally echo the conflicts mentioned in the previous sections. Such conflicts foremost appear to affect the students' regular work with Storyspace.

Conclusion

In this chapter I analysed the use of a hypermedia programme for teaching non-linear research in a university course. The course is new and hypermedia use is an experiment. It is a diversification experiment. Teachers try not to steer hypermedia use and hope that students will develop unexpected and diverse uses. I interpreted this as an attempt to postpone closure of the meaning of hypermedia use. Did the diversification experiment succeed and lead to the emergence of unexpected hypermedia uses for non-linear research?

I distinguished three clusters of factors that are relevant to hypermedia use and described their likely effect on its use. The clusters are the context of production (i.e. software constraints), the context of use (i.e. implications of the course design and teacher influences) and the context of the user (i.e. student attitude towards and experience with computers, and past educational training). Some factors reinforced the same use of hypermedia. Others counteracted each other. For example, the software was text-oriented, while the research subject was about visual media. Where factors push and pull towards different directions, I hypothesised, unexpected uses are likely to occur. But I was wrong. The examples of unexpected uses given by the participants cannot be attributed in a straightforward manner to such conflicts. Instead, students mostly coped with conflicting influences on hypermedia use by complying with one and temporarily ignoring the other.

Of special interest was whether teachers would succeed in not steering hypermedia use and thus in postponing closure. The teachers did not instruct students how to technically handle the hypermedia programme. But in a modest manner they did steer the way it was used for organising research findings. For they, of course, did have a preference for certain hypermedia structures and could not non-communicate. The students were on the look out for their teachers' norms. This degree of steering seems unavoidable in a dependent teacher-student relationship. Overall, however, the teachers steered little. At the start of the course they made explicit that there are no fixed norms on how to use hypermedia for research. They emphasised that it would be a process of 'shaping while doing'. Indeed, the lack of guidance sometimes frustrated students, up to the last week of the course. This indicates that the students had little clarity about the teachers' expectations of use and that therefore teachers were successful in postponing closure. Although dis-closure caused some unease, it triggered frequent reflection on how to use hypermedia and what non-linear research entails. It led to intense learning by all concerned. Did dis-closure also lead to diverse and unexpected hypermedia use? It appears so. Most unexpected uses would probably not have emerged if the teachers had prescribed beforehand how to handle the programme and how to use it to organise research findings.

Notes

1   The social experiment is characterised by user involvement (i.e. planned feedback) and its societal objective (Slack e.a. 1998).

2   That is, a reflexive practice where there is no intention to steer the direction of sociotechnical change.

3   Open questions were designed, tailored to each respondent category and to the three moments in the course. They lasted between half an hour and an hour and a half. I thank my two colleagues, Marc van Lieshout and Roland Bal, who assisted me during the first series of interviews. Together with Wiebe Bijker, they also gave valuable comments on an earlier draft of this chapter.

4   Their names are fictitious.

5   D08.01 User Requirement Analysis IMMICS (1996), D08.02 Functional Specifications for IMMICS (1997), ELECTRA project, TELEMATICS APPLICATION Programme of the European Commision.

6   Apart from learning being problem-based, students set their own personal learning goals, self-exploratory behaviour is stimulated, prior knowledge of students is activated, and they follow an individual trajectory. Students regularly discuss their progress and findings within their student group.

7   PBL issues are incidentally referred to. For example, asked about the educational objectives of the project, the project leader answers: to promote self-exploratory behaviour in studying complex issues and to promote co-operative teamwork. (source: the project leader's answers to the Kluge e.a. (1997) questionnaire)

8   *Oorlog in een kijkdoos. Media en Visuele Beelden.* 1997-1998 Faculteit der Cultuurwetenschappen/Cultuur- en Wetenschapsstudies, Blok 3.3.V. Universiteit van Maastricht.

9   Additional research would be required to determine which 'user model' is embedded in these guidelines, apart from research on the transformation, which the guidelines underwent in developing Storyspace.

10   'Wysiwyg' stands for 'What you see is what you get'.

11   To paste a film fragment in a text you have to copy the film to the same folder as the one where the document is located. If you then import it, you get only the first still of the film. You then have to click on the film to load it.

12   E.g. because the meaning of the links between information entities varies, the line of argument can be difficult to trace in all but the simplest structures.

PART III
COMPARATIVE ANALYSES

12 Setting of Multimedia Use

TINEKE M. EGYEDI, MARC VAN LIESHOUT,
WIEBE E. BIJKER

Abstract

This chapter compares the settings in which multimedia is used. Of interest are features of the educational and the project setting. The question addressed is whether these features explain the (lack of) multimedia use in education. Different angles of approach are taken. The cases discussed in the preceding chapters were carried out under different circumstances but there are many similarities in the conditions of multimedia use and project development, for example, in respect to project incentives and teaching environments. These similarities, as well as the most salient differences, are examined. The educational and project settings partly explain why the use of multimedia lags behind expectations. The answers range from lack of funding and the marginalisation of teachers to too narrowly defined policies on educational multimedia.

Introduction

Hawkridge (1983: 217) foresaw that in the year 2000 governments would continue to spend funds on hardware and courseware in schools but that these funds would be insufficient for universal provision. He pointed to three specific conditions that would delay the provision of computers in schools: lack of money, of courseware and of improved ways of using computers in schools. We are now entering his prophetic year. Does his forecast hold true?

In this chapter we examine the present conditions for multimedia use and project development. That is, we focus on features of the setting of multimedia use. Our framework consists of Eurelings' discussion on the state-of-art of educational multimedia (chapter 2, this volume). Examples are drawn from the case studies presented in preceding chapters. The

Table 12.1 Overview of cases

Case's main actors	Key features	Objectives
Language course for children (ch. 4) Marketing division of telecom company; children; university unit; teachers	Distance language course offered to ten children; one course; duration 40 teaching hours (originally 60 hours); only conversation (originally writing, spelling, talking).	To create an ISDN multipoint connection for electronic white-board use; to show its marketability to head quarters (cf. strategic choice of children)
Cable-School (ch. 5) Cable-modem provider; schools; teachers	Implementation of server network for exchanging teacher worksheets among schools; offering access to internal/external networks by cable modem.	Cable company aims to get a foothold in the public domain (to broaden its market) by offering educational content on a server; to develop an electronic network for schools.
Spice Girls (ch. 6) Four enthusiastic female computer users	Survey of daily uses and experiences of enthusiastic female computer and networks users.	To understand what triggers females to use computers and electronic networks.
Bornholm Distance teaching (ch. 7) Bornholm and mainland educ. Institutes; public authorities; students; teachers	Distance teaching networks between the Bornholm island and mainland educ. institutes through a virtual classroom.	To explore the economic prospects of distance teaching for island inhabitants and expand the island's educational offerings.
Multimedia use Norway (ch. 8) Government and educational bodies	Discusses national policy and national initiatives for sharing information about multimedia use in education.	N/A
Telepoly (ch.10) Swiss polytechnics; evaluation committees; students; teachers	Establishment of ATM-network for distance teaching between two (later three) institutes.	First: to explore economies of scale (cost-effectiveness) of electronic distance teaching. Later: to explore pedagogical aspects of distance teaching.
IMMICS (ch. 9/11) Teachers; faculty media lab; students; university; European partners	Use of hypermedia software in a new university course about visual culture; creation of image library; embedding media-lab in the faculty. Discussed at course level and as an innofusion process.	To train in the use of hypermedia; to learn doing research on the use and meaning of images; to consolidate the multimedia-lab.

Innofusion (Appropriation – Configuration – Translation)	Social Learning Control – Experimentation	Success – Failure
Appropriation hardly occurs. *Configuration* of children to 'adult', predictable users. *Translation* of the medium by children into 'playing field'.	Strictly controlled experiment; no room to explore unforeseen uses; innovative behaviour of children is controlled by technical means; strategic marketing considerations predominate the entire project.	The project is communicated as a 'success'; all actors share this notion of success; judged on its technical and pedagogical results it is a failure.
Appropriation of e-mail/ Internet; appropriation of worksheets by teachers fails. *Configuration* of school setting fails. *Translation* of the school server into a communication device.	Initially tightly controlled project, later room for experimentation due to lost interest of cable company; hardly support for teachers; open learning space: no deadlines, no evaluation procedures.	Interest of initiator (cable company) fades; teachers are left to fend for themselves; server is hardly used for exchanging worksheets; e-mail and Internet use increase.
Appropriation / translation of computer as/to a comm. device (e.g. chatting). *Configuration* by information content: divers use of Internet over time.	Free experimental setting; by exploring, new uses and behaviour develop; learning by doing.	Girls focus on information content; successful appropriation of multimedia facilities into daily practice; the home is an important starting point.
Appropriation is difficult due to lack of 'political' support. *Configuration* of virtual classroom fails: ordinary classroom setting is copied. No *translation* to specific distance teaching setting.	Technological design restricts room to experiment. Pedagogical elements are not integrated in the project design. Cost-efficiency considerations determine set-up; technical and pedagogical adaptations are neglected.	No economic benefit for Bornholm; the trial is disappointing from an educational perspective. An a-symmetry in educational service between island and mainland develops.
Appropriation at the national level through informative web-sites (e.g. consulted by parents and teachers)	N/A	N/A
Appropriation by some teachers. *Configuration* of teaching occurs ('show' element introduced). *Translation* to new uses (electronic documents on Internet).	Initially strictly controlled technical design (stable ATM-connection); later a move towards exploring educational issues; learning process takes place in respect to teaching conditions.	Successful realisation of stable technical infrastructure; successful prolongation of experiment (in moderated form); failure in realising cost-effective-ness.
Appropriation by students in a new research approach. Initial *configuration* of students' hypermedia uses by prior educ. Training ('linear'). *Translation* of text-oriented to multimedia software.	Very open and explorative setting which leads to uncertainty among students about whether they do their work right; choice of software is determined by educational objectives (choice for partly outdated software).	Successful in stimulating explorative multimedia use; successful in positioning the new course and the new media lab in the faculty.

features of the educational setting are treated thematically. We start with features of the education sector. We proceed, in turn, with a discussion of the degree to which multimedia is adapted for educational purposes, non-educational aims of multimedia projects, developments in project objectives, institutional incentives for non-innovative projects, the neglected role of teachers and multimedia content.

Table 12.1 provides an overview of the main features of the cases discussed in Part II. The table serves as a point of reference for the reader of chapters 12, 13 and 14.

Dissolving Boundaries in Education

The educational settings described in the preceding chapters are diverse. In one case a telecom company organises an ad hoc course for nine, 10-year-old children. In another instance a commercial party initiates a trial for cable modems in which primary and high schools participate. Four cases take place within and between institutions for higher education and universities. One case looks at the combined influence of the home environment and school in the way female teenagers use computers. The last case concerns computer use in schools and its relationship to national initiatives. Thus, although the empirical material consists of a limited number of cases, it addresses a wide range of educational settings. What, then, do we mean by 'the education sector'? Is it an institutional sector, a competitive market, or a diffuse societal phenomenon?

The pillar of traditional education consists of institutions such as kindergarten, primary and secondary school, centres for vocational training, and universities. Together they represent what we refer to as the formal education sector. In Europe this sector has been under great strain these last two decades. Means have been sought to cut the costs of education and impose efficiency measures (for example, by re-organisations). New ideas for productivity and output are introduced, and institutions are partly subsidised accordingly. For example, with regard to the universities today, the Dutch government only covers the teaching costs of students who pass their exams. Such cost-cutting measures take place while competition between subsidised institutions (for example, through ratings of schools) and institutions outside formal education increases. Examples of potential external competitors are commercial training centres and company divisions that provide in-house business training. But other subsidised organisations, such as the local and regional authorities, also offer competitive courses (for example, job creation programmes). Within this network of organisations higher education in particular is developing into a quasi-competitive market, that is, into a service sector that is run on a quasi-commercial basis. In this respect, the institutional boundaries of formal education are dissolving.

Nordli (this volume) argues that, where multimedia is concerned, 'learning by doing' may well overtake 'learning by training'. 'Learning by doing' can occur elsewhere than in educational locations. For example, if we want to learn how to use the Internet, we can learn it at home through trial and error or through a television course. We can learn it by following a course at the community centre or 'learn by doing' at work and with the help of colleagues. We can learn it in Cybercafés– or we can follow a course at a formal educational centre. Learning is not restricted to formal education and other educational centres: it takes place in different locations and spheres of life (work and leisure, public and private).

Does a similar dissolving of boundaries apply to the age of learning? Formal education specifically targets children, adolescents and young adults. At present, many policy documents refer to the notion of life-long learning, which disregards age. It is positioned as a new policy issue. But, in itself, it is nothing new. It is not new for those who follow a television course on Japanese cooking, attend a trade union lecture about the new pension law, or try to get an extra degree in bookkeeping in their spare time. Even taking future multimedia developments into account, there is no principle difference between electronic and paper course books, or between paper-based Open University courses and electronic courses on the Internet. The novelty may lie in the accessibility, multimedianess and inter-activity of Internet-based courses. But this has a bearing on the potential added value of multimedia to life-long learning; life-long learning itself is not a new phenomenon. Thus, from the perspective of age as well as location, education is – and always has been – a diffuse societal phenomenon.

Education is becoming a competitive market, a future which Hawkridge describes as a 'Learner's Hell'; it was and still is to a high degree an institutional sector; but it is a diffuse societal phenomenon as well. When policy makers express concern about the slow uptake of ICT in education, they refer to formal – and for youngsters, partly compulsory – education. In the following we adopt this policy focus and examine what extra insight learning environments such as the home may yield to the formal education environment.

Educational Multimedia?

The core-problem of multimedia in education is how to integrate it within the learning environment. Using Eurelings' terms (this volume), *learning with ICT* poses the most immediate challenge. (*Learning about ICT* is a temporary and subsidiary matter, *and learning through ICT* benefits from experiences with *learning with ICT.*) Generic tools as well as specific educational tools are relevant. The latter have changed character. Used foremost as a teaching tool, they are increasingly used as a learning tool. Parallel to this, multimedia have become more 'empty', asynchronous, and student-controlled, and the information environment less pre-structured ('richer', complex and more authentic). Eurelings does not overly stress the need to develop more and better educational multimedia, as would be expected. Instead, she observes that the design of learning environments is becoming the focus of attention. It is the positioning of the tool within the learning environment that makes multimedia into an educational tool.

If we look at the cases, none of the projects aim at developing new educational software. The technologies consist of pick-and-mix systems. In all but one instance the virtual absence of integration of multimedia into the educational setting is salient. For example, there are three distance-teaching projects (Telepoly, Telecom course and Bornholm). One project experiments with an ATM connection that connects one lecture room with another, distant one. The other experiment concerns a (multi-point) ISDN infrastructure for an out-of-school language course for children. The third uses a videophone link to connect classrooms. In all three cases (enhancement of) the didactic context is not the primary project objective. Little pedagogical attention is paid to the creation of a new learning environment. In the Telecom course and the Bornholm project the teachers' ambitions in this direction are totally by-passed by project constraints. In the Cable-School project, where teachers at different schools have access to each other's electronic worksheets, the problem is of a different nature. The whole idea of worksheet sharing among teachers does not match with the teaching practice and working culture (i.e. teacher autonomy). The project creates no social context for sharing. The teachers' fear that their worksheets will be criticised is not taken into account.

The above examples indicate that little attention is paid to the setting of multimedia use. The exception to the rule is the IMMICS project. In this project a hypermedia programme is used to teach non-linear research. The project pays some attention to the pedagogical aspects of multimedia use and to the wider educational setting. For example, the teachers maintain that co-operation among students is important. Co-operation between students on hypermedia documents is therefore part of the course design. Furthermore, in the faculty where the course takes place, the first steps are made in the development of an electronic learning (and teaching) environment.

If these projects are anything to go by, the state-of-the-art of educational multimedia is disappointing. The projects use generic multimedia tools and 'insert' them in an education setting. There is little student control. The educational content is generally pre-structured. The teaching practice continues largely without adaptations. Pedagogical concerns play a minor role. The exploration of technical uses colours the projects. The primacy of developing a learning environment in which multimedia is integrated seems far off. Do the cases reflect the general state of integration of multimedia in education? Yes, they do.[1] Few projects pay systematic attention to localising multimedia in a pedagogically sound way. Instructional theory on multimedia use appears to be way ahead of praxis. There are several explanations why praxis lags behind. These explanations are examined in the next sections.

Non-Educational Aims in Multimedia Projects

Foremost, multimedia projects in education appear to be a matter of successfully handling, negotiating and advocating multimedia promises. Concerned are unspecified promises of technology for education. In the grey area between promise and practice the educational side of the projects tends to fade into the background. The cases show that most multimedia in education projects do not have an educational focus. Only the IMMICS project has an explicit educational objective (i.e. to develop a learning environment which is integrated with multimedia information). The initiators of the other projects have different motives. In one case, the project is used to improve the position of a company division in relation to headquarters. The decision to start the education project is, like the decision to use young children, based on market considerations (Telecom course). In another case, the project is actually a means of exploring the market. The education field is a stepping-stone for the cable company's follow-up activities in the public service sector (Cable-School). In these company-driven projects the field of education is a deliberate and strategic choice. Education always has good connotations, and is thus suitable for the purpose of window-dressing. Because of this, educational aims also pop up in 'non-multimedia in education' projects (e.g. Kerr 1998). But even the projects that are not motivated by company interests and are initiated by educators need not be motivated by didactic considerations. For example, the distance learning project between technical institutes (Telepoly) was initially set up to cut the costs of education. Only at a later stage of the project, when new actors arrived on the scene, were pedagogical issues examined.

Whatever the 'true motive' that underlies the above projects, the stated project aims have little immediate relevance for education (for example, ISDN experiment, cable-modem trial, and ATM experiment). They focus on getting a working system in place.

The Project's Head and Tail

Commercial project aims remain consistent. In the Telecom course project strategic objectives coincide entirely with operational ones. The project ends the very moment the strategic objective is realised. Analogously, the commercial party in the Cable-School project drops out once its initial aims are met. Whereas, in projects where the educational setting is more prominent and the role of commercial third parties negligible, initial objectives and ultimate emphases differ. In IMMICS, the project starts out as a faculty-wide activity and ends up as a course. In Telepoly, the cost-saving objective recedes into the background; ultimately, the project is evaluated on its pedagogical merits. Typically, these projects are part of an on-going, lengthier change process within an institution or within a more permanent network of actors. Both examples suggest that where new actors become involved, a redefinition of project aims becomes likely. Mourik (this volume), however, argues that whether a redefinition of aims occurs or not, depends on whether new actors do or do not strongly affiliate with the original project (i.e. their degree of inclusion). If not, project aims remain stable (see, for example, the Telecom course). Indeed, this explains the change in project aims of both IMMICS and Telepoly. For example, in the case of Telepoly the new actors had a high degree of inclusion, that is, they had a strong interest in the educational aspects of the project, which explains why the strategic objectives were reformulated accordingly.

Institutional Incentives for Verification Experiments

Earlier we asked why there is a gap between the theory and praxis of multimedia integration in education. One explanation is that lack of integration is a natural consequence of the non-didactic motives of many projects. A second explanation could be that projects that are more likely to include pedagogical issues, namely those that are situated in formal educational settings, are susceptible to a change in orientation during the project. This leaves little room for the development of a pedagogically sound integration trajectory. There is another aspect that may explain the lack of multimedia integration in teaching and learning practices. In many projects the conditions under which they take place trigger quick fixes. Projects have a limited time-span – apart from those that manage to organise a string of follow-up projects (e.g. Telepoly). The funds are limited. The restrictive conditions favour pilots with modest aims, for example: to verify the workability and technical feasibility of certain multimedia. Egyedi (chapter 11, this volume) speaks in this respect about verification experiments, and contrasts them to experiments that aim at developing new uses (diversification experiments). An extreme example of a verification experiment is the Telecom course, where children were supposed to demonstrate the success of an ISDN-based language course at a fair. The project management had no real interest in the course itself. Its only interest was that the system worked (or, rather, looked as if it worked).

Also, multimedia projects funded by public authorities typically aim at verification. Let us, for example, take a look at the European Commission's call-for-tenders procedure regarding EU projects. The projects are selected on the basis of expected, circumscribed results. These results must justify funding. In order to secure the desired results and safeguard the desired progress, conditions are laid down and intermediate progress reports are required. For example, IMMICS is one of the educational multimedia projects of the ELECTRA consortium. One of the Commission's conditions for funding ELECTRA was that the projects would reflect on education. This would seem a highly relevant condition in respect to multimedia integration in education. Furthermore, one would expect that the EU review system would assist in keeping this issue high on the agenda of the ELECTRA projects. But, overall, it has not worked out that way. The main reason is that the EU system of deliverables demands tangible products (reports and working systems). It contains a bias towards technical outcomes that can be easily demonstrated. It triggers verification experiments. There is little or no place for pedagogical considerations. Furthermore, the projects are bound to a tight time-schedule. The limited time available to teachers and technical staff leads to an ad hoc approach and prevents a more balanced reflection on educational requirements. Consequently, such projects seldom lead to the integration of multimedia use. The institutional context of EU-projects does not support such a process.[2]

The Marginalised Teacher

If we take a look at the people involved in projects, there are two main categories. There are the operational actors, that is, those who work with the system such as teachers and students; and there are the actors who have a strategic interest in and significance for (the results of) the project. The latter category may include the project's evaluation committee and the European Commission.

Teachers play a central role in the educational setting, whether as mediator, coaches or lecturers. However, in multimedia projects they are often treated as subsidiary actors. Their significance for project design and implementation is hardly recognised. The extra facilities for teachers participating in multimedia projects are meagre. Teacher involvement usually takes place on a voluntary basis. Technical support is minimal. They rarely receive any significant training, exceptions aside (e.g. Aune & Sørensen, and Egyedi, chapter 9). Thus, the integration of multimedia in educational curricula is not facilitated. There are numerous examples. In the Telepoly project the quality of distance teaching depends solely on the teacher's understanding of the situation and on her/his voluntary efforts. In order to fit the tight project schedule of the Telecom project, teachers have to severely curtail their programme for the language course. In the Cable-School project, teachers are supposed to share and exchange worksheets but they are not treated as central actors. They are not consulted on system development, neither are they part of the strategic forum. The strategic actors themselves tend to lose interest once the basic technical infrastructure is in place (e.g. Cable-School and Telepoly).

Thus, the influence of the operational domain of teaching on the strategic domain of decision making is modest – to say the least. Teachers are assigned a marginal role in the examples discussed above, which contrasts strongly with their actual and potential role as users of multimedia and as producers of multimedia uses (e.g. Egyedi, chapter 9). More will be said about the pivotal role of teachers in chapter 13.

What Learners Learn and How

As noted, pedagogy is not a main issue in most projects. Educational content and style of teaching are subjugated to the technical medium. Students and pupils are targeted as end-users of multimedia rather than learners (– or in the Cable-School case: as end-users rather than teachers). This makes the educational setting in which multimedia is used less relevant. Implicitly, the projects focus on 'learning about multimedia' instead of 'learning with multimedia', which is the more ambitious aim. It is the latter area, on the translation of multimedia into an educational tool, something on which policy makers seem to have no grip.

So, the end-user learns how to handle the multimedia application or the nature of mediated communication. If this is indeed the primary focus of multimedia projects in education, there is no need to situate the projects in an educational setting. Then, other learning environments such as the home, the work environment, the cybercafe and the public sector are equally informative settings (e.g. Van Bastelaer *et al* 2000; McBride 1988; Williams *et al* 2000).

One of the chapters in this volume focuses on the way a group of teenagers (computer-fascinated girls) learns how to use computers (Nordli). Their school is just one of settings of learning. The study demonstrates the importance of the home environment. The girls have access to the family computer. They learn to handle it as a multimedia machine and develop a liking for it through leisure activities. Pre-school learning starts in an unorganised manner with games, asking parents and trial and error. The Internet is first used as a hobby. Its use develops to collecting information for homework, communication (chatting and sometimes e-mail), and designing own homepages. Only at a later stage do they receive computer training at school. In this study, the person of the user-learner is the unit of analysis. The person's social identity as a girl, a pupil etc., partly defines her uses. Her home use of computers is also an aspect of her identity. By centring on user characteristics as the unit of analysis, and not on the setting of use, the pedagogy of 'learning about ICT' becomes a less prominent issue. (Egyedi, chapter 11, speaks in this respect of the 'context of the user' versus the 'context of use'.) Not the teaching strategies, but the learner's strategies are of interest, and the latter are not tied to a specific setting. Within this perspective, Aune's categorisation of home users and learning strategies are important (Aune 1996; see Nordli, this volume). Her categories apply to the home setting as well as the school setting, and could be applied to, for example, the cybercafe setting as well.

But let us turn from education as a 'diffuse societal phenomenon' to the 'formal institutional setting'. Nordli's study of the influences that contribute towards computer fascination shows that multimedia content (for example, pictures of pop stars) is an important vehicle for acquiring multimedia skills. This brings us back to the problem of the educational context and content of multimedia projects in the education setting. Even if the scope of an educational project boils down to 'learning about multimedia', then too, a didactic presentation of its content remains important to reinforce use and develop user skills. For example, the students interviewed by Egyedi (chapter 11, this volume) all had a fairly positive attitude towards the Internet when they started using it – as Eurelings notes, this is a common occurrence with new media. But three out of four were disillusioned with the information they could find, and have stopped surfing out of curiosity. Likewise, the teachers in the Cable-School project (shared worksheets on the web-server) did not use the common worksheets in their classroom, because they had little added value (Slack, this volume). In contrast, for the students who studied telecommunication, the ATM experiment in Telepoly had immediate relevance for their studies (Rossel & Buser, this volume). The functioning of multimedia was, as it were, part of the course subject. For them even technical breakdowns were interesting. Such examples indicate that medium content, next to the students' learning strategies, largely determines if appropriation of multimedia use takes place and how.

Conclusion

Certain features of the educational and project setting limit the possibility of integrating multimedia in education and 'learn with multimedia'. Hawkridge (1983: 217) correctly predicted lack of money. The case-studies also point to: the lack of pedagogic aims in projects, the primacy of technical objectives, time constraints, institutional incentives for verification experiments and technical feasibility trials, lack of attention to multimedia content, and the marginalisation of teachers in projects. Overall, teachers receive little support. Commercial interests and the politics of strategic stakeholders override pedagogic concerns of teachers. Limited funding does not allow for teacher training. Most teacher-evangelists contribute in their leisure time. Within these constraints, multimedia uses develop.

Policy developers tend to focus on formal education and treat it as a semi-commercial market. A shift in this perspective is warranted, for learning occurs in other settings as well. Thus, education is also to be understood as a diffuse societal phenomenon. Pedagogical trends and the dissolving boundaries of formal education suggest a policy framework which is not restricted to the formal education setting and teaching strategies, but focuses instead on learning strategies, regardless of the setting in which the learner learns.

Notes

1   These findings are largely in accord with those of, for example, the ELECTRA projects (EU-funded projects that concern ICT use in education and took place in 1997). See Eurelings e.a. 1998.
2   We will not go into the rhetorical question, which may come to mind how well defined educational practices are apart from multimedia.

13 Multimedia Innofusion

TINEKE M. EGYEDI, MARC VAN LIESHOUT,
WIEBE E. BIJKER

Abstract

This chapter examines processes of multimedia innofusion. It focuses on mechanisms that promise to lead to a more widespread, innovative use of multimedia in education. First, the concepts of appropriation, configuration and translation are specified. These concepts are then applied to the cases discussed in Part II. The analysis shows that, although the overall degree of innofusion is modest, there are various ways in which it may take place. The findings illustrate, for example, that innofusion occurs along lines of multimedia production as well as multimedia use. Further, the authors make a distinction between mechanisms intrinsic and extrinsic to the immediate setting of multimedia use that propel innofusion. This distinction points to ways in which the uptake of multimedia in education can be improved.

Introduction

There is a general feeling that multimedia has much to offer but that it is used too little. The diffusion of multimedia uses is slow and the manner in which it is used shows little innovation (Eurelings, this volume). The term 'innofusion', introduced in chapter 3, captures both these aspects. In order to further multimedia innofusion in the field of education, attempts are made to raise the educator's awareness. A multitude of private and government-funded projects takes place. Internationally, experiences are documented and disseminated. The propagation of multimedia practices is considered to be essential for innofusion. For example, European Union projects must indicate in what way their results are transferable to other educational settings. This emphasis on transferable results would seem to be a good strategy for spreading multimedia use in education. Why, then, is the outcome disappointing? Is it that project experiences and results are not so easily transferable? Is it that processes of innofusion and social learning do not proceed along the paths laid down in government policies?

In what manner can innofusion of multimedia in education be encouraged? To answer this question, we need to understand the processes of sociotechnical change concerned and increase our insight in mechanisms that drive innofusion. Little is known about this area. Theory is scarce, and case studies that clearly illustrate innofusion processes are few. Both are required to deepen our insight. In this chapter we first develop a conceptual framework that highlights instances of innofusion. Specific innofusion processes are focused on: appropriation, translation and configuration processes. Each sets off a different aspect of multimedia innofusion. The framework is applied to the cases. (For an overview of the main features of the cases presented in Part II, see table 12.1.) Next, we turn to mechanisms that drive and hamper innofusion.

Conceptual Framework

The term 'innofusion' refers to continued innovation during technology diffusion (Fleck 1988). In chapter 3 we breakdown the notion of innofusion into three complementary concepts. The first is *appropriation,* a concept that refers to processes that lead to material, cognitive and institutional ownership of multimedia. The second is *configuration*, and refers to constraints of multimedia on user behaviour. The third is *translation*, and draws attention to ongoing processes of sociotechnical change. Together they clarify different aspects of innofusion. That is, the same phenomenon may give rise to three complementary interpretations. See Box 13.1.

The three concepts are interrelated. The focus in appropriation processes is on change at the *recipient's* end (i.e. on the actor who undergoes change). The concept of configuration focuses on change at the end of the *'sender'* (i.e. the actor who tries to impose certain behaviour). The translation perspective focuses on changes brought about by the *'intervener'* (i.e. the actor initiating change in on-going processes; in some cases this actor may also be sender or recipient). Each perspective emphasises different actors and actor roles in the innofusion process, corresponding to a different vantage point in time (see Figure 13.1). The notion of configuration focuses on change that is meant to follow from the design of the artefact (i.e. the inscription process) at time t1. The *prospect* of change is central. The notion of translation focuses on *ongoing* changes, namely on the social shaping that takes place between t1 and t2. The notion of appropriation takes a *retrospect* view on change. For example, given the current situation (t2), to what degree has multimedia been appropriated (since t1)?

Figure 13.1 The time perspective (t) of the concepts of configuration, translation and appropriation

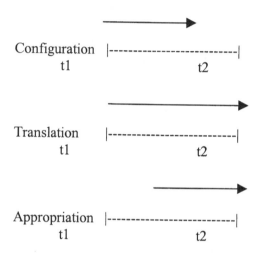

If one looks at 'multimedia in education' in terms of a market, on the face of it the three perspectives neatly address the players in the market. Configuration takes place on the side of multimedia producers; appropriation occurs on the side of the users; and the perspective of translation covers the activities of intermediate users like project managers, who adapt multimedia to fit the context of use. They are complementary in respect to the actor constituencies on which they focus. But a categorisation along the *user - producer dimension* of innofusion oversimplifies matters. The concept of innofusion already warns us against assigning the processes of innovation and diffusion to specific phases, actors and loci (see also chapter 3). Therefore caution must be exerted in the way the user-producer dimension is applied. The distinction between users and producers may well need to be reviewed, if – as the concept of innofusion implies – users are also a source of multimedia innovation.[1] In the following we will determine whether this is the case.

Box 13.1   Innofusion analysis of Telepoly

Lecturing is an effective way to disseminate information to large groups of students. A pedagogical consideration that petitions for face-to-face lectures instead of, for example, a written course, is that students process information better if they have the possibility to interact with teachers. Face-to-face interaction is mimicked in the Telepoly distance teaching project by two-way audio and visual channels. Furthermore, electronic documents and the use of broadcasted blackboard/whiteboard substitute the paper course books and the use of the blackboard, respectively.

In Telepoly, selective substitution characterises the translation of face-to-face lecturing to distance teaching. The system design is based on the idea that teaching consists of communication between teachers and students. The translation is restricted to the physical properties of communication, that is, to communication of sound and vision. From this point of view, if the system allows interaction between students and teachers, the system is a success.

But the system changes the teaching environment in a way that also affects teacher-student interactions. The design constrains their behaviour and, as such, configures the education process. For example, the students at the virtual site hesitate to come forward and pose a question to the lecturer via the shared microphone. They filter their questions more carefully. In addition, the camera angle determines their view of the 'real' site, which affects eye-to-eye contact between teachers and students. The students at the 'real' site, on the other hand, postpone their questions until after the lecture because they feel that 'virtual site' students need the broadcasting time. In other words, the multimedia system leads to unwanted configuration of the education setting.

To minimise the differences between face-to-face interaction and mediated interaction, the most malleable element in the mediated setting must adapt (see also Mourik, this volume). In the Telepoly case, the teacher is the most likely person to compensate for a lack of interaction. Two of the lecturers do this successfully. They appropriate the media in a way that helps to enhance their teaching (e.g. they adapt by slowing down their speech, addressing the camera, and by providing additional demonstration material on the Internet). They create a learning environment that localises the media and partly turns the tables with regard to the determinant of the teaching situation. But their less successful colleague lecturers are, as it were, extensions of the technical system instead of vice versa.

Innofusion of Telepoly's multimedia practice cannot proceed without first addressing a number of problems. Analysed from the angle of 'translation', we see that a pure communication approach to distance teaching does not suffice. It does not take account of local circumstances. The angle of 'configuration' illustrates how infrastructure design may lead to decreased interaction between students and teachers. This is likely to hamper future diffusion of this particular multimedia set-up. The 'appropriation' angle exemplifies the process of local adjustment to multimedia, and the educational innovations which the disparity between technical design and local setting may give rise to.

In respect to the object of innofusion, multimedia, our analysis is not restricted to the technology at stake. Such a restriction would bypass many of the social mechanisms that underpin innofusion. Moreover, the social shaping approach pursued here emphasises how strongly the technological artefact is embedded. Therefore, we take multimedia to comprise, next to multimedia technologies, developments in technological content, contexts of use, multimedia practices, multimedia projects and, on a more general level, meanings of multimedia. All of these elements play a part in multimedia innofusion.

Appropriation

'Appropriation' refers to multimedia 'ownership'. For example, in the process of acquiring multimedia skills the individual user becomes the 'owner' of these skills. During the multimedia project, the project and the organisation mutually adapt. An equilibrium develops in which the project acquires a certain position within the organisation. The organisation becomes, as it were, the 'owner' of a specific multimedia project and of the multimedia practice concerned. This practice may become exemplary and find followers outside of the organisation. The network of actors, within which the organisation operates, can thus become the 'owner' of a multimedia practice that originated elsewhere.

The degree of 'ownership', or appropriation as we will henceforth call it, is relevant to multimedia innofusion, firstly, because it indicates the degree to which multimedia has had an impact on actors and educational processes. That is, it says a great deal about the effectiveness of the previous diffusion process. It may provide clues for improving the nature of multimedia diffusion. Secondly, it indicates the degree to which uses and practices have become stable. Since stable practices are a constant potential source for spreading multimedia uses, the degree of appropriation says something about the likelihood that such practices will have their own innofusion impact on their educational environment.

There are two dimensions that help identify signs of appropriation. The first is the degree to which sociotechnical change has materialised. Examples are changes in a project's problem definition, the development of new organisational rules on multimedia use, and adaptations to the technical configuration. The second dimension concerns the degree to which change was focused, that is, whether the change was of an isolated, local nature or more diffuse. For example, a change in project objectives may indicate appropriation by the project group. If multimedia is very much embedded in a wider system, a change in project objectives indicates sooner organisational appropriation. These two dimensions are used below to categorise and compare the different forms of appropriation described in the cases. The section is structured according to actor level: end-users, educational locus and institutional setting, respectively. Box 13.2 summarises the main forms of appropriation.

Forms of Appropriation

Salient is that, overall, *end users* have little difficulty using multimedia. Students and teachers may have initial problems and be frustrated by the technology but they soon learn how to adapt to and handle it. The stage where "technology is adapted to everyday life" and vice versa is called *domestication* (Aune 1996: 93). In some cases new uses develop. Multimedia may be used in unforeseen ways (e.g. in the Telecom course the children played tricks on the teacher with the sound-responsive camera). Or the way users handle multimedia content can be innovative (e.g. the way students visualised their research findings in hypertext structures the IMMICS project). In some cases, multimedia use becomes trivial. This paves the way for more diverse uses of multimedia (e.g. designing homepages in the Girls & multimedia case). Diversification of use is sometimes an integral part of the project (IMMICS). More often it is a spin-off of the project (e.g. individual e-mail use by teachers in the Cable-School project). The cases show two special forms of diversification. In the Girls & multimedia case the computer is also used for personal and intimate matters (e.g. electronic diary) – that is, 'personalisation' of computer uses. The second, related form of diversification is its use for leisure activity ('entertainment'). Examples are using the school's computer lab during off-school hours (Girls & multimedia) and playing with the multimedia facilities of the language course (Telecom course).

The degree to which multimedia is appropriated by *the educational setting* differs. In most cases pedagogical and educational integration is marginal, as was noted in chapter 12. It requires, for example, special adaptation of the physical learning environment (e.g. higher chairs in Telecom course; development of multimedia lab in IMMICS); special preparation of teaching material and a different style of teaching (e.g. Telecom course, Bornholm and Telepoly); a different manner of evaluating learning (e.g. new rules for evaluating computer-based documents in Girls

& multimedia and IMMICS); and a change in educational culture (Cable-School). In all projects a continuous adaptation and refinement of the technological set-up and project objectives take place. Adaptations are often introduced ad hoc. They are immediate answers to unforeseen mismatches between multimedia and its setting of use. The adaptations may not suffice. For example, despite adaptations the technical system seriously hampered learning in the Bornholm case.

Box 13.2   Forms of multimedia appropriation

* Material ownership

End-user appropriation
* Domestication
* Trivialisation of use
* New uses
* Diversification of use
          Personalisation
          Entertainment

Educational appropriation
* Physical localisation
* Adaptation of teaching (e.g. style and material)
* Pedagogical integration

Institutional appropriation
* Management support
* Multimedia facilities (crystallisation points)

Actor network appropriation
* Cumulative appropriation

To a certain extent, all educational settings localise multimedia and appropriate it. One of the more pronounced examples of localisation is IMMICS. Here a text-based system is used for visual media, and hypertext is used to learn non-linear research. IMMICS is an example of innovative multimedia use. It is innovative use of software in education. But this is not the same as pedagogical innovation. What is conspicuously lacking in all the cases is the use of technology in a way that sets off a preferred didactic approach. In cases where teachers voice pedagogical concerns, their attempts are curtailed by funding organisations (e.g. government in the

Bornholm case, and technology providers in the Telecom course and Cable-School project), and they do not have the power to change matters (e.g. because of a shift in power from educators to technical operators, Telepoly). In the projects, the procurement of computers and infrastructural facilities (i.e. material ownership) overrides educational concerns (i.e. cognitive ownership).

The degree to which *institutional appropriation* of multimedia takes place varies strongly. It largely depends on the attitude of higher management. Where higher management supports the project or the teachers involved in multimedia, institutional appropriation benefits (e.g. IMMICS). Where support for it is lacking, wider use within institutions is limited (e.g. Telepoly and Cable-School). Wider multimedia use also depends on *material crystallisation points* (Egyedi, chapter 9, this volume): once a temporary provision such as a virtual classroom becomes a permanent provision, its use is likely to outlive the duration of the project. The Bornholm case confirms this: although, in retrospect, investments in distance-teaching facilities turn out to be more expensive than sending a teacher, the costs have been made and distance teaching continues. Another example is the build up of a multimedia lab in IMMICS. These are semi-permanent manifestations of institutional appropriation of multimedia.

A last category of appropriation discussed here is one in which actors in the *actor network* benefit from the experiences of other actors. Some multimedia projects build on earlier projects (e.g. Telepoly). Often, new actors get involved along the way (e.g. new schools in Cable-School). Sometimes the experiences of the project group are applied to new markets (e.g. Cable-School). In EU projects, partners exchange project experiences (e.g. IMMICS). In these examples, appropriation takes place in a cumulative manner by overlapping actor constituencies of parallel and successive projects. This is a form of *social learning* and can be an important vehicle for diffusion of multimedia use in education. But, as was noted in the introduction, the results have not lived up to expectations.

Appropriation and Innofusion

At all levels, a higher degree of appropriation increases the possibility of multimedia innofusion. Acquiring multimedia skills is relatively unproblematic. In order to lead to the innofusion of individual multimedia uses, the multimedia content must be worthwhile (chapter 12). Some end-users, such as teachers, are also producers of multimedia practices. These intermediaries are crucial for localising multimedia, demonstrating and advertising its added value for education, and innofusing multimedia practices in education. But in most projects the conditions required to exploit their role of intermediary are not met. Localisation of multimedia uses is marginal. Overall, it occurs too ad hoc and shows too little pedagogical integration to provide a stable basis for innofusion.

Currently, innofusion strategies of governments mainly focus on exchanging multimedia experiences between organisations (actor-network level). They stimulate more projects, not better projects. A focus on institution-wide appropriation of multimedia practices promises to be a more effective strategy, in particular if these practices and projects centre on pedagogical integration of multimedia. The insight gained by such projects and their effect on the intra-institutional innofusion of multimedia practices is a stepping-stone for diffusing multimedia practices education-wide.

Translation

The term 'translation' refers to the transformation of a situation, an artefact, a problem definition etc. from one state to another. It is a change brought about by or attributable to an individual, a group, an institution or an actor network. We focus here on the way meanings are redefined. There is some overlap between the translation and the appropriation perspective, since each appropriation process also involves a degree of translation. Limited educational appropriation of multimedia can, for example, be interpreted as insufficient attention being paid to translating off-the-shelf multimedia technology to a specific context of use. From the vantage point of 'translation', this is understood in terms of insufficient influence of teachers and instructional designers as intermediary translators in multimedia projects. Most translations that occur during projects are ad hoc translations. See Box 13.3. These are short-term responses to immediate pressure from inside or outside the project. Below, we highlight the influence of more strategic translations on multimedia innofusion in education. We focus on the influence of long-term translations (at actor-network level) on short-term translations (at project level).

Box 13.3   Examples of ad hoc local translations

- The technology infrastructure in the Telecom course changes from a decentralised system to a centrally controlled system and, on a more abstract level, from an adults' system to a children's system.
- The teachers in the Cable-School project redefine the project aims in terms of their own situation. Instead of reaping the fruits of the electronic exchange of worksheets with other teachers, they feel that putting their course material on the web makes them more vulnerable to the criticism of colleagues and parents.
- The symmetrical set-up of distance teaching in the Bornholm case changes to an asymmetric distribution of education between institutes.
- In the Girls & multimedia case, the girls' perception of other computer users changes; first, the latter are thought of as individualistic people, later they are viewed as sociable people.
- User requirements in the Telecom course shift from spontaneous to disciplined children.
- Technical support for the IMMICS project evolves from external to in-house faculty support.
- The institutional locus of the project changes from a faculty-wide activity to a course (IMMICS) and from a self-regulating project to a dependent project (Telepoly).

Long- and Short-Term Translations

Different kinds of long-term translations affect the multimedia projects. Some are based on technological change; others involve, for example, changed ideas about teaching and learning. Some translations involve perceptions that are shared society-wide; others concern changed views in a specific actor network. If these views are held by important people or become more widely accepted, they exert pressure towards conformity. Multimedia projects are expected to take these long-term views into account.

A society-wide translation, for example, is the shifted meaning of the computer from a calculator and a text processor to a multimedia processor, and from a stand-alone to a networked device. All our cases take account of these developments in one way or another. The relevance of networked devices is prominent in projects for distance teaching and the networked use of common educational resources (Telecom course, Telepoly, Bornholm, Cable-School). The overall perception is that electronic networks reduce both distance and location of the educational service to negligible variables. Indeed, the impetus of these projects is based on the supposed insignificance of the locality, and the competition between educational institutions to which this is expected to lead. However, the distance-teaching projects show that geographical location and accompanying organisational, technical and cultural differences remain significant. In the projects, they lead to different kinds of asymmetries between participants and institutions (e.g. Bornholm, Telecom course, Telepoly, Cable-School). Thus, although the long-term translation towards a networked set-up of educational provisions has strongly shaped some project designs, experiences contest the underlying assumption that networking provides equal opportunities to co-operating institutions.

Eurelings mentions trends in the field of education, long-term translations of a pedagogical nature, that are widely endorsed (chapter 2, this volume). Examples are the shift from teacher-oriented to student-oriented learning and, related to this, from a collective to an individualised and flexible learning environment. Whether these issues play a role in projects depends on whether the actor network linked to the project pursues such educational issues. In most cases it does not (e.g. Bornholm). But it does play a prominent role, for example, during final stage of the Telepoly project. Here, the actor network consists of parties who are to evaluate the project. The Telepoly project starts out with a techno-economic focus, which, at the time, draws few comments. During the project the constituency of the actor network changes, however, and pedagogical issues acquire more emphasis. In the final stage, the evaluators criticise Telepoly for providing real-time distance teaching; in retrospect, they would have preferred the participating institutions to provide flexibility with regard to the moment that students take their courses. In other words, Telepoly's actor network is first caught up in the technological promise of multimedia, and later in pedagogical translations of technology. Its influence on the project is inconsistent. Inconsistency also shows up in other projects (e.g. IMMICS). Innofusion of educational multimedia would benefit if actor networks would consistently prioritise pedagogical considerations.

Translation and Innofusion

Strategic and operational actors, education-oriented actors included, share their belief in the value of technology. They share a technology-oriented frame of mind. Technology-based views strongly affect the design of multimedia projects in education. Most projects are founded on such views.

The danger is that these views become paradigmatic and that signs of mismatches with educational praxis are not recognised. Many of the problems encountered in projects can be interpreted as one-sided technological translations of educational practices. The consequence is that multimedia innofusion will proceed along technological paths rather than education-specific areas of application. Where diffusion occurs, diffusion of technology without pedagogy appears to be the rule.

Configuration

'User configuration' refers to the way technology shapes user behaviour. It does so by means of behavioural scripts. These scripts are embedded in the technological design. They are based on the designer's model of the user. Configuration refers to the constraints on multimedia use that follow from the way the multimedia products are designed (producer domain) and then combined and adapted to suit local requirements (user domain, i.e. users as co-producers of multimedia). Technological constraints are usually difficult to overcome. They are 'hard' compared to, for example, teacher instructions about multimedia use during a course. Most of the constraints on multimedia use that are part of the educational design are malleable in the sense that they are more easily changed. We refer to these as 'soft' constraints. User configuration can thus ensue from the technology (technological design), its educational setting (localised design), and the educational practice that develops around multimedia use (process of use). The scripts that affect user behaviour may be implicit or explicit; they may materialise in a technological or social design (e.g. user procedures); and they may invite or compel compliant user behaviour (i.e. represent soft or hard constraints). Box 13.4 contains examples of constraints on user behaviour.

User Models and Models of Use

Sometimes the designer's model of the user remains implicit: the design does not force compliant user behaviour. Examples are the 'collaborative teacher' model in the Cable-School project, and the 'adult user' set-up of the Telecom course, where the model of the user and user behaviour diverge. Usually, such divergence is unwelcome and because it may endanger the project's progress, additional constraints are invoked. In the Telecom course, for example, teacher control over the children's behaviour is increased by technical means. Most projects cannot accommodate divergent behaviour. There is no room to experiment with multimedia. IMMICS is an exception in this respect. In this project, students are encouraged to overcome the constraints of the hypertext programme and experiment with new uses. This project further demonstrates that conflicts may arise between user models in the technological and educational design. For example, the hypertext software is not designed to incorporate visual data, whereas the use of visual data is essential in the course. As Egyedi argues in chapter 9, more research is needed to determine whether such conflicts are a source of innovative multimedia use.

Technology-based models of multimedia use depart from the assumption that the technology is unproblematic and that it works. Praxis shows that there are always problems, and that teachers and students must adapt their behaviour to compensate for technical failings. Exceptions aside, models for teaching and learning with multimedia are the same as those in settings where no multimedia is used. No separate scenarios are elaborated for teaching and learning with multimedia.

Box 13.4   Examples of configuration: 'Hard' and 'soft' constraints.

- A number of children in the Telecom course cannot get an ISDN-connection, which prevents their participation in the course.
- The hypertext application used in IMMICS forces students to cope with the research material in a certain way.
- With regard to multimedia content, the male gender model embedded in many computer games keeps female users at bay (Girls & multimedia).
- In the Bornholm distance-teaching set-up, student and teacher behaviour is configured to fill the gaps and connect the loose ends of the technical system.
- EU requirements for funding projects encourage technically oriented projects (chapter 12).
- The broadcasting nature of Telepoly's distance teaching 'softly' configures teachers to behave as entertainers (i.e. television show as model of use).
- In the educational setting, the attitude and expectations of teachers trigger specific user behaviour (Girls & multimedia, IMMICS).
- In Telepoly a strong top-down belief in the success of the project prevents bottom-up hesitations from being expressed.
- Distance teaching requires more-disciplined students.

Configuration and Innofusion

Most of the cases address a multimedia project. The initial project proposals indicate how those involved expect multimedia to be used. The proposals promise innovative uses, that is, novel educational uses, and sometimes the diffusion of these uses. The cases show that expected multimedia uses are based on a mixture of abstract, unspecified scenarios of technology use and concrete educational scenarios. The latter are grafted on previous, 'non-multimedia' teaching experiences. This mixture leads to a modest degree of multimedia technology diffusion among those involved in the project; but it leads to very little educational localisation. Because technical configuration processes dominate, few innovative educational multimedia uses develop.

Mechanisms Driving Innofusion

Multimedia innofusion in education may be modest and primarily technically oriented, nevertheless, the cases indicate a number of possibilities for more widespread and education-oriented innofusion. Below, we examine the mechanisms that drive innofusion and appear to be generally applicable to other educational settings. We distinguish *extrinsic factors*, namely, those that lie outside the immediate sphere of influence of the actors concerned and represent external conditions for innofusion; and *intrinsic factors*, namely, those that drive innofusion from within (e.g. teacher and institution). The most salient factors are discussed. Others are summarised in Box 13.5.

Extrinsic Factors

An important drive to introduce multimedia is the fear of lagging behind internationally. It leads to the bundling of national efforts in the field of education. Countries are installing web-sites to diffuse experiences and teaching material (e.g. Swiss virtual campus, Norwegian School Net, UK National Grid). Aune & Sørensen (this volume) illustrate that such web-sites may address a wide audience, teachers and parents included. Moreover, multimedia can be a means to retain or improve the educational

---

Box 13.5   Examples of mechanisms driving innofusion.

• The fear of lagging behind and losing a 'share of the education market' spurs on multimedia innofusion at sector level.

• The call-for-tenders procedure is an effective way to 'innofuse' multimedia within and across organisations. It triggers teachers to mull about ways to incorporate multimedia in teaching (e.g. IMMICS).

• Teachers are crucial as intermediary users and producers of multimedia, and, as such, a driving force for multimedia innofusion.

• The support of strategic actors for multimedia initiatives facilitates intra-institutional innofusion (e.g. Telepoly, IMMICS, Teaching Transformed).

• Students play a modest intermediary role with regard to multimedia innofusion in formal education (e.g. vicarious learning, exemplars). They appear to play a larger role in other learning settings (e.g. the home environment).

• The manifest nature of and continuity inherent to material and educational crystallisation points (e.g. multimedia lab and curriculum, respectively) facilitate intra- and extra-institutional diffusion of multimedia practices.

• Multimedia content and pedagogic multimedia use (i.e. evident added value) are intrinsic drivers for innofusion, but are not exploited as such by policy makers.

---

institution's position as national and international competitors. The perception – or actual treatment – of education as a competitive market causes the spreading of multimedia uses (i.e. mostly unfocused multimedia uses). Furthermore, teachers and students view computer training as an asset. Many students believe that multimedia proficiency will improve their chances on the labour market. This 'demand-pull' leads to further diffusion of multimedia in education.

Intrinsic Factors

Eurelings mentions that most students like using new media. But for how long? Some students turn their back on the Internet because they are disappointed in the information they can find (Egyedi, chapter 11). In contrast, the information found on the Internet is one of the reasons why teenage girls like the Internet (Nordli, this volume). Thus, multimedia content can be a leverage for use. It may trigger other computer uses. For example, the teenage girls diversified their computer use from fun uses only to 'serious' uses too. The right content can thus be an intrinsic mechanism of multimedia diffusion within the same person. Likewise, the teachers in the Cable-School project may not have used multimedia much for collaboration, but they started using e-mail as a result of their acquaintance with it.

Two cases point to a high degree of intra-institutional multimedia innofusion (Rossel & Buser; Egyedi, chapter 9). The institution described by Rossel & Buser counts 30 individual multimedia initiatives and 5 major distance teaching projects. In Egyedi's study, intra-institutional innofusion is directly related to the initial phase of IMMICS. The project leads to several new multimedia supported courses and to the set up of a multimedia lab. The lab works as a material crystallisation point for the diffusion of multimedia uses. The curriculum, in which multimedia plays a significant role, can be understood as an educational crystallisation point. Both encourage diffusion of multimedia practices.

All the cases illustrate that multimedia innofusion – i.e. both innovation *and/or* diffusion – proceeds along lines of use and production. Individual teachers are crucial as intermediary users and intermediary producers of multimedia uses. The teachers' use of multimedia is a precondition for multimedia innofusion in education. Ultimately, teacher-entrepreneurs and the 'evangelism' of individual teachers are the source of innofusion (Slack, this volume). They are a driving force for multimedia innofusion – where they receive room to manoeuvre.

Conclusion

The net effect of multimedia policy on multimedia innofusion in the field of education is limited. The problem is not the lack of initiatives and projects. Indeed, the call-for-tenders procedure among and within institutions is an example of an effective means of triggering multimedia activity at all levels. It is one of the main extrinsic drivers for multimedia diffusion, second only to the fear of educational centres of lagging behind in multimedia developments and losing their 'market share' to competitors. But the criteria to sponsor these initiatives generally foster verification experiments, and not the diversification experiments which are needed to bring about innovative multimedia practices. The European Commission, for example, assesses project outcomes in terms of their transferability, a requirement that counteracts the urgent need to localise multimedia use and integrate it as part of the learning environment. Learning thrives on meaningful multimedia content, and not on the technical feasibility of the supportive infrastructure.

Multimedia innofusion proceeds along the lines of use and production. Teachers play a pivotal role as intermediary multimedia users *and* as producers of multimedia practices. At present, innofusion in formal education depends on the intrinsic drive of such intermediaries to use and localise multimedia.

Lastly, let us stand still by what should be 'innofused'. It is not our aim to promote the sales of multimedia equipment and services. Our aim is to contribute to 'learning about' and 'learning with' multimedia. We would like to see their useful application. This means the pedagogical use of multimedia.

Note

1   We thank Harro van Lente for pointing this out.

14 Social Learning in Educational Multimedia

MARC VAN LIESHOUT, TINEKE M. EGYEDI,
WIEBE E. BIJKER

Abstract

Many projects on educational multimedia do not live up to their expectations. Technology and education are apparently difficult to mix. Proposals to improve the present situation either reflect on the technological base or on the educational context. Social learning in multimedia offers an approach that combines both perspectives. Based on the reflexive character of contemporary processes of change, it entails two ideal-typical forms of social practices: the mode of experimentation and the mode of control. This chapter provides for an analysis of the cases presented in part 2, in terms of their match with either one or both modes. Control and experimental aspects are analysed, leading to various points on the spectrum between both ideal-types. Then, we shift perspective form analysis to a pro-active orientation: what do the projects contribute to notions about successful or failing practices? Though success is more attractive than failure, the analysis of practices that are perceived to have failed, render useful insights for constructing guidelines of best practices. Accepting exploratory settings that may lead to failure guides the establishment of good practices.

Introduction

Today's society is commonly referred to as a 'learning society'. This does not only refer to learning as such (in the sense of the school as a learning environment) but also to the reflexive construction of society Reflexive modernity gives rise to processes that we label 'social learning' (cf. Chapter 3). In this chapter we explore the concept of social learning in greater detail, on the basis of the cases that have been presented in Part II. We demonstrate that the concept contributes to improving our understanding of the dynamics of multimedia in education.

The two modes of social learning that were identified in chapter 3 are elaborated in more depth. The 'mode of experimentation' and the 'mode of control' address different societal practices. These modes are 'ideal-types'. In daily practice, a mix of both modes will be found. Analysing the projects that were studied in this volume enables a further clarification of the content of each of both modes. We then discuss the correlation between the modes of experimentation/control and successful or failing practices. First of all, we question whether any such correlation can be demonstrated, then we continue to discuss the content of the correlation. The final section discusses how the findings contribute to guidelines for establishing good practices of innofusing educational multimedia.

Social Learning in Educational Multimedia

In general, learning is perceived as a beneficial activity. It is better to know than to be ignorant, and the more knowledge the better. Social learning may in a similar – but intuitive – manner perceived as a beneficial learning of society. In relation to technology, one might point at the learning processes that society experiences in embedding technology in a social practice. Social learning seems to indicate progress: we have learnt which factors are important in the process of socio-technical change. In chapter 3, we discriminated between two 'kinds' of social learning. Firstly, social learning can be taken as analytical concept that enables a specific analysis of social practices. The peculiarities of the analysis follow contemporary social-shaping theories. Secondly, social learning can be granted the status of an action-oriented (or: pro-active) concept in which analysis and action go hand in hand. The latter relates to creating the situation as-we-would-want-it-to-be. This is no easy task, given the heterogeneity of the process of change. It also assumes knowledge of individual or institutional preferences with regard to the objectives to be realised.

It is our conviction that we should prevent a too quick and too automatic merging between the 'situation as it is' with the 'situation as we would want it to be'. So, we start with the analysis of how reflexivity is constituted in the cases under study without anticipating to final objectives to be realised. To address this analysis we elaborate the modes of experimentation and the mode of control in such a way that the reflexive aspects of the process of change come to the fore.

The Mode of Experimentation

The social-shaping approach of technology presumes that technology may be studied as a social phenomenon. The interpretation of the phenomenon changes over time and with the actors involved. To take the computer as an example, it may be clear that the interpretation of what the computer stands for has changed considerably over the years. From a machine that needed a room of considerable size and that was only accessible by the high priests of technology, it has changed into a processor that can be found everywhere at very modest cost. The interpretation of what a computer *is*, thus changed over time. It also varies with the actors involved. For the one it is an intelligent calculator, for the other it is a communicative device (Nordli, this volume, chapter 6). The societal role of the computer is, thus, never unambiguously defined. Its role is open to change, and whenever closure occurs, this may always be re-opened.

Instead of focusing on the technological artefact that gives rise to a specific socio-technical constellation (e.g. multimedia PCs), the socio-technical practice itself may serve as a starting point (e.g. the introduction of a multimedia PC in a classroom). In case of educational multimedia the seamless web around educational multimedia is formed by educational institutes, educators, local and national public authorities, students, their parents, private enterprises that develop educational multimedia, research institutes that research and evaluate the process of introduction of multimedia, etc.. It is not possible to delineate explicit boundaries around the web to indicate who are part of it and who are not. The network of relations and actors can only be constituted by following the actors involved and by interrogating their relations with other actors, i.e. by researching the meanings, interpretations, experiences, money, skills, etc. they exchange. This amalgam of interactions spans the socio-technical practice. It is difficult to predict the behaviour of the network by reference to some inner logic of the network. The network is heterogeneously constituted, and dependencies may change, thus affecting the course of events. On the other hand, not everything changes at once. Some patterns may evolve that constrain the kind of possible exchanges within the network. These patterns may determine the 'rules of the game', i.e. the rules that implicitly determine what is allowed and what is prohibited, or –

less stringently – what belongs to be accepted ways of acting and what are considered to be not or hardly accepted ways of acting.

The *mode of experimentation* is one such manifestation of the rules of the game. It represents a socio-technical practice that can be recognised according to a specified set of characteristics. These characteristics relate to a way of acting that takes the open-endedness and non-determinacy of the process of innofusion as a starting point. We do not strive to present a complete set of characteristics that constitutes this mode of experimentation. Above all, this mode functions as a heuristic device that guides our thinking about processes of social learning. We proceed in a rather pragmatic way: we offer good arguments for the following list of characteristics that – taken together – give rise to the mode of experimentation:

- open to change;
- permanent reflection on the process of change;
- absence of external objectives to be realised;
- minimum of boundaries and constraints;
- experimentation as normal mode of operating;
- open style of management.

Open to change The mode of experimentation identifies socio-technical practices that are principally open to change. This is not to say that these practices are rigorous promoters of change, but that the practice shows a benevolent attitude towards change. Change is not seen as something to be avoided, neither as something to be promoted for the sake of change itself. The attitude towards change may best be circumscribed as a 'laissez faire' attitude.

Permanent reflection on the process of change Within this 'laissez faire' attitude a variety of reflexive elements are present. The process of change is closely monitored and somehow fed back into the socio-technical practice. This implies a general awareness of 'what is going on', without however, the objective of steering or guiding the process of change in a pre-determined direction. It is not 'control' that is exercised, (see under) but mere observation. This implies that much of what is observed may go unnoticed and be without consequences.

Absence of external objectives to be realised Monitoring a process renders data. Depending on the context in which these data are interpreted, the information that is derived from the monitoring process is more or less valuable. The monitoring is meant to deliver information about how things are developing: are we still on schedule? are the objectives still within reach? should we intervene, and if so, how? In case of the mode of experimentation these kind of objectives – i.e. objectives that indicate the realisation of some or other final goal, for instance a product to be delivered – are absent. There is no definite end goal, no final objective waiting to be reached at the end of the project. The kind of objectives to be reached within the mode of experimentation are predominantly directed at process characteristics: is the practice still evolving in a way that is satisfactory for the participants; is it still open and non-constrained; does it still endorse and stimulate learning and experimenting?

Minimum of boundaries and constraints   In line with the absence of external and product-oriented objectives is the characteristic that constraints and boundaries are minimised: the innofusion process is as open as possible. There are no predetermined expectations. The 'laissez faire' attitude is complemented by an 'anything goes' approach. Experimenting means being able to go in whatever direction surfaces, or whatever challenges one imposes on oneself. The practice reconfigures itself according to the flow of events.

Exploratory experimentation   The mode of experimentation deserves its name because of the important role of experimentation within this mode. Here, experimentation is meant in a rather playful manner. It has the connotation of 'anything goes', 'playing around', and discovering 'what's in it?', in short, they are aimed at exploring the yet unknown. These are all very open and unconstrained aspects of experimenting. Most multimedia products allow for such a disposition towards the product to be taken in, and stimulate a 'learning by doing' approach. Multimedia products invite you to discover what they contain, how they are structured, what kind of information they entail, to explore them. The mode of experimentation is set up around these open characteristics of multimedia products. It proclaims strategies as 'learning by doing', 'learning by using', 'learning by trying', 'learning by mimicking' (Sørensen 1996), etc. as part of exploratory experimentation. Learning means acquiring skills and competencies in using the multimedia products and what can be done with them.

Open style of management   Finally, we argue that the mode of experimentation endorses a specific style of management. In a sense, since anything goes, no predetermined objectives have to be met, and your approach is as good as mine, the mode of experimentation is based on an open style of dealing with people. This is not to say that formal responsibility is shared amongst all participants. When we take educational institutes as an example, there is no reason to suggest that the mode of experimentation changes anything about the formal structure of the institute. In managing the innofusion process, however, the style of management takes the specifics of the experimental situation into account. It might collect data to be fed back into the innofusion process, but it does not control the flow of information. It also does not prescribe the way the innofusion process should evolve. It adopts a 'wait and see' attitude towards what is going on.

The Mode of Control

Having dealt with the mode of experimentation in an extensive way, we can restrict the discussion of its counterpart – the *mode of control* – by focusing on differences between both modes. The mode of control is – just like its counterpart – a crystallisation of 'rules of the game' that constitute a socio-technical practice. The practice under consideration can be recognised by a set of characteristics that take the goal-directness of the process of innofusion as a starting point. This is not to say that the goal to be reached is only defined in terms of output figures (like the number of people using an educational tool, the level of satisfaction reached, the number of applications used, the difference between expected and real uses). Objectives may also relate to manners of using, innovative forms of using etc. The main difference with the mode of experimentation is the structure of the practice under consideration. Much more attention is paid to supervising and controlling what is going on, with the explicit purpose of redirecting the course of events when a mismatch with the planned course occurs. As few aspects as possible should be left open and out of control.

The mode of control is identified by a number of characteristics. The following list is meant as pragmatic starting point for researching the cases presented in the preceding chapters on their contribution to social learning:

- semi-open to change;
- permanent reflection on the process of change;
- purposeful experimentation;

- explicit boundaries and constraints;
- control as normal mode of operation;
- hierarchical style of management.

Semi-open to change By this we mean that the practice is open towards change, but that, at the same time, this openness is constrained by the objectives that have to be met. Not all is possible, not all may happen, and not all situations are acceptable.

Permanent reflection of change The monitoring, surveillance and evaluation practices play an important role in this mode. They are meant to deliver timely information about how the innofusion process proceeds, and whether specific actions should be undertaken. Thus, the reflexive practices are not open-ended but are constrained by how they contribute to guiding and steering the process of change in pre-determined directions.

Purposeful experimentation The control structure that is part of the mode of control does not forbid experimentation as such. Experimentation within this mode bears the characteristics of purposeful experimentation. Based upon a pre-set notion of what situation should be realised, and how this situation should be realised, experimentation is meant to deliver information about the process of innofusion. The innofusion is directed at realising a set of predetermined objectives. Purposeful experimentation is often part of contemporary projects with educational multimedia, since they are generally aimed at introducing some specific practices of use.

Explicit boundaries and constraints The term 'control' has its roots in the verb 'contra-rotulare' that indicates the checking of two roles against each other (Beniger 1986, p. 8). So, it checks whether everything still proceeds as planned. A script must be followed that entails all practical information for the situational set-up, the checks and balances and the requirements that must be met in the end. Not 'anything goes'; freedom of acting exists within the boundaries and constraints that are indicated as the borderlines of the innofusion process. This binding of the innofusion process still leaves plenty of room for innovative practices to emerge, as long as they fit within the imposed boundaries and constraints.

Control as normal mode of operating The mode of control implies that control is part of daily practice. So, the reflexive practices themselves are also supervised, evaluated and monitored. There may be several layers of reflexive practices that all serve to monitor and check each other. In one of the studies in Part 2, for instance, as many as seven distinct layers of evaluation were discerned, surrounding one single project (Egyedi, this volume, chapter 9). Any system of checks and balances gives rise to adding another level of checks and balances to the pile already existing. There is not a 'natural' boundary for the amount of control layers that might be erected around a project. The kind of control structures may differ, as well as the way they are used. The only thing that needs to be guaranteed is the internal consistency between the various checks and balances, but this only implies another check or control procedure.

Hierarchical style of management Objectives have to be set, goals have to be defined, planning procedures have to be developed. All these aspects point in the direction of a clear command and control structure, in which lines of responsibility are clearly indicated and unambiguous. Of course, command and control may be dispersed over a variety of entities and actors. It need not be a centrally co-ordinated command and control structure. But even in case of a distributed chain of command and control, it must be clear who gets what kind of information, for what kind of purposes, from whom. This needs a certain kind of hierarchy in the management of the information flows, the evaluation of the flow events, and the decision about what to do if specific events occur.

Experimentation and Control in Practice

The projects that have been presented in part two of this volume cover a variety of initiatives and activities within educational settings. They are illustrations of how educational practices evolve around the introduction of multimedia. The sample of studies represents a variety of approaches of innofusion of educational multimedia. Five out of seven studies are project-based, i.e. they represent a usually time and space constrained activity that has a beginning and an end. The sixth study analyses the introduction of multimedia on three different levels: the policy-level (macro) the institutional level (meso) and the individual, teacher-oriented level (micro); the seventh one is a survey of attitudes and behaviour of a specific group of multimedia users: young girls fascinated by computers. In the following analysis the last study is only marginally discussed The analysis is focused on the five project-based studies, viz. the language course, Cable School,

Bornholm teleteaching, Telepoly and IMMICS and the review of the Norwegian situation.

Evaluation of Educational Practices

The mode of experimentation and the mode of control form each others antipodes. The presented characteristics of both modes have been combined in the five dimensions of the following scheme. This scheme enables a relative position of projects on a scale of experimentation vis-à-vis control. The scaling is not an absolute one. The respective positions serve mainly to indicate a qualitative judgement about the various projects. In figure 14.1 the various dimensions used for the qualitative analysis are presented.

Figure 14.1 Dimensions of mode of experimentation vis-à-vis mode of control

Mode of Experimentation	Dimension	Mode of Control
Open to change	-------- *dominant attitude* --------	Semi-open to change
Process oriented	-------- *goal/objective* --------	Product oriented
Absence of boundaries	-------- *environment* --------	Presence of boundaries
Exploratory experiment	-------- *mode of practice* -------	Purposeful experiment
Open, process-oriented	-------- *style of management* --------	Hierarchical, closed

The only dimension missing in the table is the permanent reflection on the process of change. Both modes show this permanent reflection, (as this is supposed to be one of the main characteristics of contemporary activities) but both differ on the focus of the reflection. These differences show up in the remaining dimensions, making the reflexive dimension by itself superfluous. In scaling the projects, we divided the line between two juxtaposing concepts in five units, ranging from "close to the one", via "indecisive", to "close to the other". Though the suggestion of a quantitative scaling of the respective projects is all too present, it is incorrect to assume an absolute balance between the projects. Figure 14.2 visualises the five dimensions of the mode of control versus the mode of experimentation. These are graphically portrayed as five axes. For example, one axis runs from 'semi-open to change' in the centre to 'open to change' at the outer end of the axis. In the figure the two ideal-typical modes of social learning are also represented: the mode of control in the middle and .the mode of experimentation at the outside. This manner of visualisation (i.e. centre-periphery) emphasises the mode of control be directed towards containment, with the mode of experimentation directed towards openness.

Figure 14.2 Presentation of the modes of control versus experimentation on the axes of the five project dimensions[1]

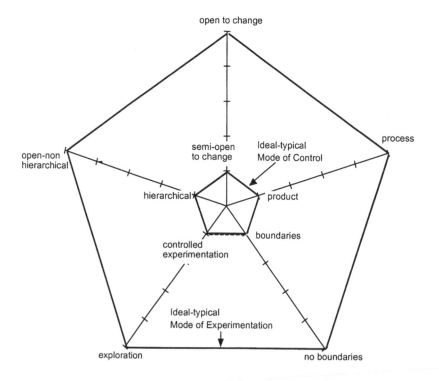

The Language Course

The language course is a clear illustration of the mode of control. In this case, social learning hints at the reflective practices in the sense of monitoring what is going on with the explicit purpose of redirecting any deviation from the (time-)schedule back to the final (and original) goal: presentation of the 'results' at the fair. But even in this case there are also illustrations of the mode of experimentation. The children are playful and spontaneous, a characteristic that originally led to the choice of children as the 'show' group. This exploratory behaviour of children led to annoyance on part of the management during the course. Educational aspects did not play a predominant role in this case. The mode of control is visible from the very beginning of the project to the very end of it. Technical control measures were needed to control social behaviour of the children. The whiteboard application was stripped and the teacher was provided with an "undo-delete" button. But these technical measures were combined with social ones: children and their family were forbidden to use the computers in ways that might damage the software (Mourik, this volume, chapter 4).

Figure 14.3 Language Course – "Controlled experimentation"

EXPERIMENTATION	Language Course	CONTROL
Open to change	•	Semi-open to change
Process oriented	•	Product oriented
Absence of boundaries	•	Presence of boundaries
Exploratory exp.	•	Purposeful exp.
Open, process oriented	•	Hierarchical, closed

An intriguing detail of this project is that it is the only project that really came to an end after its final date. As Mourik remarks: "From one day to the other there were no more lessons. For the children the end of the project came as a shock" (Mourik, p. 80). From the perspective of inno-fusion this is very unusual, and almost impossible. Since we deal with *socio*-technical practices, there is always something that resides after the official ending of the project. The fact that it proved possible to have this clear-cut ending of a project supports the interpretation of this case as a form of the mode of control. The project was not started from an educational objective. It was above all a validation of technical skills and proficiency on part of the company. Still, at least originally, the experiment had educational purposes as well. Mourik argues that these purposes were needed to bind the educational centre of the company and the teachers of the university to the objectives of the marketing division (MCD) that initiated the project. However, in the end, the teachers and the educational centre had sacrificed all their educational purposes on behalf of meeting the deadline of the fair. They took over the problem definition of the management. The same can be said of the technical evaluations, firstly performed by the hardware company MW, later by the data network technician. All evaluative practices – important from the perspective of social learning – were matched with the evaluative framework of the MCD. The MCD stayed in control from the very beginning to the very end of the project.

The Cable School

In this case the dynamics that surrounded the introduction of an educational network in the respective schools are indicated in a straightforward manner. In the beginning of the case description it is stated that there is a clear division "between the provision of technological infrastructure and pedagogic content. In some cases this has led users to generate their own content and to use the technology in potentially unanticipated ways". (Slack, this volume, chapter 5, p. 83). Within the Cable Schools, a mode of experimentation comes to the fore, mainly due to a shift in interests of the provider of the technological base (at the same time the facilitator of content to the network). Since the strategic importance of the educational network seemed to be fulfilled for the company after a while, interest in filling the educational space vanished. This left the educators on their own. Teachers performed their own evaluation of the possible uses of the network, and came to the conclusion that filling the database with worksheets might backfire on their own position. Since no incentives were provided for delivering worksheets, this hardly happened (except for the worksheets delivered by experts from the SCET – the Scottish Council of Educational Technologies).

Figure 14.4 Cable School – "Submissive experimentation"

EXPERIMENTATION	Cable School		CONTROL
Open to change	•		Semi-open to change
Process oriented		•	Product oriented
Absence of boundaries	•		Presence of boundaries
Exploratory exp.		•	Purposeful exp.
Open, process oriented		•	Hierarchical, closed

Interestingly, there are many clues in the description of the project that point in the direction of a free experimental environment for the project. Local authorities accepted the project as an experiment (Slack). Slack remarks that "the system became the focus of innovation initiated by individual teachers, usually in isolation" (Slack, p. 97). Even in managing the experiment, "meetings that did exist were used for the management of the system as an experiment" (Slack, p. 96). And it was hoped that a *de facto* standard for submitting documents would arise spontaneously (Slack). Within this free-floating space, a formal evaluative framework was absent. There were no formal deadlines to be met, no formal responsibilities that had to be dealt with, no agreed objectives. The socio-technical practice that was resurrected around the available infrastructure and on base of facilitated uses, can be characterised as a *submissive* practice: a playing ground to be used, an experimental setting with no other purpose than to experiment and wait to see where it would lead to. This was only possible due to how the most important strategic actors (the company, the board of schools, the local authorities) faced the experiment: it doesn't hurt to try.

Bornholm Teleteaching

The initiative to introduce teleteaching to the island of Bornholm was originally meant to contribute to an economic upheaval on the deprived region of Bornholm. Due to external deliberations, the initiative got a new twist: by connecting Bornholm to a number of mainland educational centres, inhabitants from the island did not have to leave the island anymore (only in one out of five initiated teleteaching courses was Bornholm the sender). This was to be realised by simply inserting a video-link between two locations, one at the sending institute, the other at the receiving institute. Technology was a mere substitution for the teacher at the receiving institute. Due to instability of the link (with the accompanying audio- and data-transmission) it forced the students at the receiving institute to become professional trouble-shooters. During meetings, when no professional assistance was provided (in the evening for instance), students had to take care of the connections themselves. Contrary to initial promises, the county of Bornholm did not supply extra finances for the experiment, which led to provisory and temporary facilities at Bornholm institutes (each time a teleteaching course was to be given, the connection had to be set up anew).

Figure 14.5 Bornholm teleteaching "Controlled experimentation"

EXPERIMENTATION	Bornholm	CONTROL
Open to change	•	Semi-open to change
Process oriented	•	Product oriented
Absence of boundaries	•	Presence of boundaries
Exploratory exp.	•	Purposeful exp.
Open, process-oriented	•	Hierarchical, closed

From the beginning, students and teachers at the receiving institutes, (mainly located at Bornholm) had indicated the need for a more encompassing approach of the teleteaching situation; they pleaded for a 'social room', implying that before and after teaching there should be opportunities for discussions and chats amongst students and teachers at receiving and sending institutes. Since all extra expenses had to be covered by the educational institutes themselves, no extras were provided during the trial. The evaluation afterwards shows that students at the island of Bornholm enjoyed the opportunity to follow courses on their own island but they complained about the lack of facilities and guidance offered by the sending and receiving institutes. The trial was taken too much as a simple substitution of teachers by technology. Attention was focused on technological aspects, but this was mainly due to the complete disregard for educational and pedagogical aspects. Teachers were not guided in what it meant to teach a virtual and a real classroom at the same time. Students discovered they had to behave in a strictly disciplined way in order to follow the teaching. It was suggested in the end that students should first pass a kind of disciplinary exam to see whether they could cope with the teleteaching situation. All these aspects contribute to a situation that does not provide for any room to play with and explore new and maybe unforeseen uses of the new setting. Especially the statements about the needed discipline for students show the Bornholm trial to be much on the side of controlled experimentation. The formal evaluation – that took almost as long as the trial itself – is another manifestation of the reflexive character of the entire trial in combination with an orientation to a controlled situation: were initial objectives met, yes or no? With respect to possibly financial benefits of teleteaching, it is interesting to note that the trial shows that displaced teaching is more expensive than sending a teacher.

Telepoly

Telepoly is embedded in an evaluative framework. Both initial contributors, EPFL and ETHZ, had their own evaluation team to accompany the distance teaching project. Evaluation of the project shows that educational aspects played a role from the beginning, but did not get much attention before the technical infrastructure was realised. It was not before the ATM-infrastructure was reasonably stable that the project got an educational twist. Given the original objective of the project, (researching cost-saving aspects of distance teaching) this may not have to be much of a surprise. With this shift in attention the experiment shifted from validating technical requirements into exploring/researching didactic consequences. Part of these didactic consequences were primarily related to the didactic of distance teaching. Part of it was related to the promise of establishing an a-synchronous learning environment. This was seen as an innovative and evolving new practice, that posed simultaneously didactic and technical challenges.

Figure 14.6 Telepoly – "Controlled experimentation"

EXPERIMENTATION	Telepoly	CONTROL
Open to change	•	Semi-open to change
Process oriented	•	Product oriented
Absence of boundaries	•	Presence of boundaries
Exploratory exp.	•	Purposeful exp.
Open, process oriented	•	Hierarchical, closed

With regard to the organisation of the reflection on the established socio-technical practice, it is interesting to note that the first uses of the ATM-infrastructure for distance teaching comprised a course on ATM. The reflective practice was built-in, and the technical and educational challenge were strictly in line. Later on, it proved to be difficult to convince teachers of other subjects to join in. For a part, motives that can also be found in the Cable School, played a role: "Telepoly was not really welcomed by many of the lecturers, as they feared losing their autonomy, being compared with their peers and even being replaced by a Telepoly broadcast from 'the other side'" (Rossel & Buser, this volume, chapter 10, p. 221). Since these actors were not included (or at least not sufficiently) in the innofusion process, they refused to co-operate. Due to the overall structure in which Telepoly is embedded, the mode of control dominates the project, though experimentation (in exploring new uses) surfaces every now and then. This exploratory use of Telepoly even leads to promises in the longer term (especially in respect to establishing an a-synchronous learning environment).

"IMMICS the Course"

In the organisation of IMMICS the course, the mode of experimentation is clearly visible. However, IMMICS also embeds aspects of the mode of control. The conflict that is sketched between the apparent absence of values on behalf of the teachers vis-à-vis the simultaneous expectations of the students about explicit norms with which their efforts should be rewarded is typical for an educational situation. The teachers refrain from value judgements about how the programme Storyspace should be used, but in the end they have to mark the results of the students. This implies an evaluative framework. This conflict, that became apparent during the course, can't be avoided in (institutionalised) education. It shows the ideal-typical form of the mode of experimentation in education to be problematic. Other factors contribute to the problem, like the time available – which is usually restricted in an educational setting – and the attitude of those involved towards experimentation (Egyedi, this volume, chapter 11). So, we can argue that the mode of control is indispensable in the innofusion of educational multimedia.

Figure 14.7 "IMMICS the course" – "Submissive experimentation"

EXPERIMENTATION	'IMMICS the course'	CONTROL
Open to change	•	Semi-open to change
Process oriented	•	Product oriented
Absence of boundaries	•	Presence of boundaries
Exploratory exp.	•	Purposeful exp.
Open, process-oriented	•	Hierarchical, closed

The mode of control invades the mode of experimentation when students themselves discover and develop norms and criteria for the use of Storyspace. Students sought for agreement about 'good practices'. They expected, more or less implicitly, that any practice could be scaled in terms of good, better, and best, and they were out to search the norms to apply. This became even more important when it showed that the teaching staff was reticent in making public a specific set of norms and values (convinced that there was no such set). Another interesting element within this case is the choice for a rather outdated multimedia application, which, one might argue, doesn't match contemporary standards. In this case, the focus was not on the most modern equipment, but on the use of an application that might serve educational purposes best. As Egyedi notices: "The latter illustrates that the use of Storyspace for non-linear research is problematic. The programme's lack of flexibility constrains the research approach." (Egyedi, p. 239). The choice for StorySpace was a deliberate one (though from a restricted set of possibilities). IMMICS represents one of the rare occasions in which the technological opportunities were balanced from the onset against the educational objectives.

Shifting attention to IMMICS as a project, sponsored by the EU as part of an on-going effort to research the introduction of ICT in a variety of educational setting at a few selected universities, the first thing to be noticed is the impressive amount of evaluative layers surrounding the entire project. First of all, this abundance of evaluative procedures underscores the reflexive attitude that was mentioned in chapter 3. IMMICS the project is a crystal-clear representation of the reflexive modernity we are experiencing today. Next to this, it also indicates the mode of control that is present within these projects. This is not much of a surprise, since any sponsor has a certain right to know what is happening with the resources that are invested. But, as Egyedi properly states, the mere presence of any evaluation procedure implies that contingent factors are at work, and that matters may turn out differently than planned. In essence, evaluation activities signify the acceptance of 'failure', provided lessons are learnt (Egyedi, this volume, chapter 9). But, at the same time, this longing for control may yield contradictory results, since some projects only flourish when left by themselves and have room to explore more than to validate preconceived ideas and notions.

The Norwegian Case: Teleteaching Transformed

The analysis of the Norwegian situation provides some interesting insights on how social learning may be embodied in policy documents and initiatives, and how this may be contrasted with the situation on the work floor itself. The various initiatives by the Ministry of Education aim at realising political/ideological objectives in line with overall Norwegian values: equal opportunities for young and old, girls and boys, rich and poor. In the case of multimedia (and ICT in general) this ideology is translated in educational objectives: learning *about* ICT must be evenly distributed throughout society. This ideology is simply imposed on the educational institutes, by providing, amongst other ways, a programme, an institute and initiatives to further the diffusion of governmental policy. The initiatives themselves (organised by the National Centre for Educational Resources) are also pretty much top-down structured. There is hardly any room for the institutes addressed to explore, experiment or diversify uses of new ICT. Though the institute is aware of interaction needs, the Schoolnet initiative is primarily an information-oriented medium that enables institutes to pick what they need. Exchange of experiences is organised as well, and is considered an important aspect of Schoolnet. Critical for the position of Schoolnet as being either part of the mode of control or part of the mode of experimentation, is in what sense the development of Schoolnet itself may be redirected due to influences from 'down under'. The entire approach fits pretty much in a top-down, hierarchically structured, rather closed process and thus gives rise to social learning in the mode of control.

The paper also discusses the way educational institutes themselves deal with new educational multimedia. Of course, schools vary in their approach. Some offer more space to experiment with the new technologies (aimed at both teachers and students), some are more restricted in how they use and diffuse multimedia within the schools. From the tales of the three schools that are presented it may be concluded that schools that offer the most flexibility in using computers (i.e. the school that offers PCs on wheels) are also the most profitable in exploring new uses *and* implementation of ICT and multimedia in educational settings. The mode of experimentation pops up in the most flexible schools, and this is correlated to the most beneficial uses of ICT/multimedia. Regarding the teachers, the paper differentiates between four different models: the traditional teacher, the lonely innovator, the supported enthusiast and the resistor. The most profitable – in terms of establishing a platform of change – is the supported enthusiast. As the examples given show, the lonely innovator may as well combine pedagogical and technological aspects of the process of change in his or her use of new educational multimedia, without much chance however, of getting his or her ideas implemented in a broader setting.

Conclusions

The six projects show different patterns of experimentation and control. The dimensions do not correlate to each other in a straightforward manner. Next to the two ideal-typical patterns, ('control' on all dimensions or 'experimentation' on all dimensions) all kinds of mixtures between both modes are present.

Figure 14.8 Visualisaton of all cases in one figure, showing the prominence of either the mode of control or the mode of experimentation in each case

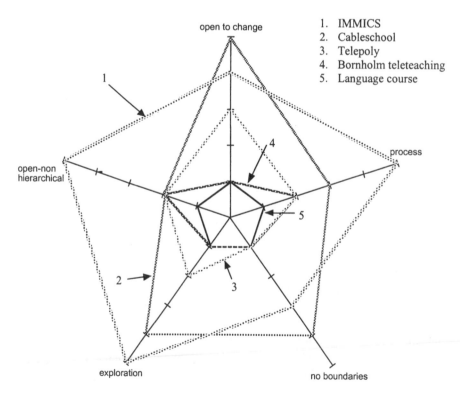

open to change

1. IMMICS
2. Cableschool
3. Telepoly
4. Bornholm teleteaching
5. Language course

open-non hierarchical

process

exploration

no boundaries

As we said before, the scaling seemingly implies an absolute evaluation of a project on the dimensions presented. This is difficult since, for instance, the scaling may vary during the project. We have presented the most dominant aspects of each project, in order to give an overall indication of the character of the respective projects.

Of all cases, IMMICS comes closest to the ideal-type of an experimental project, in which the control procedures are minimised. The educational purpose is to create a 'learning by doing' environment, in which students learn by experiencing what it means to use a flexible and adaptable multimedia tool. IMMICS has a self-reflective element: the course to which IMMICS belongs teaches students about the impact of various media; the tool to learn about this is 'multimedia'. The language course reflects best the ideal- type of a controlled project. Educational objectives were originally part of the problem definition of the project, but these were abandoned in favour of meeting a deadline. Priority was given to the technical lay-out of the project. The other cases, combine aspects of both modes, where Cable School lean towards to experimentation, Telepoly and Bornholm lean towards to control.

The 'laissez faire' approach within Cable School – as this is reflected by the fact that it is open to change, there are hardly any boundaries set on the project, and it has an exploratory setting as a mode of practice – suggests that Cable School has created an environment that is open to *learning by doing* and *learning by trying*. The style of management is, however, rather hierarchical and closed, which prohibits an institutionalised way of sharing what is learnt. The experimental setting that informally arose after the initiator of the project (the cable company) withdrew, did not include a reflexive layer that embeds what is learnt.

The structure of Telepoly is reflected in the presence of boundaries that determine what may be done within the project. Within these boundaries, Telepoly is rather open. During the project, the openness increased and allowed for exploring new and combined uses of the technological infrastructure. Due to its rather strict evaluative organisation, learning was guaranteed by the reports of the evaluation committees. In this reporting format (which is typical for a mode of control) institutionalised learning is postponed until the report has been published and subsequently debated. The informal learning (how to use the tools that are offered) goes on outside the formal evaluative framework. In the case of Telepoly, there was not much opportunity to embed this informal learning in the project.

The status of the Bornholm experiment is best reflected by the assumption that teleteaching could be realised by simply offering technical facilities as replacement for a real teacher. The original intentions of the Bornholm county officials, i.e. the realisation of Bornholm as knowledge and educational expertise centre, would have introduced many more instances of an experimental situation. By supplanting the teacher under the condition that no educational or pedagogical issues were at stake, the situation became much more directed towards the realisation of a technically stable infrastructure. As with Telepoly, this imposed demands on unqualified staff to become trouble-shooters. No feedback occurred that endorsed a change in this situation.

Finally, the Norwegian case, shows how policy documents can easily face an implicit control structure, even when the intention is different. The realisation of facilities for schools – without their clear and unconditioned support – would indicate a far more open approach – allowing for exploratory experimentation – than a top-down structured approach that still leaves space for exchange of experiences etc. With regard to the different styles of teaching, it is interesting to note how some teachers are able to start from pedagogical objectives and relate them to teaching material; these 'computer enthusiasts' might be more supported, by an open and exploratory setting.

The Success of Good Practices

The most important feature of a project is whether it may be conceived as a success or a failure. Has it lived up to its expectations or did it fall short? Did it deliver insights and experiences that were hoped for or did the results 'fade away' during the process? By attributing success or failure we must be aware however, that these are in the eyes of the believer. Success is constructed: actors declare an event to be successful, depending on their definition of the situation. Since the problem definition of actors may vary, so may their notion of success in a specific situation. Success, in other words, is not pre-given or unambiguously formulated, but is the result of a process of negotiation about success and failure. The same reasoning fits *mutatis mutandi* the notion of failure.

A second aspect must be added. In general 'successful ending of a project' hints at the fact that preconceived objectives have been met. Having delivered a successful project enhances the credibility of those who have performed the project. They have – apparently – been successful in controlling all external factors, they have kept the project on track to some extent. When it comes to projects that hinge on activities based on rather unproblematic knowledge, this may be a proper way to proceed. The implementation of an electronic network within an organisation while using off-the-shelf technologies, for instance, may be termed successful when it is delivered on time, according to the specifications that have been agreed upon. The (social) learning in this situation points at corroborating old knowledge in new situations. The added value of the experiment is, then, the fact that this practice is apparently comparable to other practices. When, on the contrary, the objectives are not met, new uncertainty has been created. New perspectives have to be added, the situation has to be thought through once more, and information is needed on why the experiment failed. This, in the end, might lead to a better understanding and to more intimate knowledge and more insight in the socio-technical constituency of which the experiment forms a part. Both aspects, i.e. corroborating the hoped-for results, or being forced to research new uncertainties due to non-corroboration, are results of (social) learning in the mode of control.

However, when it comes to projects that are meant to explore new avenues or to research new opportunities, uncertainty is a built-in characteristic of these projects. Criteria for success are more difficult to address. Instead of focusing on *output* one could focus on *process* aspects: did everybody contribute to exploring new uses and new situations, did new uses pop up, and if so, were they stimulating new practices of use, were new ideas developed, was the interaction between the participants stimulating and creative, etc. Within an exploratory setting, it is more difficult to be precise in advance about what constitutes success or failure.

Finally, since we are dealing with the introduction of multimedia in educational settings, actors may differ in their attribution of success and failure, depending on whether they concentrate on technology, the educational setting or a combination of the two. One and the same project may be successful in technological terms while being a failure in educational terms or vice versa. What remains to be explored is whether there is a correlation between success and failure, the mode of experimentation and control, and technology and education.

Successful Practices

In the studies presented in this volume it is difficult to draw demarcation lines between those projects that are broadly looked upon as successful and those that are generally judged as failures. First of all, we only have a small sample. Generalising over these few projects is quite impossible. Secondly, given the various grounds on which a project can be termed successful, one and the same project may be successful from one perspective and a failure from another one. In our sample, most projects show a manifold relationship with success and failure. We discuss some of them.

To start with, few of the studies report the project to be a success from an educational point of view. Given the fact that projects are directed at introducing educational multimedia in educational settings this may come as a surprise. There is an overall predisposition towards realising a technological infrastructure that might be conditional for teaching and learning. In the case of Cable School for instance, Slack reports that "Cable-School provided the information infrastructure, but its success would have depended on a change in the practices of teachers, in particular in making their teaching documents visible to other schools on the system." (Slack, this volume, chapter 5, p. 101). With regard to Telepoly it is mentioned that "The challenge was to make this ATM-network operational, not to create the perfect teaching environment, nor to build a new teleteaching concept." (Rossel & Buser, this volume, chapter 10, p. 220). In the Bornholm case, a similar focus can be found: "The main attention was devoted to make the video-technique and the data-transmission work." (Hansen & Clausen, this volume, chapter 7, p. 149). All three cases purport the presupposition that a technological infrastructure (electronic networks, communication protocols and the like) is prerequisite for teaching and learning. They also suggest that both can be disentangled: the creation of a technological infrastructure is a different kind of challenge than the creation of an adequate educational environment based on technological tools. There is no need to include deliberations about educational purposes in the design of a technological infrastructure. Bornholm, Cable School and Telepoly all represent a perspective on technology as a *generic, enabling tool*. Success means that the technological infrastructure is established according to a predetermined set of specifications. In case of Telepoly, establishing a stable ATM-link between two – and later three – centres was the original goal. Once this was realised, the technological challenge was fulfilled, and space was created for educational experimentation. In case of Cable School, the organisation and logistics of the server was of prime importance to the company that was vital to/a key component in the project. And in case of Bornholm, the aim was the realisation of a technological counterpart of an ordinary classroom situation.

Most projects we studied did not pay much attention to the educational problems they encountered. The only project that is termed successful from the perspective of educational objectives is IMMICS. Even in this project, success is not explicitly addressed but is presumed on the basis of the realisation of normal educational results (the course was successfully ended by the students; evaluation showed the positive and negative attributions of the course as these were perceived by the students; this is, however, part of normal practice within the institute that houses IMMICS). We might add that IMMICS is the only project in which success was not determined by the realisation of a new piece of technology. Technology (Storyspace as multimedia-programme to be used in the educational setting) was off-the-shelf technology that was only slightly moderated for use in the media-lab of the course. Educational objectives were predominant. Technology was only important in how it contributed to realising the educational objectives. As Egyedi states, in IMMICS the course was established as an open learning environment without pre-determined norms and values in respect to the use of educational multimedia within the course (the use of Storyspace). Egyedi phrases this as a deliberate attempt to postpone closure and to sustain interpretative flexibility. Her analysis shows that teachers were rather successful in postponing agreement about 'best practices', i.e. the hardening of a specific interpretation of the use of Storyspace (Egyedi, this voume, chapter 11). The cases of Bornholm and Telepoly show that teachers' attitude is the key to successfully using an electronic learning environment. Awareness for the needed shift in teaching style is prerequisite for the successful use of the medium. Some teachers were rather successful in adapting to the needs of the new medium, others were not. The new medium required a different style of addressing the public (it needed a 'broadcasting style'). Teachers differed in their opinion about the effect of the new technology on the quality of their teaching. They agreed about the importance of being aware of the new pedagogical constraints that were imposed by the technology. One teacher successfully integrated electronic documents in his course, thereby extending his course into an a-synchronous mode.

Success also depends on the 'definition of the situation'. Sometimes success is defined in *strategic* terms (creating successful conditions for realising new opportunities), sometimes in *operational* terms (having realised concrete objectives in a specific setting). The definition of success in strategic (as contrasted with operational) terms is clearly visible in the language course. The marketing department declared the project to be a success, because the department was successful in convincing headquarters that the project *was* a success. Besides the apparent self-reflexivity in this line of reasoning (some would say: the use of a circular style of argumentation), this definition of success is interesting since, as Mourik notes, all actors eventually shared the problem definition of the marketing department: "The reason for the attribution of 'success' to the multimedia network is that a closure occurred with regard to the interpretative flexibility in the project." (Mourik, this volume, chapter 4, p. 81). Within Telepoly, the interpretative flexibility to which Rossel and Buser refer, encompasses, amongst other things, the successful co-operation between culturally diverse institutes (the French-speaking EPFL and the German-speaking ETH Zürich). The fact that the decision to continue the experiment has been positively taken (though in a probably minimal format), is another indicator of the strategic success of the project. Within the Cable School the situation is more difficult to evaluate. On the one hand it seems as if the company has been rather successful in using the Cable School experiment for attracting attention and broadening their portfolio. On the other hand, the re-organisations that took place within the company might indicate a feeling of discomfort in this respect. Finally, IMMICS is successful in its development from a university project into a faculty course.

The definition of success in operational terms is more difficult to envisage in the studies. An exception is Telepoly where it is argued that the provision of a stable ATM-link between the adjacent educational centres was eventually successful, and where the information gathered during the project is seen as a worthwhile contribution to knowledge about the distance teaching concept. The definition of success relates to realising a stable (i.e. reliable) link. In Bornholm, success in operational terms is linked to the realisation of a technological counterpart of a classroom situation. This only was partially successful. And within 'IMMICS the course' the educational use of the created multimedia environment was also declared a success, at least in terms of fitting the course in a problem-based teaching and learning environment.

Contrary to Success: Failing Practices

Within all projects failure is as much part of the praxis as success. Just as success is in the eye of the believer, so is failure. What is termed a failure by the one, might be termed a success by another. The absence of success points at failure, the absence of failure points at success.

The studies show failure to be prominent when it comes to meeting educational objectives. In both Telepoly and the Cable School it is reported that the project failed to convince teachers that they should use the supplied infrastructure. In both projects teachers feared that the infrastructure might backfire on their autonomy as teacher; teachers also feared that the infrastructure might facilitate evaluations of their teaching skills by outsiders. Another kind of failure that is mentioned in Bornholm, Cable School and Telepoly alike, is the failure to teach teachers how to perform properly within the provided configuration. In case of Bornholm and Telepoly the problems relate to distance teaching skills that differ from teaching skills needed in an ordinary class situation. Only teachers who were aware of the prerequisites of the medium were able to present interesting lectures (Rossel & Buser, this volume, chapter 10). The absence of a virtual social space hindered students in feeling at ease in the distance classrooms (Hansen & Clausen, this volume, chapter 7). In both situations it was mainly left to the teachers to decide how they dealt with the new situation. No encompassing pedagogical framework was available to guide them in their teaching with the new medium. In case of the Cable School, Slack reports that teachers were reluctant to deliver worksheets to the server, since this enabled outsiders to judge their teaching skills. As a matter of fact, hardly any worksheets were prepared by the teachers, although this was central/a key to the original objectives of Cable School. The language course was a failure in educational terms as well. Instead of 60 hours, only 40 hours of teaching remained, instead of teaching all elements of a language (amongst which grammar, spelling, speaking, writing), the course was restricted to mere communication in a straightforward, purposeful way (being able to answer questions about what they had learned). Researching the effectiveness of this form of teaching compared to more traditional forms (of distance teaching) was cancelled because of time constraints. Only 'IMMICS the course' seems to escape the notion of failure in reaching educational objectives, according to the actors involved (teachers, members of the media-lab, and students).

With regard to the technological infrastructure and educational multimedia, the projects show a dispersed pattern. In case of Cable School, worksheets are hardly used, in case of the language course the whiteboard is brought under control of the teacher, the infrastructures of Bornholm and Telepoly are difficult to stabilise, and IMMICS shows students struggling with the restricted facilities available in Storyspace. But none of these problems are seen as a failure of the entire project. Some problems are cumbersome, and must be overcome in due time, but in some cases the problems are regarded as a fact of life and simply taken for granted.

Educational Multimedia and the New Pedagogy

When it comes to the use of educational multimedia a question we have to answer is whether this is somehow related to the new pedagogy, i.e. a pedagogy based on the constructionist perspective. In case a criterion of success would be an explicit showing of this new pedagogy, then four out of five projects – with IMMICS as exception – must be termed a failure. None of the projects explicitly addresses the new pedagogy. At most it might be argued that awareness for the new pedagogy is present in some of the projects, but even then it does not play a very dominant role. We might add that the overall perspective, as for instance elaborated in the cybergirls-study, supports the new pedagogy in a sense of experience-oriented learning. In terms of learning strategies this comes close to trial and error, a strategy that is visible in the activities of the girls. With respect to the study on the Norwegian teachers, one of the motives of change within the curriculum is the expected need to change the curriculum due to external – societal – influences. The accompanying ideology is top-down structured and 'released' in the educational field. It may be a visionary ideology from one point of view, the present-day situation in Norwegian education – as experienced by the teachers – does not yet encompass this ideology. Generally speaking, the studies show that educational multimedia are used in an instrumental manner, i.e. they are supplanted in the educational practice as this exists without reference to a change in learning styles (learning *with* multimedia). The consequences of the use of educational multimedia may be such that they support a change in teaching and learning styles, but the overall dynamics in the presented projects show a rather conservative approach towards the possibly pedagogical consequences of new educational multimedia. This needs not come as much of a surprise in a situation where most of the initiatives are essentially technologically based. IMMICS might serve as counter-example: it is interesting to observe that the educational multimedia used in this project do not meet contemporary standards of multimedia – from a technological point of view – and are technologically speaking even outdated. This might indicate a dominance of non-technical motives, such as educational ones, within this project. But even then, it is important to realise that IMMICS fits the overall educational perspective of the institute in which it is embedded, and that IMMICS does not form an exception to the dominant pedagogical approach within this institute. In that sense, even IMMICS can not be labelled more pedagogically challenging than the other projects, though it fits 'modern' ideas about the new teaching better than the other projects.

Constructive Guidelines for 'Good Practices'

Good practices are intuitively related to success. They seem to embody rules of the game that – if followed – will most probably lead to the successful implementation and use of (in our case) educational multimedia. The previous discussion on what constitutes success did, however, show the problematic aspect of an unambiguous definition of good practices. Following the reasoning of the foregoing section, good practices should be symmetrically tackled in respect to success and failure. Just as guidelines may be distilled from successful events, failed experiences also contribute to guidelines for good practices. But not all good practices relate to the same kind of experiences. It matters whether they relate to the mode of control or to the mode of experimentation. When a project is initiated while specific objectives have to be met, good practices will typically address quality control aspects. In the case of experimental, exploratory settings, good practices entail other characteristics that fit the exploratory setting best. Finally, good practices may be formulated with regard to the technological setting, the pedagogical setting, or a combination of the two.

Figure 14.9 Dimensioning of good practices (++: combination often found; -- combination seldom found)

	Mode of Control	Mode of Experimentation
Technology-oriented projects	++	-
Education-oriented projects	+	+

At least a fourfold differentiation between good practices thus evolves as figure 14.9 summarizes. This 'dimensioning' of good practices is meant to underscore the variety of characteristics and constitutive aspects that give rise to the formation of guidelines for good practices. Depending on the context and the objectives to be realised, the emphasis might shift from one dimension to another one.

The dimensioning of good practices is guided by what we found in the cases. Another step is needed to arrive at what we think should be part and parcel of good practices. We proceed with the more action-oriented perspective on social learning.

At present, the situation is as follows:

- the focus within most projects we studied, is on success rather than on failure; failure is considered not to contribute to lessons to be learnt, but a waste of time, resources and energy;
- the focus is on the mode of control rather than on the mode of experimentation; when dealing with technological projects, the mode of experimentation is almost entirely absent;
- most projects we studied, are technology-oriented; hardly any projects were educationally-oriented; a mix of both perspectives (both education *and* technology) has not been found in the projects under study.

Moving from this situation 'as-it-is' towards the situation 'as-it-should-be' we want to argue that the following pro-active social learning processes are called for:

- In order to retain a balance between success and failure – considering that both success and failure are the result of the perception and interpretation of actors – it is needed to add qualifiers of failure to what constitutes good practices. These qualifiers are important to warn for what might be avoided, and to highlight the localised and contextual aspects of innofusion processes.
- In order to retain a balance between a controlled approach of the innofusion process that imposes constraints on what is acceptable and what should be avoided, and an exploratory approach that leaves room for all kinds of uses and experimentation with educational multimedia, the process of the innofusion should be cast in a mode of experimentation. This balance should stimulate that new and unforeseen uses are explored.

• In order to retain a balance between a technological perspective and an educational perspective, awareness of educational changes that may be promoted by introducing multimedia in educational settings must increase. Much of the educational innovative potential of multimedia goes as yet unnoticed, due to the often too strict and exclusive focus on multimedia as a technological tool.

Having given this general social learning lesson, flowing from the more pro-active approach towards educational multimedia, it must be emphasised that the specifics of the innofusion process will always depend on the kind of objectives one has. We do not intend to present a prescriptive format for the organisation of these innofusion processes; we merely want to draw attention to some aspects that are over-emphasised while others hardly receive attention.

To give a few examples of over-emphasis: the approach in Bornholm focused to much on technology and neglected the need for a so-called social space; the fact that technology by itself does not replace a teacher was not fully appreciated, and thus the technology presented many obstacles. It also presented obstacles because of the instability of the technological configuration itself, which forced teachers and students themselves to become trouble-shooters. The Norwegian contribution addresses the need for exploratory settings when comparing different school systems, and by this the apparent neglect of these settings in contemporary approaches. It is suggested that schools that allow for exploratory experimentation will benefit most from the opportunities offered by the new educational multimedia. This would be in line with the establishment of good practices as these evolve from the IMMICS case, where priority is given to educational objectives. Bornholm, Cable-school and Telepoly show that failing practices (a failing preparation for the new teaching situation) may give rise to the formulation of new pedagogical requirements, i.e. to guidelines to be followed in order to establish good teaching practices. The language course shows that controlling children was necessary in order to prevent them exploring unforeseen uses of the new technology. Only by technically constraining the children's behaviour was the project kept on schedule. In the meantime, these unforeseen uses might have led to new and profitable innovations with regard to the educational setting that was created by the project.

Conclusions

The innofusion process of educational multimedia is far from optimal. A starting point to organise good practices encompasses a mix of control and exploration, and a mix of technology and education. Control is needed to survey and evaluate what is going on, to offer clarity of responsibility, to motivate by showing innovative uses, and by offering a platform to exchange ideas and experiences. Exploration is needed since educational multimedia are no *'one size fits all'* products. Their possible uses have to be explored, they have to find a place in new settings. The mix of technology and education provides a potential synergy between technology and education. The technological foundation of educational multimedia enables the support of specific pedagogical approaches, such as activating didactic, student-centred learning. Up till now, these 'slogans' have hardly been included in the design of educational multimedia, and projects to experiment with this synergy are rare. Social learning in multimedia presupposes the mixed combination of education, technology, control and exploration to be a foundation for good, better and, perhaps, even best practices.

Note

1   We would like to thank Robin Williams for suggesting this representation to compare the various cases.

15 Conclusions and Recommendations

WIEBE E. BIJKER, TINEKE M. EGYEDI,
MARC VAN LIESHOUT

Introduction

In the seventies, Ivan Illich wrote a visionary book called *Deschooling society*. This book evokes images of a learning shop, situated between the bakery and the grocery. Behind the counter an elderly lady passes her wisdom on to her customers. If necessary, she helps them find and interpret additional sources of information. Illich's visions highlight the importance of an integrated kind of knowledge and the accessibility of such knowledge to the person in the street. These two elements are also essential in the current debate on education. Society needs citizens who have cognitive and social skills. While knowledge of facts is less important, the capacity to find and cope with information now has high value. Information is everywhere. Each self-respecting city square has electronic information pillars. Service centres and Internet cafés are daily increasing in number. Finding one's way in the information society is a precious skill.

'Deschooling society' refers to de-institutionalised learning. It can come in different versions. A contemporary version is 'life-long learning'. The latter notion has gained new significance through the Internet. To a certain degree, the use of the Internet dissolves the boundaries of the 'schooled' setting, or as we call it: formal education. In the future, it may provide the backbone for a 'deschooled' approach to education. But whether this will occur depends on how society appropriates the Internet. At present, praxis and theory still diverge. The reasoning pursued in policy documents is that, once the information infrastructure is universally accessible and multimedia use common practice, everyone will learn from whoever they like, at any time, any place. Comparable expectations have been voiced with regard to multimedia use in the 'schooled' educational setting. But despite high hopes, the promise of multimedia has not been met. The innofusion of multimedia uses and practices is limited. It depends almost solely on the intrinsic motivation of individual teachers.

313

Furthermore, our analysis showed that multimedia projects are generally regarded as successful, but rarely so in terms of educational objectives. It is not yet evident in what manner multimedia do support new pedagogical approaches. Pilot projects are carried out to develop new multimedia uses. But, as the case studies show, these focus on the control and verification of multimedia uses rather than on experimentation and the diversification of uses.

Conclusions

When integrating the findings of the cases, a not-too-bright-a-picture emerges of multimedia use in education. The main conclusions are summarized in table 15.1.

Table 15.1 Summary of conclusions

Education	
	1. Learning *about* multimedia occurs in different settings – also in non-educational settings.
	2. Technology and education are often treated as separate entities instead of constituents of one sociotechnical practice.
	3. Education does not benefit from multimedia 'integration' if integration means implanting a technical infrastructure and *subsequently* turning to pedagogical issues.
	4. There is little room for exploration and experimentation in multimedia projects.
	5. Teachers play too marginal a role in multimedia projects.
	6. Structural support for teachers who participate in projects or who (want to) use multimedia for teaching on their own initiative is lacking (time, facilities, training).
	7. Multi-disciplinary teams benefit project design and development, provided there is a balance of influence among team members.
	8. There is a need for an evaluation framework which enables a cross-comparison of project processes and results.

I n n o f u s i o n	1. Multimedia innofusion – combined innovation *and* diffusion – proceeds along lines of multimedia use and production. 2. Teachers are crucial as intermediary users and intermediary producers of multimedia, and are the driving force of multimedia innofusion – particularly where they have space to manoeuvre. 3. Material and educational crystallisation points (e.g. a multimedia lab and a clear curriculum) facilitate intra-institutional diffusion of multimedia practices. 4. Multimedia content and pedagogic multimedia use (as added value) are intrinsic drivers for innofusion, but are generally not recognised as such by policy makers. 5. The call-for-tenders procedure is an effective extrinsic driver of innofusion within and across organisations – but it presently thrives on the voluntary efforts of individual entrepreneur-teachers. 6. The fear of lagging behind and losing a 'share of the education market', is an extrinsic driver of innofusion at sector level – but it often leads to unfocused, non-integrated multimedia activity by schools and institutes.
S o c i a l L e a r n i n g	1. All projects are a success (depending on the criterion applied); they differ, however, on the degree of collective learning that ensues. 2. Reflexivity is inherent to multimedia projects, whether formalised in evaluation procedures or not. 3. There is a correlation between a technical or an educational focus, and the mode of control or experimentation in social learning, respectively. This implies that more emphasis on educational considerations leads to diversified multimedia uses. 4. Social learning through control and through verification experiments has little to add to innofusion of multimedia practices in education – it will merely lead to an increasing number of similar experiences. 5. The institutional evaluation context of EU projects misses an important source of social learning: failure and experimentation in embedding multimedia.

In general, we see a neglect of the educational goals *per se* and accordingly a lack of attention to the potentially positive synergy between multimedia and innovative teaching. This lacuna can be traced down to the policies that intend to stimulate educational multimedia use, to the design of multimedia projects and to their results. A naïve technological determinist view is clear – if the technical infrastructure is in place, the rest will follow...

Recommendations

These conclusions can be recast in terms of policy recommendations, as summarised in box 15.1.

Box 15.1   Summary of recommendations

- The opportunity to learn from failure should be part of research programmes, implementation programmes, and individual project designs.
- Projects should reserve time for experimentation and failure; this increases diversified multimedia use and social learning.
- Projects, which focus on experimentation and diversification of multimedia uses, broaden the collective experience with multimedia in education, and thus enhance social learning.
- To enhance social learning, the project design should show a balance between the "mode of experimentation" and the "mode of control".
- Even for projects that are mostly in the "mode of control", monitoring and evaluation should pay explicit attention to the *process* of experimentation.
- An evaluation framework should be designed in order to increase social learning.
- Innofusion of new technologies always involves various groups; pro-active and strategic enrollment of a wide variety of social groups should be part of any technology development and demonstration programme.
- To achieve education-wide multimedia innofusion, teachers need to be supported in their role of intermediary users and producers of multimedia uses; they should be offered multimedia training, technical support and time.
- Teachers and instructional engineers should be involved from the start; they should be members of the multi-disciplinary project team.
- Concrete crystallisation and translation points should be conceived as means of supporting intra- and inter-institutional diffusion of multimedia uses.
- The call-for-tenders practice should also be applied within organisations.
- Multimedia projects should start with educational objectives and the design of an overall learning environment.
- Learning strategies in non-educational fields should be studied to clarify differences between formal and non-formal learning, and thus to contribute to an understanding of the possibilities of life-long learning.

The key recommendation is to better recognise that more is learned from failure than from success. New technologies are sooner adopted when accompanied by social learning strategies. That implies a dual and reflexive learning process: technology is further shaped and tuned to its application contexts, and these contexts are adapted in order to accommodate the technology. This process comprises elements of a technical, social and cognitive nature. It requires adaptation of the technical infrastructure and organisation, and the development of individual knowledge and skills. The next step is to recognise that social learning occurs best if the right balance is struck between the mode of experimentation and the mode of control: if a project is open enough to allow for unplanned changes, social learning increases. Such openness implies tolerance for 'failure', for only if projects are allowed to fail, will they be sufficiently open to change. The crucial final step in the argument is then, of course, that the project design must allow for proper monitoring, evaluation, and learning of 'failure'.

A second general recommendation is to recognise that in the development, implementation, and application of technologies various groups are involved – not only the standard "producers" and "users." Experiences of failure often occur when specific groups adopt a technology without, at least partly, reshaping it. Had the input of these groups been better accommodated, the technology might have been transferred more successfully. In the field of educational multimedia, this leads to the recommendation to include teachers more consciously, more seriously, and from the start.

A third class of recommendations is based on case evidence that multimedia form and content are inextricably intertwined. The technological determinist view that the mere introduction of multimedia technology is enough to generate proper educational content is false. Only if educational aims are part and parcel of a multimedia innovation project, can one hope to realise an integrated application and make multimedia work for education. It is equally necessary to think explicitly about the technological aspects of pedagogical innovation. Thus, strategic thinking about integrated development of education and multimedia technology includes the design of concrete measures to transfer these practices within the organisation or across organisations. Crystallisation points "anchor" such developments within an organisation. Translation points may help their transferal to other organisations.

Bibliography

Akrich, M. (1992), 'The De-Scription of Technical Objects', in W.E. Bijker and J. Law (eds), *Shaping Technology / Building Society, Studies in Sociotechnical Change*, MIT Press, Cambridge, MA, pp. 205-224.

Andersen, E.S. and Lundwall, B-Å (1988), 'Small national systems of innovation facing technological revolutions: an analytical framework', in C. Freeman and B-Å. Lundwall (eds), *Small countries facing the technological revolution*, Pinter Publisher, London, pp. 9-36.

Andriessen, J.H.E. (1996), 'The why, how, and what to evaluate of interaction technology: a review and proposed integration', in P.J. Thomas (ed), *CSCW Requirements and evaluation*, Springer Verlag, London, pp. 107-124.

Aune, M. (1992), *Datamaskina i hverdagslivet, En studie av brukernes domestisering av en ny teknologi*, STS-report 15, Centre for Technology and Society, Norwegian University of Science and Technology, Trondheim.

Aune, M. (1996), 'The Computer in Everyday Life: Patterns of Domestication of a New Technology', in M. Lie and K.H. Sørensen (eds), *Making Technology Our Own? Domesticating Technology into Everyday Life,* Scandinavian University Press, Oslo, pp. 91-120.

Aune, M. and Sørensen, K. H. (2000), 'Teaching transformed?', this volume.

Barras, R. (1990), 'Interactive innovation in financial and business services: The vanguard of the service revolution', *Research Policy,* vol. 17, pp. 1-14.

Beck, U. (1992), *Risk society: towards a new modernity*, SAGE Publications, London. (Originally published as Beck, U. (1986), *Risikogesellschaft: Auf dem Weg in eine andere Moderne*, Suhrkamp Verlag, Frankfurt am Main.)

Beck, U., Giddens, A. and Lash, S. (1994), *Reflexive modernisation: Politics, tradition and aesthetics in modern social order*, Polity Press, Oxford.

Befring, E. (1995), *Dataspill forklart for akademikere. Nye medier – nye underholdningsformer*, Hovedoppgave i medievitenskap University of Oslo.

Beniger, J. (1986). *The Control Revolution*, MIT Press, Cambridge, MA.

Berg, A.J. (1996). *Digital Feminism*, STS-report 28, Centre for Technology and Society, Norwegian University of Science and Technology, Trondheim.

Bijker, W.E. (1995), *Of bicycles, bakelites, and bulbs – Towards a theory of sociotechnical change*, MIT Press, Cambridge, MA.

Bijker, W.E., Hughes, T.P. and Pinch, T.J. (eds) (1987), *The social construction of technological systems*, MIT Press, Cambridge, MA.

Bijker, W. E. and Law, J. (eds) (1992), *Shaping Technology / Building Society. Studies in sociotechnical change*, MIT Press, Cambridge, MA.

Boettcher, J. (ed) (1993), *101 Success Stories of Information Technology in Higher Education*, Mc Graw Hill, New York.

Brosveet, J. and Sørensen, K.H. (2000), 'Fishing for fun and profit? National domestication of multimedia: The case of Norway', *Information society*, (in press).

Brown, E. and Chignell, M.H. (1995), 'End-user as developer: Free-form multimedia', in E. Barett and M. Redmond (eds), *Contextual Media, Multimedia and interpretation*, MIT Press, Cambridge, MA, pp. 189-211.

Callon, M. (1986), 'The Sociology of an Actor-Network: The Case of the Electric Vehicle', in M. Callon, J. Law and A. Rip (eds), *Mapping the dynamics of science and technology*, MacMillan, London, pp. 19-34.

Committee on MultiMedia in Teacher Training (COMMITT) (1996), *Teaching and Learning for the Future*, Enschede.

Coopers & Lybrand (1996), *Evaluation of the Teaching and Learning Technology Programme*, Higher Education Funding Council for England, Bristol. (Summary available at http://back.niss.ac.uk/education/hefce/pub96/m21_96.html)

CTU (1996), *Evaluering af fjernundervisning på Bornholm, Bilag III, Analyse af de teknologiske og organisatoriske effekter af fjernundervisningsforløbet på Bornholm*, Center for teknologistøttet uddannelse, Copenhagen.

Dewey, J. (1933), *How we Think: A Restatement of the Relation of [Reflective] Thinking to the Educative Process*, D.C. Heath, Boston, MA.

Dierkes, M., Hoffman, U. and Marz, L. (1996), *Visions of technology, Social and institutional factors shaping the development of new technologies*, St. Martin's Press, New York.

Dijkstra, S. and Merrienboer, J.J.G. (1997), 'Plans, Procedures, and Theories to Solve Instructional Design Problems', in S. Dijkstra, N. Seel, F. Schott and R.D. Tennyson (eds), *Instructional Design: International Perspectives*, Erlbaum, Mahwah, New Jersey, pp. 23-47.

Dillemans, R., Lowyck, J., Perre, G. van der, Claeys, C. and Elen, J. (1998), *New Technologies for Learning, Contribution of ICT to innovation in education*, Leuven University Press, Leuven, Belgium.

Dosi, G. (1982), Technological paradigms and technological trajectories', *Research Policy*, vol. 11, pp. 147-162.

Dosi, G., Freeman, C., Nelson, R., Silverberg, G. and Soete, L. (eds) (1988), *Technical change and economic theory*, Pinter Publisher, London.

Eurelings, A.M.C., Bal, R., Bemelmans, Y.A.T.W., Egyedi, T. and Vander Steene, W. (1998), 'Euregional collaboration as a motor for innovation of education with information technology', *Proceedings BITE Conference, 'Bringing Information Technology to Education: Integrating Information & Communication Technology in Higher Education'*, March 25-27, 1998, University of Maastricht, the Netherlands, pp. 92-102.

Eurelings, A.M.C. & Ronteltap, C.F.M. (1996), *User Requirement Analysis POLARIS*, Telematics Application Programme report D10.01, European Union, University of Maastricht.

Evalueringscentret (1996a), *Evaluering af fjernundervisning på Bornholm (Evaluation of distance teaching on Bornholm), Evalueringsrapport,* Evalueringscentret, Copenhagen.

Evalueringscentret (1996b), *Evaluering af fjernundervisning på Bornholm, Bilag I, Selvevalueringsrapporte,* Evalueringscentret, Copenhagen.

Evalueringscentret (1996c), *Evaluering af fjernundervisning på Bornholm, Bilag II, Studenterundersøgelse,* Evalueringscentret, Copenhagen.

Fleck, J. (1988), *Innofusion or diffusation: the nature of technological development in robotics,* Edinburgh PICT Working Paper No. 4, Edinburgh University, Edinburgh.

Forskningsministeriet (1996), *The Info-Society for all – the Danish Model,* Danish Ministry of Research and Information Technology, Copenhagen.

Freeman, C. and Perez, C. (1988), 'Structural crises of adjustment: business cycles and investment behaviour', in G. Dosi, C. Freeman, R. Nelson, G. Silverberg and L. Soete (eds), *Technical change and economic theory,* Pinter Publisher, London, pp. 38-66.

Gansmo, H. J. (1998), *Det forvrengte dataspeilet, En kvalitativ studie av hvordan ungdomsskolejenter forstår datateknologiens muligheter i dag og i fremtiden,* STS-report 36, Centre for Technology and Society, Norwegian University of Science and Technology, Trondheim.

Giddens, A. (1990), *The consequences of modernity,* Polity Press, London.

Goodyear, P. (1997), 'Instructional Design Environments: Methods and Tools for the Design of Complex Instructional Systems', in S. Dijkstra, N. Seel, F. Schott and R.D. Tennyson (eds), *Instructional Design: International Perspectives,* Erlbaum, Mahwah, New Jersey, pp. 83-112.

Goodyear, P. (1998), 'New Technology in Higher Education: Understanding the Innovation Process', *Proceedings BITE Conference, 'Bringing Information Technology to Education: Integrating Information & Communication Technology in Higher Education',* March 25-27, 1998, University of Maastricht, the Netherlands, pp. 107-136.

Hammond, N. et al. (1992), 'Blocks to the effective use of information technology in higher education', *Computer Education,* vol. 18 (1), pp. 155-162.

Hansen, E. and Perry, D. (1993), 'Barriers to collaborative performance support systems in higher education', *Educational Technology,* November, pp. 46-52.

Håpnes, T. and Rasmussen, B. (1991), 'What makes computer science an all-male business?', in I. Eriksson, B. Kitchenham and K. Tijdens (eds), *Women, work and computerization,* North Holland, Amsterdam, pp. 395-407.

Håpnes, T. (1996), 'Not in Their Machines, How Hackers Transform Computers into Subcultural Artefacts', in M. Lie and K.H. Sørensen (eds), *Making Technology Our Own?,* Universitetsforlaget AS, Oslo, pp. 121-150.

Håpnes, T. and Rasmussen, B. (1997), *Internett – jentenett?? Ungdomsskolejenters databruk og datainteresser*, Report 7/97, Centre for Womens' Research, Norwegian University of Science and Technology, Trondheim.

Hawkridge, D. (1983), *New Information technology in Education*, Croom Helm, London.

Hertog, J.F. den, and Wee, E. van der (1982), 'Gebruikersparticipatie, uitgangspunten bij het inschakelen van gebruikers in automatiseringsprojecten', *Informatie*, vol. 24 (3), pp. 141-151.

Holden, M.C. and Wedman, J.F. (1994), 'Future issues of computer-mediated communication: The results of a Delphi study', *Educational Technology Research & Development*, vol. 41 (4), pp. 5-24.

Illich, I.(1976), *Deschooling society*, Penguin, Harmondsworth.

IMMICS (1996), *Project planning 1996-1998, Action Plan Phase II: Functional Design*, August 1996 - January 1997, Faculty of Arts and Culture, University of Maastricht, the Netherlands.

Jacobs, D. (1996), *Het kennisoffensief*, Samson Bedrijfsinformatie, Alphen aan den Rijn/Diegem.

Jæger, B. and Storgaard, K. (eds) (1997), *Telematics and rural development*, Proceedings of an International Workshop on the Danish Island of Bornholm, Research Centre of Bornholm, Rønne, Denmark.

Jæger, B. and Hansen, F. (1999), 'Multimedia in Denmark – an Overview', in R. Williams and R. S. Slack, *Europe Appropriates Multimedia, A study of the National Uptake of Multimedia in Eight European Countries and Japan*, NTNU, Centre for Technology and Society, Trondheim, pp. 83-121.

Jonassen, D., Mayes, T. and McAleese, R. (1993), 'Amanifesto for a constructivist approach to uses of technology in higher education', in T.M. Duffy, J. Lowyck and D.H. Jonassen (eds), *Designing environments for constructive learning*, Springer, Berlin, pp. 231-248.

Kerr, S.T. (1981), 'How Teachers Design their Materials: Implications for Instructional Design', *Instructional Science*, vol. 10, pp. 363-378.

Kluge, A., Hornke, L.F., Denis, B., Detroz, P., Daniëls, J., Baaren, J. van der, Egyedi, T. and Eurelings, A. (September 1997), *Evaluation Guide Part 2, A guide for the evaluation of the workpackages in the ELECTRA project*, European Union Telematics Application Programme, ELECTRA project.

Koschmann, T.D., Myers, A.C., Feltovich, P.J.M. and Barrows, H.S. (1994), 'Using Technology to Assist in Realizing Effective Learning and Instruction: a Principled Approach to the Use of Computers in Collaborative Learning' *The Journal of the Learning Sciences*, vol. 3, pp. 227-264.

Koschmann, T. (1995), 'Medical education and computer literacy: Learning about, through, and with computers', *Academic Medicine*, 70(9), pp. 68-71.

Koschmann, T. (in press), 'Tools of termlessness: Technology, educational reform, and Deweyan inquiry', to appear in T. O'Shea (ed), *Virtual Learning Environments*, Lawrence Erlbaum, Mahwah, NJ.

Kvande, E. & Rasmussen, B. (1991), *Nye kvinneliv. Kvinner i menns organisasjoner*, Ad Notam forlag AS, Oslo.

Lauvdal, T. (1994), *Pedagogikk, politikk og byråkrati. Om statlig styring av grunnskolen og reformintensjoner i den statlige forvaltning på grunnskoleområdet 1969-1991*, PhD-dissertation, University of Trondheim, Trondheim.

Lauvdal, T. (1996), *Makt og interesser, Strying og forhandlingssystem i skolesektoren*, Scandinavian University Press, Oslo.

Latour, B. (1987), *Science in action, How to follow scientists and engineers through society*, Open University Press, Milton Keynes.

Lente, H. van (1993), *Promising Technology: the dynamics of expectations in technological development*, Eburon, Delft.

Lente, H. van and Klooster, E. van 't (1997), *Multimedia in Onderwijs en Onderzoek, Enquete Multimedia & CWS*, Internal report, Faculty of Arts and Culture, University of Maastricht, February 5, 1997.

Lie, M. (1997), 'vett i pannen, stål i ben og armer – Teknologiens bilder av kjønn', *Kvinneforskning*, 97(2), pp. 37-49.

Lie, M. (1998), *Computer Dialogues, Technology, Gender and Change*, Report 2/98, Centre for Womens' Research, Norwegian University of Science and Technology, Trondheim.

Lie, M. and Sørensen, K. (1996), *Making technology our own? Domesticating technology into everyday life*, Scandinavian University Press, Oslo.

Lieshout, M. van (1999), 'The digital city of Amsterdam: between public domain and private enterprise', in B. van Bastelaer and C. Lobet-Maris (eds), *Social Learning regarding Multimedia Developments at a Local Level: The Case of Digital Cities*, University of Namur, Namur, pp. 101-149.

MacKenzie, D. (1996), 'Economic and Sociological Explanations of Technological Change', in D. MacKenzie (ed), *Knowing Machines, Essays on Technical Change*, MIT Press, Cambridge, MA, pp. 49-65.

MacKenzie, D. and Wajcman, J. (eds) (1985), *The social shaping of technology – or how the refrigerator got its hum*, Open University Press, Milton Keynes.

Moonen, P. and Kommers P. (1995), *Implementatie van Communicatie- en Informatie- technologieën (CIT) in het Onderwijs*, Universiteit van Twente, 1995/1997.

Mulder, K.F. (1992), *Choosing the corporate future, Technology networks and choice concerning the creation of high performance fibre technology*, Dissertation, University of Groningen, the Netherlands.

National Committee of Inquiry into Higher Education (1997), *Higher Education in the Learning Society*, Dearing Report, HMSO, London. (http://www.leeds.ac.uk/educol/ncihe/)

Nelson, R.R. and Winter, S.G. (1977), 'In search of a useful theory of innovation', *Research Policy*, vol. 6, pp. 36-76.

Nissen, J. (1996), 'Det är klart att det är grabbar som håller på med datorer! Men varför er det så?', in E. Sundin and B. Berner (eds), *Genus, teknik og social förandring: Från symaskin till cyborg*, Nerenius & Santèrius förlag AB, Stockholm, pp. 141-162.

Nissen, J. (1997), 'The hacker culture and masculinity', in V. Frissen (ed), *Gender ITC and everyday life, Mutual shaping processes*, European Communities, Belgium, pp. 230-250.

Nordli, H. (1998), *Fra Spice Girls til Cyber Girls, En kvalitativ analyse av datafascinerte jenter i ungdomsskolen*, STS-report 35, Centre for Technology and Society, Norwegian University of Science and Technology, Trondheim.

Oshima, J., Bereiter, C. and Scardamalia, M. (1995), *Information-access characteristics for high conceptual progress in a computer-networked learning environment*, Paper at Conference on Computer Support for Collaborative learning, Bloomington, USA.

Pinch, T. and Bijker, W. E (1987), 'The Social Construction of Facts and Artifacts: or How the Sociology of Science and the Sociology of Technology Might Benefit Each Other', in W.E. Bijker, T.P. Hughes and T. Pinch (eds), *The Social Construction of Technological Systems*, MIT Press, Cambridge, MA, pp. 17-50.

Pugh, S.L. (1996), 'Using Case Studies and Collaborative Computer-Assisted Communicaton to Support Conceptual learning in a Teacher-Education', *Educational Technology*, November, pp. 30-38.

Rockman, S (1992), *Learning from Technology: A Perspective on the Research Literature*, Congress of the US, Office of Technology Assessment.

Rasmussen, B. and Håpnes, T. (1991), 'Excluding women from the technologies of the future?', *Futures*, vol. 23 (10), pp. 1107-1119.

Rip, A., Misa, T. and Schot, J. (eds) (1995), *Managing technology in society – The approach of constructive technology assessment*, Pinter Publisher, London/New York.

Rowland, G. (1992), 'What do Instructional Designers Actually do? An Initial Investigation of Expert Practice', *Performance Improvement Quarterly*, vol. 5 (2), pp. 65-86.

Salomon, G. (1992), 'Effects with and of Computers and the Study of Computer-Based Learning Environments', in E. de Corte, M.C. Linn, H. Mandl and L. Verschaffel (eds), *Computer-based learning Environments and Problem Solving*, Springer Verlag, Leuven.

Scardamalia, M., and Bereiter, C. (1992), 'An Architecture for Collaborative Knowledge Building', in E. de Corte, M.C. Linn, H. Mandl and L. Verschaffel (eds), *Computer-based learning Environments and Problem Solving*, Springer Verlag, Leuven.

Scardamalia, M., and Bereiter, C. (1996), 'Computer Support for Knowledge-Building Communities', in T. Koschmann (ed), *CSCL: Theory and Practice of an Emerging Paradigm*, Erlbaum, Mahwah, New Jersey, pp. 249-306.

Scardamalia, M, Bereiter, C, McLean, R.S., Swallow, J. and Woodruff, E. (1988), 'Computer Supported Intentional Learning Environments', *Journal of Educational Computing Research*, 5, pp. 51-68.

Schagen, K. (1998), *Review report IMMICS*, Faculty of Arts and Culture, University of Maastricht.

Seel, N.M. and Dijkstra, S. (1997), 'A Historical Snapshot on the Growth of Instructional Design', in S. Dijkstra, N. Seel, F. Schott, and R.D. Tennyson (eds), *Instructional Design: International Perspectives*, Erlbaum, Mahwah, New Jersey, pp. 17-22.

Silverstone, R. and Hirsch, E. (eds) (1992), *Consuming Technologies. Media and information in domestic spaces*, Routledge and Keagan Paul, London.

Sjøberg, S. and Lie, S. (1984), *"Myke" jenter i "harde" fag?*, Universitetsforlaget, Oslo.

Sjøberg, S. (1985), *Elever og lærere sier sin mening*, Universitetsforlaget, Oslo.

Slack, R., Williams, R. and Jaeger, B. (forthcoming), Social Learning in Multimedia: An overview of Experiments in Multimedia, *Information Society* (accepted).

Smith C. and Mayes, T. (1995), *Telematics Applications for Education and Training: Usability Guide*, EU report, version 2.0.

Spilker, H.S. (1998), *GirlsROM: A ROM of one's own? The construction of femaleness in multimedia*, STS working-paper 12/ 98, Centre for Technology and Society, Norwegian University of Science and Technology, Trondheim.

SSB (1995), *Bruk av EDB i skolen*, Statistisk Sentralbyrå, Oslo.

Stuedahl, D. (1997), *Jenter og informatikkstudie – en rapport om jenters studiesituasjon ved Institutt for informatikk UiO*, Institutt for informatikk, University of Oslo.

Sundvoll, A. and Teigum, H.M. (1997), *IT i skolen 1997. Del 1, Tilstandsundersøkelse i skolene: Hovedresultater og dokumentasjon*, Working paper 97/42, National Bureau of Statistics, Oslo.

Sætnan, A.R. (1998), 'Flexible technology vs. organizational stalemate – The story of PREOP', in K.H. Sørensen (ed), *The spectre of participation, Technology and work in a welfare state*, Scandinavian University Press, Oslo, pp. 189-219.

Sørensen, K.H. (1996), *Learning technology, constructing culture, Socio-technical change as social learning*, STS-report 18, Centre for Technology and Society, Norwegian University of Science and Technology, Trondheim.

Sørensen, K.H., Aune, M. and Hatling, M. (2000), 'Against linearity. On the cultural appropriation of science and technology', in M. Dierkes and C. v. Grote (eds), *Between understanding and trust: The public, science and technology*, Harwood Academic publishers, Amsterdam, pp. 237-257.

Tennyson, R. (1997), *Automating Instructional Design, Development and Delivery*, Springer Verlag, Berlin.

Turkle, S. (1984), *The Second Self, Computers and the human spirit*, Simon and Schuster, New York.

Turkle, S. (1988), 'Compuational retirence: Why woman fear the intimate machine', in C. Kramarae (ed), *Technology and woman's voices, Keeping in touch*, Routledge and Keagan Paul, New York/London.

Turkle, S. (1996), *Life on The Screen, Identity in the Age of the Internet*, Weidenfeld and Nicolson, London.

Undervisningsministeriet (1996), *Evaluering af fjernundervisning på Bornholm, Bilag IV, Komparativ økonomisk analyse af fjernundervisning til Bornholm og forlagt undervisning fra Handelshøjskolen i København til Bornholms Erhvervsskole*, Undervisningsministeriet, økonomiafdelingen, Copenhagen.

Undervisningsministeriet (1997a), *Informationsteknologi og uddannelse (Information technology and education)*, Danish Ministry of Education, Copenhagen.

Undervisningsministeriet (1997b), *Nyhedsbrev 5*, Danish Ministry of Education, Copenhagen.

Valcke, M. (1996), *Flexible learning materials to adapt to the characteristics of distance education learners*, Expertise Centre for Educational Technology, Open University, Heerlen, The Netherlands.

Weges, H.G. and Wessels, L.H.M. (eds) (1997), *ICT gebruik en COO binnen de Letteren en Cultuurwetenschappen: Mogelijkheden tot innovatie en samenwerking*, Verslag Consortiumdag Letteren en Cultuurwetenschappen 18 september 1997, Consortium Innovatie Hoger Onderwijs, Open Universiteit, Heerlen.

Winner, L. (1988), *The Whale and the Reactor: A search for limits in an Age of High Technology*, University of Chicago Press, Chicago.

Woolgar, S. (1991), 'Configuring the user – the case of usability trials', in J. Law (ed), *A sociology of monsters – Essays on power, technology and domination*, Routledge and Keagan Paul, London, pp. 58-99.

WTR (1995), *Trends en visie 1. Bestuurlijk document Informatietechnologie in het Hoger Onderwijs*, 2 vols., Otto Cramwinckel, Den Haag.

Wynne, B. (1995), 'Technology assessment and reflexive social learning: Observations from the risk field', in A. Rip, T. Misa, and J. Schot (eds), *Managing technology in society – The approach of constructive technology assessment*, Pinter Publisher, London/New York, pp. 19-36.

Zucchermaglio, C. (1993), 'Toward a Cognitive Ergonomics of Educational Technology', in T.M. Duffy and J. Lowyck (eds), *Designing Environments for Constructive learning*, Springer Verlag, Berlin, pp. 249-261.

SLIM publications

Sørensen, Knut H. (1996), *Learning technology, constructing culture. Socio-technical change as social learning*, STS working paper no 18/96, Centre for technology and society, University of Trondheim.
Version available on the web at:
http://www.rcss.ed.ac.uk/SLIM/public/phase1/knut.html

Williams, R. (1997), 'The Social Shaping of Information and Communications Technologies', in H. Kubicek, W.H. Dutton and R. Williams (eds), *The Social Shaping of Information Superhighways: European and American Roads to the Information Society*, Campus Verlag and St Martin's Press, Frankfurt and New York, pp. 299-338.
Version available on the web at:
http://www.rcss.ed.ac.uk/SLIM/public/phase1/SSICT.html

Williams, R. and Slack, R. (eds) (1999), *Europe Appropriates Multimedia: A study of the National Uptake of Multimedia in Eight European Countries and Japan*, Senter for Teknologi og Samfunn (Centre for Technology and Society), Report No. 42, Norwegian University of Science and Technology, Trondheim, Norway. ISSN 0802 3581 42
Available on the web at:
http://www.rcss.ed.ac.uk/SLIM/public/nationals.html

Jaeger, B., Slack, R. and Williams, R. (forthcoming), 'Europe Experiments with Multimedia', *The Information Society Special issue on Multimedia*.
Available on the web at:
http://www.rcss.ed.ac.uk/SLIM/private/phase2/SocExp.pdf

Lobet-Maris, C. and Bastelaer, B. van (eds) (1999), *Social Learning Regarding Multimedia Developments at a Local Level: The Case of Digital Cities*, CITA, University of Namur, Namur.
Available on the web at:
http://www.ed.ac.uk/~rcss/SLIM/private/I-studies/BvB/digitalcities.html

Rossel, P. (1998), *Cross-cutting perspectives on the social learning of multimedia in the organisation*.
Available on the web at:
http://www.rcss.ed.ac.uk/SLIM/private/crosscutting/PR/PRorgsum.html